MW00352237

New Centers of Global Evangelicalism in Latin America and Africa

This book shows that new centers of Christianity have taken root in the Global South. Although these communities were previously poor and marginalized, Stephen Offutt illustrates that they are now socioeconomically diverse, internationally well connected, and socially engaged. Offutt argues that local and global religious social forces, as opposed to other social, economic, or political forces, are primarily responsible for these changes.

Stephen Offutt is Assistant Professor of Development Studies at Asbury Theological Seminary. His work has been published in a number of peer-reviewed journals, including the *Journal of Contemporary Religion*, the *Journal for the Social Scientific Study of Religion*, *Pneuma: The Journal for the Society of Pentecostal Studies*, and *Sociology of Religion*. He has contributed to edited volumes such as *The New Evangelical Social Engagement*, *Sociology of Religion: A Reader*, and *The Blackwell Encyclopedia of Globalization*. Offutt also writes for popular audiences, with work appearing in magazines such as *Books & Culture: A Christian Review* and *Prism*.

New Centers of Global Evangelicalism in Latin America and Africa

STEPHEN OFFUTT

Asbury Theological Seminary, Wilmore, Ky.

CAMBRIDGE
UNIVERSITY PRESS

University Printing House, Cambridge CB2 8BS, United Kingdom

One Liberty Plaza, 20th Floor, New York, NY 10006, USA

477 Williamstown Road, Port Melbourne, VIC 3207, Australia

4843/24, 2nd Floor, Ansari Road, Daryaganj, Delhi - 110002, India

79 Anson Road, #06-04/06, Singapore 079906

Cambridge University Press is part of the University of Cambridge.

It furthers the University's mission by disseminating knowledge in the pursuit of education, learning and research at the highest international levels of excellence.

www.cambridge.org
Information on this title: www.cambridge.org/9781107435216

© Stephen Offutt 2015

This publication is in copyright. Subject to statutory exception and to the provisions of relevant collective licensing agreements, no reproduction of any part may take place without the written permission of Cambridge University Press.

First published 2015
First paperback edition 2017

A catalogue record for this publication is available from the British Library

Library of Congress Cataloging in Publication data
Offutt, Stephen.
New centers of global evangelicalism in Latin America and Africa / Stephen Offutt.
  pages   cm
ISBN 978-1-107-07832-1 (hardback)
1. Evangelicalism – Latin America.   2. Latin America – Church history.
3. Latin America – Social conditions – 1982–   4. Evangelicalism – Africa.
5. Africa – Church history.   6. Africa – Social conditions – 1960–   I. Title.
BR1642.L29039   2014
270.8'3–dc23   2014027969

ISBN 978-1-107-07832-1 Hardback
ISBN 978-1-107-43521-6 Paperback

Cambridge University Press has no responsibility for the persistence or accuracy of URLs for external or third-party internet websites referred to in this publication, and does not guarantee that any content on such websites is, or will remain, accurate or appropriate.

To Amy,
Addy, Emily, & Gabi

Contents

Map and Tables

Preface and Acknowledgments

The blisters on my hand were open, and sweat was running freely down my face. It was the aftershock, though, that caused us all to pause. I leaned on my shovel and glanced warily first up the hillside and then across the valley, at the San Salvador volcano.

The date was January 12, 2001. An earthquake had ripped through El Salvador the previous day, creating landslides and destroying houses across much of the small, mountainous country. In Santa Tecla, the town in which I lived, a landslide covered almost the entire neighborhood of Las Colinas. The hundreds of ensuing aftershocks caused the volcano to bellow ominous plumes of dust.

I came to El Salvador as part of a socially conscious tech startup company. One of our Salvadoran colleagues, who I will call Juan, lived in Las Colinas. He was out running errands when the earthquake hit. His wife, two small children, and a niece visiting from Guatemala were at home.

Juan was a member of a small evangelical church. I joined his fellow congregants as they climbed up onto the landslide with shovels in hand. We began to dig down into his house; we were one of several gaggles of people gathered over buried houses in the neighborhood. We had collectively suspended our belief in the new reality that the landslide had brought. But hope was fading as we pressed on in the glaring sun, and what our shovels found after hours of digging forced us to confront and accept our worst fears. Juan's family added four to the tally of more than 550 landslide victims in Las Colinas that day.

The scene in Las Colinas recalls and transforms the image Roger Lancaster (1988) painted of Central American religion in his remarkable prologue to *Thanks to God and the Revolution*. Lancaster imagines large, moving statues of Marx and Jesus on opposite ends of the square in Managua, Nicaragua. As they oppose each other, the crowd in the square comes to embody the synthesis of ideology and religion. Lancaster uses the rest of the book to show the ways this works for different Central American faith communities.

By the dawn of the twenty-first century, the region's guerrilla movements had been incorporated into the political process, and the region's religious movements were in rapid flux. Las Colinas served as a different kind of public square and a different locus of activity. A local congregation was a first responder to a natural disaster. Full of pragmatism, fear, fortitude, and personal loss, congregants arrived well before the massive international aid machine got on the ground; they even arrived ahead of the national government's plodding response. The local congregation would later become part of a global faith-based disaster response, showing that it too had international ties. But in those first moments, it was simply a group of people responding to physical and emotional pain in very practical ways – ways that hinted at subtle religious changes that would become more amplified over the next decade and a half.

Two and a half years after the earthquake, I left El Salvador and returned to graduate school to learn more about the changes occurring to evangelicalism, not just in Latin America but also in Africa, where I previously lived, and quite possibly in other parts of the world. This book is the result of that journey.

I have had immeasurable help along the way. Four people deserve special mention for their intellectual influence on this project and on me. During the dissertation phase at Boston University, Nancy Ammerman advised my work and grounded my view of religious communities in sound theoretical principles. Peter Berger served on my committee; he became an invaluable conversation partner about how to interpret global evangelical and Pentecostal movements. Robert Wuthnow also provided guidance and insights into how to think about and investigate religion and transnationalism. He was extremely gracious in the time that he gave me, both when I worked for him and after. Finally, Grace Goodell served as a mentor at the Johns Hopkins University's School of Advanced International Studies (SAIS), where I earned my master's degree. She has provided intellectual depth, friendship, and wise council from the beginning of this project to the end.

Institutions matter when one undertakes intellectual inquiry, and I have had the privilege of being associated with some of the world's best places to study religion and globalization. At Boston University, the Center for Religion and World Affairs (CURA) and the Center for Global Christianity & Mission were important places of discourse. At SAIS, the Social Change & Development Seminar transformed all of the students who participated. I found a home at Princeton University's Religion and Public Life Seminar for several years, and I benefited from the experience I had at the University of Notre Dame's Center for Religion and Society. Finally, Wheaton College's Human Needs and Global Resources program and the E. Stanley Jones School of World Mission and Evangelism at Asbury Theological Seminary have both provided conversation partners from all over the world. Were it not for the opportunity I have had to participate in these communities, this study would not have been possible.

People fill institutions and provide them with meaning. I had the privilege of interacting in these venues with Dana Robert, Emily Barman, Laurel Smith-Doerr,

John Stone, Roman Williams, Mia Diaz, Judy Dean, Marc Chernick, Riordan Roett, Gretchen Ansorge, Nicole Behnam, Joe Boesch, Paul Giacomini, Elinor Haider, Michelle Hecker, Ron Johnson, Dano Jukanovich, Janet Kilian, Kathy Latek, Alice Lin, Paticia MacWilliams, Eileen Pennington, Meredith Vostrejs, Kurt Sanger, Jen Seltzer, Susan Starnes, Nick Szechenyi, Justin Tyson, Omri Elisha, Jim Gibbon, Becky Hsu, Conrad Hackett, Michael Lindsay, Rebekah Massengill, Christina Mora, LiErin Probasco, Larry Stratton, Christian Smith, Kraig Beyerlein, Bob Brenneman, Cole Carnesecca, Mike and Ines Jindra, David Sikkink, Brandon Vaidyanathan, Mark Amstutz, Sandra and Paul Joireman, Paul Robinson, Ryan Juskus, George Hunter, Kima Pachua, Eunice Erwin, Gregg Okesson, Russell West, Steve Ybarrola, Art McPhee, Jay Moon, and David and Lisa Swartz. There were many others who intersected with my life and work in these places; I have tried and inevitably failed to list those who I meaningfully intersected with on topics related to this book.

A word of gratitude must also go to those who welcomed me and provided me with enormous assistance in my field sites. In El Salvador, a special thanks must go to Hilda and Raul Bojorquez. Indeed, it is because of them that I am able to pen the final additions and corrections of this manuscript in the same quarters I inhabited when I first lived in El Salvador. Others who have been important include Alejandro Amaya, Terri Benner Dominguez, David Bueno, Ron Bueno, Adonai Leiva, Andy Liu, Moises Mejia, Ruth Padilla DeBorst, Kevin Sanderson, and Ana Silvia Valencia. In South Africa, Michael Cassidy, Calvin Cook, Johannes Erasmus, Oya Gumede, Jurgens Hendriks, Aidan and Robyn Hillebrand, Gareth and Jane Killeen, Barry Noel, Sandra Pillay, Tuso Siziba, and Ron Steele were extraordinarily gracious. Both of these cultures and communities provided an open and inviting space for the data-collection part of this project.

Various types of assistance eased the considerable transition that the manuscript underwent as it moved from dissertation to book. Tim and Emily Wank provided living and office quarters; 1712 was a memorable venue in which to work. Kevin Hughes served as a research and writing assistant. My visit to see him in Nicaragua helped put my two case studies in further context. Rebekah Smith helped design the map in Chapter 1. There were also several key informants in both of my research sites that put up with a great number of e-mail messages and efforts to verify or double-check claims that are made in this book. I thank them for their patience.

Funding sources for this work must also be acknowledged. These include Boston University's Graduate Research Abroad Program, the Hauser Center for the Study of Non-Profits at Harvard University, the Center for Religion and Public Life at Princeton University, and awards from the Religious Research Association and the Society for the Scientific Study of Religion. Without such funding, this work would not have been possible.

The team at Cambridge University Press also deserves a word of appreciation. Thanks to Lew Bateman for seeing the value in this work and providing needed guidance. Richard Wood has been enormously helpful throughout the process, going above and beyond any normal level of responsibility. Shaun Vigil has also lent a needed hand. I count it a privilege to work with such professionals. Any errors or problems that appear in the book are of course my own.

Thanks must also go to the *Journal of Contemporary Religion*, the *Journal for the Scientific Study of Religion*, and *Pneuma: The Journal for the Society of Pentecostal Studies*. Some pages in this book first appeared in articles published by these journals, and each has graciously allowed for them to be reprinted here.

Most importantly, I wish to thank my family. My grandparents have shown a keen interest in my work and have been a source of encouragement. My parents have been tireless supporters of everything I have done, and this project is no different. They were involved in some of the early efforts to organize the data. My three daughters – Addy, Emily, and Gabi – have come along at different stages of this project and have kept its overall importance in perspective. My wife, Amy, has been my most important intellectual partner. She shared in the field visits, tirelessly listened to different iterations of the book's argument, sharpened my ideas, and helped refine their presentation. For all of these things and so much more, I say thank you.

Abbreviations

AE	African Enterprise
AFM	Apostolic Faith Mission
AG	Assemblies of God
AIC	African Independent Churches
AIDS	Acquired Immune Deficiency Syndrome
ANC	African National Congress
ARENA	The National Republic Alliance
BGA	Billy Graham Association
CAFTA	Central American Free Trade Agreement
CAM	Central American Mission
CCC	Campus Crusade for Christ
CCI	International Christian Center
CCMN	Cell Church Missions Network
CELAM	Conference of Latin American Bishops
CIA	International Center of Praise
Comisal	Committee for Salvadoran Missions
CONESAL	Salvadoran Evangelical Association
COSATU	Congress of South African Trade Unions
DGACE	General Directorate of Attention to the Community Living Abroad
EFSA	Evangelical Fellowship of South Africa
ES	El Salvador
FMLN	Faribundo Marti National Liberation Front
GDOP	Global Day of Prayer
GDP	Gross Domestic Product
HIV	Human Immunodeficiency Virus
IFCC	International Federation of Christian Churches
IFP	Inkatha Freedom Party
MDG	Millennium Development Goals

NCE	New Center of Evangelicalism
NGO	Nongovernmental Organization
NUPSA	Network of United Prayer in South Africa
PAC	Pan Africanist Congress
PCN	Party of National Conciliation
PDC	Christian Democratic Party
SA	South Africa
SABC	South African Broadcasting Corporation
SACC	South African Council of Churches
SACLA	South African Christian Leadership Assembly
SACP	South African Communist Party
SAMS	Southern African Missiological Society
SWAPO	South West Africa People's Organization
TBN	Trinity Broadcasting Network
TEASA	The Evangelical Alliance of South Africa
UNDP	United Nations Development Program
WCD	World Christian Database
WCE	Western Center of Evangelicalism
WEA	World Evangelical Alliance
WV	World Vision
ZCC	Zion Christian Church

Introduction

Oya-Hazel Gumede and Mario Vega represent a new kind of global evangelical. Oya-Hazel grew up in apartheid South Africa. The product of a teenage pregnancy, she was raised by her grandmother in a township called Gezinsila, which literally translated to "wash your filthy dirt." Tragedy marked her life: her mother died of HIV/AIDS, and her father, whom she did not know well, and two of her brothers became victims of the violence that marks post-apartheid South Africa.

In the midst of these hardships, Oya-Hazel had a teenage conversion experience to Pentecostal Christianity. Even before her conversion, Oya-Hazel decided she did not want to become trapped by the spiraling consequences of unwise decisions. She thus opted not to become sexually active as a teenager, a decision that ran counter to the norm in her neighborhood. Oya-Hazel also did well in school and fondly recalls the days her grandmother slaughtered a chicken to celebrate a good report card. Oya-Hazel's newfound faith community reinforced the life decisions that she was making and provided a new spiritual dimension that further motivated her. Buttressed as she was by faith and an instinctive avoidance of constraining social entanglements, Oya-Hazel came of age at the dawning of the new, democratic South Africa, where exciting opportunities opened up before her.

Now in her early forties, Oya-Hazel's intellectual gifts, charisma, and growing pedigree have given her entrée into the cohort of upwardly mobile black South Africans who are helping to craft a new nation. Oya-Hazel's professional activities in South Africa include becoming engaged and involved in the South African executive administration, through working in the office of then First Lady Zanele Mbeki (wife of former South African President Thabo Mbeki), and serving as an advisor for various government ministries. Oya-Hazel has also remained deeply engaged in her faith community, serving as the dean of a church's local Bible Institute and on boards of various Christian organizations across the country. More globally, she has represented South Africa at the United Nations, often represents South Africa at international conferences, and travels into Africa for different business ventures. In 2012 she was named to the Forum of Young Global Leaders, which is part of the World Economic Forum. She traveled to Mexico to participate with other "young leaders who share a commitment to shaping the global future" (Forum of Young Global Leaders 2012). Even in her professional circles, Oya-Hazel freely identifies herself as a follower of Jesus.

Mario spent his childhood in San Salvador, El Salvador's capital city. He was shy and introverted as a child, and when Mario reached his teen years he fell into the wrong crowd. Mario began to use drugs, and by the time he was sixteen he was selling drugs. Eventually Mario's cousin confronted him and took him to church. Mario soon converted to evangelical Christianity, leaving the drugs behind.

Five years later, God told Mario to become a pastor. Mario obeyed, and the church he served grew quickly. Then, when the mother church of this independent Salvadoran denomination, Elim, had a leadership crisis in the late 1990s, they called Mario to become the head pastor. This ushered Mario into a position of public prominence: Elim is currently one of the ten largest churches in the world, with a congregation of roughly 110,000 people. And when the FMLN, a left wing political party that was formerly a coalition of guerilla organizations, won the 2009 presidential elections in El Salvador, Mario delivered the prayer at then President-elect Mauricio Funes's inauguration. Such intersections with political and social spheres are now part of Mario's regular routine.

Evangelicalism has grown rapidly across much of the Global South over the past century. The movement changes as it grows, just as the national and international contexts around it continue to evolve. New converts now maintain a different relationship with mainstream society. Even those who have grown up within the movement are finding new expressions of the faith as they seek to navigate their contemporary contexts. The stories of Oya Hazel and Mario demonstrate these changing trajectories and dynamics, and they reflect the new environments in which they live.

As this evolution takes place, the "new centers" of evangelicalism (NCEs) are becoming socioeconomically diverse, better connected internationally, and increasingly socially engaged. Evangelical leaders and entrepreneurs in these contexts are busily building organizations on a grand scale: booming megachurches in middle class suburbs now balance the numerous storefront churches that continue to dot the poorer sectors of society. No longer content to simply tend to their own flock, such congregations engage in significant social ministries and will on occasion even partner with the state. Evangelicals are also broadening their horizons geographically; their institutions now have transnational identities, and their members cross national borders with regularity. Taken together, these trends and activities are recreating evangelical identity, and they are reorienting the movement's social and political location.

Why are these changes occurring, and what are the consequences? A number of paradigms are competing to explain the emergence of global evangelicalism and the broader category of global Christianity. Scholars have linked evangelicalism's global expansion to U.S. military interests, U.S. cultural influence, or both. Others have framed the growth as a prominent component of religious fundamentalism's emergence across the globe. A third school of thought posits that the Pentecostal explosion is the religious extension of modernity into cultures that have heretofore resisted it. A fourth perspective argues that the massive demographic shifts within global Christianity have wrested control of the religion away from the West. In this conception, Christianity is dominated by new faces, and it is primarily a faith of the Global South and East. All of these paradigms have merit, and they are carefully considered in Chapter 1. Few, however, shed great insight on the internal dynamics of global evangelicalism that interest this study, nor the religious motors of change that drive them.

Robert Wuthnow (2009) has recently introduced a fifth paradigm that captures part of this picture. Wuthnow shows the extent to which global flows of goods, people, services, and communication exist within Christianity and argues that these flows connect Christians in different parts of the globe. He further demonstrates that Christianity's growth in the post-colonial Global South is happening in concert with expanding global flows to these regions; it is not happening, as has been claimed elsewhere, because agents of Western Christianity have withdrawn from these regions. To buttress his argument, Wuthnow points to American churches' increased religious spending, increased numbers of full-time missionaries, the explosion of short-term mission teams, and heightened interest in humanitarian causes across the world. All of these represent mechanisms by which American religious influence, buoyed by the country's considerable cultural and economic power, is being felt beyond its own borders.

Wuthnow's interest is, however, primarily in showing the global outreach of American churches. He stops short of making key claims about the kind of impact and change that such activities might be having in NCEs. In some respects, I pick up the story where Wuthnow left off, but I reframe his global flows as one of a number of religious social forces, both international and local, that are changing the reality of faith communities in two particular places: El Salvador and South Africa. Put differently, I identify the global and local religious forces at work in NCEs, the impacts that they have, and how the trends they initiate are being played out.

El Salvador and South Africa are particularly interesting cases for a number of reasons. There are striking similarities between the two: the evangelical movement has thrived in both countries and now constitutes at least a quarter, or in El Salvador's case at least a third, of their national populations (IUDOP 2009; Johnson 2014; Pew Forum 2011; Teichert 2005). El Salvador and South Africa also have surprisingly similar histories over the past half century. This has made them comparable politically and economically as well as religiously, as Elisabeth

Wood (2000) has demonstrated. And yet the contrasts between the two are many. African and Latin American cultures are clearly distinct, and as the evangelical faith is integrated into each, different dynamics within the same global movement emerge. The legacy of different colonial histories, one Spanish and the other British and Dutch, also persists. Finally, geopolitical locations still matter; sharing a hemisphere with the United States has implications for El Salvador that South Africa need not address. These comparable yet contrasting dynamics make the two cases excellent fodder for a cross-continent analysis of a global religious movement.

OLD TIME EVANGELICALISM

The term "evangelicalism" is notoriously difficult to define and overlaps considerably with terms like Pentecostalism and Christianity. I explain the meanings of each more fully in the following chapter, but put briefly, evangelicals have a high regard for the Bible and feel compelled to share the "Good News," or the "evangel" of Christ's death and resurrection. Pentecostals share these beliefs but emphasize the work of the Holy Spirit and have enthusiastic worship practices that not all evangelicals share.

Pentecostal evangelicalism is the strain that dominates today's NCEs, and it has a history of multiple beginnings. John Wesley's Aldersgate experience in 1738 and the 1906 Azusa Street Revival in Los Angeles are important moments in Pentecostal history. So too are independent manifestations of the Spirit that occurred in locations across the Global South. India, Chile, (Sepulveda 2011), Uganda (Cassidy 1989), and South Africa (Elphick & Davenport 1997) are just a few of the locations that witnessed their own "manifestations of the Spirit." These events soon became interlinked, and a truly global religious movement emerged.

Classical Pentecostal denominations were a critical early component of today's evangelical communities. These include but are not limited to the Assemblies of God, Four Square Gospel Churches, Apostolic Faith Mission, Church of the Nazarene, and the Church of God in Christ. Such denominations originated in, or were heavily influenced by, the 1906 Azusa Street Revival and from there spread quickly around the world.

Classical Pentecostalism is, however, only part of the story. In some regions of the globe, they are predated by ancient Christian communities of non-Western origin (Sanneh 2003; Walls 2002). Local manifestations of the evangelical movement were often rooted in these longstanding traditions. In other areas, Western missionaries made inroads into local cultures, planting mission churches and starting other types of non-Pentecostal, evangelical congregations. Even today's main-line churches had a role to play, as Anglican, Lutheran, Presbyterian, Methodist, and Baptist denominations created a context in which an evangelical faith could be cultivated and nurtured. None of these actors experienced the kind of growth witnessed within classical

Pentecostalism, but they were critical to establishing the early context of the global evangelical movement.

It was thus that the foundations of NCEs had been laid by the late nineteenth and early twentieth centuries, although Asian, African, and Latin American evangelicals remained remote outposts of their global faith community throughout the first half of the twentieth century. In these developing country contexts, evangelicals were particularly poor, uneducated, marginalized, and reclusive. They were considered to be the "yahoos" of society as they conducted noisy, sometimes chaotic religious events in public spaces and avoided, or were denied access to, mainstream social institutions. Such a popular religious movement had little appeal to educated and more powerful members of society; these more sophisticated sectors tended to either chuckle at evangelical antics or look upon them with disdain.

Post–World War Evangelicalism

The post–World War II period brought both consistency and change. Much of evangelicalism's identity remained the same, but this was a period in which accelerated expansion occurred. In Latin America, reasons for (and rates of) growth were different from country to country, but it was nonetheless a region-wide phenomenon. In Africa, the time line for classical Pentecostalism was different: the Azusa Street Revival denominations gained a stronger early foothold, especially in southern Africa, but they also generated splinter groups that came to be known as African Independent Churches (AICs) (Anderson 2004). Partly because these splinter movements did not stay within the broader faith community of the earlier groups, strong growth did not occur within evangelical Pentecostalism beyond its early establishment. Growth did, however, accelerate again roughly a decade later than it did in Latin America (Martin 2002). That this expansion coincided with the rollback of formal colonial structures is interpreted by many as no accident. The end of formal colonialism began with the emancipation of Ghana in 1957 and concluded with the end of apartheid in South Africa in 1994. The number of African Christians increased perhaps a hundredfold during these years.

A larger evangelical population enabled the movement to have more clearly identifiable but always flexible characteristics. The first and most obvious of these was that evangelical growth occurred predominantly in poor neighborhoods and villages. Evangelical conversions often occurred in moments of crisis, frequently brought on by severe poverty, intense social conflict, or both. The movement as a whole represented a "walkout" on society (Martin 1990), essentially inviting marginalization and oppression from the dominant religious and cultural groups. Converts thus tended to be those with little to lose even when evangelicals grew to be upwards of 10 percent of national populations. Poverty, after all, was (and is) rife throughout the Global South and certainly far more prevalent than even the largest religious movements. But it was during this period that humble evangelical churches became fixtures in slums and poor villages across the developing world.

A second prominent feature of evangelical communities during the Cold War was their flat, relatively egalitarian social networks. Conversion to evangelicalism often included extrication of individuals from (usually the bottom of) religious and social hierarchies. The lay-driven congregational forms of evangelicalism were not based on such vertical relationships, even if significant power was wielded by the local pastor. As Martin (1990) noted, local evangelical pastors may wield power autocratically, but the organizational structure in which they do so causes centralized authority to be spread out and multiplied. Gender relationships within nuclear families were reordered among new converts (Brusco 1986), and scholars of that time period went so far as to say that many men were essentially domesticated when they became evangelicals. Such results may well be a motivating factor for women's central role in the spread of evangelicalism. The general effect led Martin (1990) to claim that the evangelical movement carried within it values of greater social equality.

Third, pre-1990 evangelicals were characterized by their ascetic practices and social withdrawal. Although not always identified as such, these two characteristics were closely connected. For evangelicals, extramarital sexual relations and any form of alcohol consumption were clearly taboo. In most cultures, dancing was also prohibited. This meant that evangelical converts stopped frequenting mainstream public spaces such as bars and canteens, opting instead for church meetings four to five nights a week. The church meetings increased social capital among evangelicals, but it often sidelined them from creating bridging relationships with actors of influence in the broader community. Add this to the fact that evangelicalism remained a minority and often a scorned religion during the time period, and it was clear that evangelical retreat to congregational life, in part made necessary by restrictions on mainstream cultural activities, set them apart from broader social events, processes, and activities.

Such social tendencies affected evangelical political life. With the exceptions of Brazil, Guatemala, Zambia, and a few other notable outliers in this respect, early evangelicals chose not to participate in existing political structures. This did not imply that they were uninterested in creating positive social change. On the contrary, they were highly interested in doing so. But they believed that converting ever higher ratios of the public to evangelical Christianity was the most effective way of ameliorating social ills such as violence, corruption, and inequality (Smith 1994).

The political process, on the other hand, was viewed as part and parcel of these kinds of problems. Evangelicals avoided political systems because of their perceived (and real) corruption; they reasoned that they could not help but become corrupt themselves if they became politically active. Based on this logic, numerous denominations even prohibited their members from voting. Extra systemic political activities, such as armed insurrection or public protest, were also generally not considered options. This was especially so for Pentecostals, who carried strong traditions of quietism and even pacifism.

When in the 1980s some evangelicals began to think differently about these issues and to seek strategies by which they could have a voice in the national political discourse, they often chose to start evangelical political parties. This strategy was only viable in countries where the electoral and political party system permitted new parties to enter the scene. Such parties allowed evangelicals to steer clear of the this-worldly corruption that surely accompanied mainstream party involvement. But most evangelical parties garnered such a small number of votes that they did not last more than an election cycle or two. There were some exceptions to this rule, of course, and as time wore on, more evangelicals realized that their primary strategy to create social change, evangelism, might need to be accompanied by political engagement to be effective. This set the stage for new strategies to be introduced after 1990.

A final evangelical characteristic of this period was an entrepreneurial bent. The impetus to create new organizations seems to be part of the evangelical DNA. New churches were springing up at remarkable rates. Some of these were the result of Western missionary initiatives, but most were not. Evangelicals in NCEs were also active in local economic entrepreneurship. One of the earliest scholars to study Latin American evangelicalism, Willems (1967), used the term "penny capitalism" to describe evangelical initiatives in Brazil and Chile. Although Willems used this term to indicate that evangelicals' ascetic behavior had only a limited impact on their economic advancement, numerous authors since then have argued for a link between present day evangelicalism and Max Weber's Protestant ethic. Indeed, Peter Berger is fond of saying that "Max Weber is alive and well and living in Guatemala." In pre-1990 Africa, however, this case was more difficult to make. The impulse to start new churches was certainly evident, but other forms of entrepreneurship were obscured by competing cultural values and practices. Still, examples could be found where entrepreneurial impulses led to modest religious and economic organizational formulations throughout the developing world.

RELIGIOUS SOCIAL FORCES

Today, a number of these characteristics no longer apply to evangelicals living in places like El Salvador and South Africa. Any effort to understand why rapid changes are occurring in NCEs must acknowledge that there are many different factors in the global, national, and grassroots environments that are spurring the evangelical movement in new directions. Global political realities, such as the end of the bipolar world system and increased religious freedoms in many national contexts, certainly play a role. So too do international and national economic trends, including reduced barriers to trade and the increased presence of multinational corporations across Africa, Asia, and Latin America. Even social trends, perhaps most notably variations in birth rates and increased transience around the world, impact the shape and nature of national faith communities.

Such political, economic, and social dynamics intersect with the *religious* social forces that are most directly affecting evangelicalism. A religious social force is one in which religious symbols, resources, actors, or organizations are in motion and are setting other (in this case religious) symbols, actors, or organizations in motion. Such forces can be global or local. They can be ideational or material. An important premise of this book is that such forces, although they do not act to the exclusion of other types of social forces, are formative in determining the direction of change in NCEs.

But where exactly do religious social forces come from? Why are they so important in creating change within faith communities? Perhaps the best method to answer such questions is to list the most prominent religious social forces currently at work in NCEs and to introduce them in categories that will help to map the terrain that they cover.

Global Religious Social Forces

There are three basic kinds of global religious social forces. Religious transnational networks that penetrate national evangelical communities like El Salvador and South Africa are the first. Evangelicals in these regions have had transnational ties since their genesis, but today's faith communities take advantage of the many globalizing trends in society to create tighter and more wide-ranging connections. Evangelical activities and relationships that cross borders include participation in the international political economy, international connections between local congregations based in the United States and other countries, and the creation and maintenance of international nongovernmental organizations (NGOs) and other ministry organizations (Reynolds & Offutt 2014). At the grassroots level, migration worldwide has rapidly increased since the early 1990s, and ease of travel and communication now allow migrants to maintain community across borders (Levitt 2007). Religious networks and organizations of all types, including evangelical ones, are deeply embedded in this larger social phenomenon (Cadge & Ecklund 2007; Ebaugh & Chafetz 2002; Levitt 2007; Sheringham 2013; Wuthnow & Offutt 2008). These and other types of transnational networks are allowing foreign influences to affect local evangelical communities from multiple directions and at multiple levels.

Religious symbols are a second global religious force. Symbols entering national evangelical communities in the Global South carry religious meaning, and they are powerful enough to reorient how faith communities think about the sacred and ultimately how they structure their social lives. They travel through the transnational networks just mentioned, or they come as free-floating signifiers, passing through mass media and other tools of global communication (Csordas 1997). One group or constellation of symbols that has particularly impacted national evangelical communities has become known as the prosperity gospel. Its message has been refined in places like Tulsa, Oklahoma, at the late Kenneth Hagin, Sr.'s Rhema Bible Institute (Harrison 2005) and has been exported all over the world. Other symbols invading evangelical communities in the Global South and East include a call to do missionary service in "the four corners of the earth," the Christ as a highly relational figure, and the conception of prayer. These symbols have served as catalysts for certain forms of social organization within and beyond national evangelical communities.

Resources, a third global religious social force, also flow into the NCEs. Such resources may be knowledge based, material, or human. They include people, products, money, services, and information. They often flow from North to South via evangelical denominations, from migrants back home to their families, from evangelical NGOs to sites of disaster or places in need of economic development, and from missionary or ministry organizations to people they wish to serve. Specific resource flows include missionaries and NGO personnel, educational material, relief supplies (such as food, blankets, and clothing), and information or knowledge about the broader world. These resources are sometimes spread more or less evenly throughout evangelical communities in places like El Salvador and South Africa; at other times, they are consolidated in the hands of leaders and used to create or maintain power. In both cases, transnational resources are helping to foment change in the Global South.

Local Religious Social Forces

When transnational networks, symbols, and resources arrive in the NCEs, they intermingle with local religious forces. Such forces often look similar to those that operate globally: local symbols commingle with global symbols and local resources complement global resources. To return to the prosperity gospel example, some sectors of African Christianity had independently developed corresponding themes of prosperity in their own understanding of the faith (Marshall-Fratani 2001; Maxwell 1999; Meyer 1998). Local and global prosperity symbols then merged, the synergy of which has had powerful cultural implications. But the prosperity gospel is not alone in seeing its formation come from multicultural negotiation of meaning. Any time religious people and ideas cross cultural borders, they encounter different meaning systems, and their own meanings must be renegotiated. This occurs daily and in manifold ways as local and global forces meet in the new centers of evangelicalism.

It is critical for those examining the impact of global forces, whether religious, political, or economic, to recognize and acknowledge that the local communities with which they interact have been socially sustainable for a very long time. Local decision making occurs on an ongoing basis. A long history of social learning predates any form of global interference. There are almost always longstanding local institutions around which civil society has been built. Local churches are often among the most important of these types of institutions, and while they certainly change in the midst of globalization, they maintain a sturdy and distinctly local identity through it all. These facts should, in fact they must, force scholars to be modest in the claims they make about globalization's mono-causal ability to create change. They should also prompt scholars to take into account locally driven dynamics of change and to examine the interaction these might have with the forces of globalization.

Within NCEs, the most important local religious social force continues to be evangelicalism's entrepreneurial spirit. This again is consistent with evangelical-ism at least since Willems's writings, but whereas in the previous era entrepre-neurs were operating with sparse local resources, evangelicals today are grabbing hold of the transnational symbols and intellectual and material resour-ces that populate their newly globalized environments to build ever larger move-ments, religious organizations, and businesses. The change in the scale of entrepreneurial products is such that it is significantly changing the institutional makeup of the faith community.

Evangelicalism is a movement that exhibits remarkable global coherence, but the diversity among national faith communities remains strong. These differences can be attributed in no small part to other local religious social forces, including the different ways such communities choose to structure social relationships, varying cultural norms that develop within religious communities, longstanding local organizations and institutions, important local religious symbols that have possibly been borrowed from religions of a bygone era, and a plurality of beliefs within the broadening tent of evangelical doctrines. In addition to the national political economies that also influence the trajectories of local faith communities, such local religious social forces work with and against the global religious social forces at work in the NCEs.

Stepping Stones of Social Change

As synergies are developed between local and global religious forces, national faith communities begin to change in size and social location. The dramatic increase in the number of evangelicals in the Global South and East has been well documented. Many believe there are more than 500 million Pentecostals world-wide (Pew Forum 2011), and their most explosive rates of growth are found in Africa, Asia, and Latin America. In Latin America, for instance, 64 million evangelicals are creating a new religious pluralism in the region (Allen 2006). In Africa, adherents of the Christian faith grew from 30 million in 1945 to an estimated 380 million in 2005 (Carpenter 2005), with particularly sharp growth in Pentecostal churches and denominations. These developments make the South more important within global Christianity (Jenkins 2002) and make evangelical communities more prominent in the national societies that house them. For these reasons, the movement's growth has grabbed headlines and captured the world's attention even as other forces spur more significant change within the communities themselves.

As these communities grow, they also increase in socioeconomic diversity. Although the majority of evangelicals are still poor, leading churches have been established in the business classes and among the university educated across the southern hemisphere. The upward trend is consistent with longstanding social theory and observation; H. Richard Niebuhr wrote that "the churches of the poor all become middle-class churches sooner or later" ([1929] 1957, 54). Niebuhr points to restrictions on consumption and an emphasis on production as the motors for such upward social mobility, and he notes that "there is no doubt of the truth of Max Weber's contention that godliness is conducive to economic success" ([1929] 1957, 54). Pentecostals and evangelicals in the Global South have demonstrated a strong penchant toward both of Niebuhr's causal mechanisms for increased wealth (Brusco 1986; Martin 1990, 2002; Smilde 2007). They have practiced a godly asceticism and possess an inspired energy that together have pushed many up the economic ladder. And although Niebuhr's analysis primarily follows historical religious developments in Western contexts, the same kinds of dynamics are just as evident in Africa. Jean Comaroff (1985), for example, has traced the movement of the mission churches from the periphery to the center of local communities, with the African Independent Churches (AICs) following suit.

The increasing size of the movement and the shift in its social location are themselves certainly new and developing features of evangelicalism. But as they are put into motion, they become powerful sources of change themselves. The social location of a movement is often a determining factor with respect to the kinds of characteristics and identity markers it maintains (Weber 1978). Likewise, the size of a movement has significant implications for the quantity of resources it contains and attracts, and it also is a determining factor in the kind of interactions that can occur with other social and political entities in society.

Size and social location thus introduce a stepladder effect to social change. In other words, these changes are part of the evolution of local faith communities, but they also become forces of change themselves.

NEW CHARACTERISTICS OF THE NEW CENTERS OF EVANGELICALISM

Although evangelicals in NCEs today maintain the basic faith identity formulated by their forebears, they have taken on important new characteristics. More than two decades have now passed since the end of the Cold War, allowing such characteristics to become firmly rooted. The following is a brief introductory description of the six most important of these characteristics. Each will be more fully explored in the book's subsequent chapters.

Exporters of Religion – NCEs have long imported religious people and products. Indeed they still do, and in higher volumes than ever before. But today evangelicals in places like El Salvador and South Africa are initiating flows of missionaries, radio programs, publications, and other goods and services that cross national as well as continental borders. Such initiatives are making the traditional networks between North and South stronger by introducing some modicum of reciprocity into the relationships. They are also forging South–South ties that have never before existed, as Salvadoran churches partner with Chinese churches, and South African churches extend networks into Argentina and elsewhere. A redistribution of initiative facilitates the redistribution of power, and it is likely to reduce the power imbalance that has long characterized relations between North and South within the structures of global evangelicalism.

Big Organizations – Whether they are planting churches, starting NGOs, or building businesses in the private sector, evangelicals in the NCEs have acquired the knowledge and resources to build remarkably large organizations. The Elim church in San Salvador, as mentioned earlier, now has more than 110,000 congregants. It is also the mother church of some forty congregations in the United States. Another Salvadoran evangelical started a school for the deaf with just $57 and the support of her local church. The school now owns its own building, has multiple teachers for each grade level, and employs cutting-edge education for hearing impaired students. It is so respected in El Salvador that the national government has consulted the school as it tries to expand its own programs for the hearing impaired. In South Africa, an evangelical has developed a consortium of companies with interests throughout Africa, the Middle East, the United States, and elsewhere. These organizations are the result of the entrepreneurial inclination already discussed, and they represent an institutional robustness that was absent in earlier epochs of the movement.

Hierarchical Social Networks – Egalitarian networks have long been a feature characterization of evangelicalism, and many relationships within the faith community have maintained their more egalitarian orientation. But the remarkable growth of some evangelical institutions has created a tiered system of networks within the movement. Larger organizations serve as platforms for their leaders to participate in national and international networks. When they do, they often leave behind the flat, associational neighborhood networks of churches that scholar Philip Berryman (1999) described. Along the dusty streets in Elim's neighborhood, for example, there are a number of storefront churches. In spite of their proximity, it is not likely that Elim's senior pastor is able to engage in an egalitarian network structure with the leaders of these small congregations. Rather, Elim and its pastor wield significantly more social power than the typical storefront church and may soon leave their lower class community for nicer facilities and more comfortable surroundings – a move that reveals how different Elim is to its current storefront neighbors.

Shifting Beliefs and Actions – Core beliefs within the evangelical movement have remained stable through the various social changes that it has undergone. However, there has been a pluralization of what evangelicals believe are the implications of the core teachings. For example, one core teaching to which there is unanimous consent is that God sent His son, Jesus, to die on the cross for the whole world because He loved the whole world. Many evangelicals continue to believe that they experience this love in their hearts, and that a relationship with Jesus provides meaning to their thoughts and actions without significant implications for their material conditions. But newer strands of evangelicalism increasingly believe that there is a material element to God's love as expressed through Christ. Most, but not all, of those who hold this belief can be found within the Word of Faith or prosperity gospel movement.

Changes and diversification in the praxis of evangelicalism are also afoot. Today, many evangelicals blend more easily into the mainstream than earlier generations. Their habit of conspicuously carrying the Bible with them during their daily routines is waning, and the differentiation in clothing between evangelicals and mainstream culture has all but disappeared. In short, evangelicals are changing the way they engage the outside world, a trend that is heightened as the movement inhabits new social locations.

Increasing Social Engagement – When converts to evangelicalism restructured their social networks by removing themselves from public spaces such as bars and dance halls, they developed a strong ethic of helping each other. They did not, however, earn the reputation of helping others. This was not entirely fair because in the early days evangelicals were simply too few and too marginalized to have a social impact. When they did reach outside their faith communities, they felt the first and by far most important step they could take was to share their faith with others.

Today, evangelicals display a reformulated understanding of social engagement. Larger congregations and less social marginalization enable evangelicals to more confidently reach beyond the four walls of their congregations. Greater resources and a more holistic understanding of the gospel are motivating them to engage directly with social needs rather than trying only to share their faith. Donald Miller and Tetsunao Yamamori (2007) have also noted the orientation to social outreach among some Pentecostals. I provide a different explanation for these developments, but regardless of how it is interpreted, there can be little doubt that while job one among evangelicals in the Global South remains saving souls, they are also serious about pursuing a broadened social agenda.

Integrated Political Engagement – Although evangelicals in some countries started their own political parties to engage in politics, most such parties met with limited success. Even evangelicals did not support them, by and large, at the ballot box. Many were defunct after one or two election cycles. Evangelicals have shifted their focus; they are now more willing to become integrated into existing political parties, processes, and institutions. The plurality of political views and methods of engagement among evangelicals bedevils efforts of easy categorization. Evangelicals can be found praying at the presidential inauguration of former leftist guerillas, working behind the scenes to bring together actors across the political spectrum, and vehemently espousing the most conservative ideologies. They can also be found participating in clientelistic relationships and accepting bribes. In many cases, class and social locations of evangelicals are greater determinants of political leanings than religious affiliation. What is clear, though, is that the perception that evangelicals ought not get their hands dirty by being active party members is fading rapidly. The political activity of evangelicals is an important part of their new approach to participation in the *polis* and of a more integrated approach to civic activity.

Together, these six characteristics show a global movement that is moving up, getting larger, and taking a more prominent place in society. Such developments beg the question: Is evangelicalism changing the societies in which it resides? Perhaps, but that is not the question raised here. Rather, this book is focused on the internal changes of global evangelicalism itself.

HOW THE STUDY WAS CONDUCTED

This study has been uniquely built on a cross-continent, in-depth ethnographic look at two countries, El Salvador and South Africa, which are located in two of global evangelicalism's new centers. In all, I conducted 118 interviews with leading evangelicals, including the heads of the evangelical alliances, senior pastors of megachurches, entrepreneurs working in the private sector, and key members of civil society. I attended church services and evangelical leadership meetings, and I lived in the homes of some of my subjects. These strategies built on the nearly five years of combined previous experience I had in these two countries.

My research uncovered variation between African and Latin American evangelicalism. Variants include the way in which evangelicals interface with power, the conceptualization of healing, the frequency and role of visions in directing faith communities, the kind of prosperity theology that is emerging, and the interface between evangelical social structure and preexisting social structures, to name just a few. However, there are also broad themes and trends within evangelicalism that look strikingly similar in the two research locations. This is true in part because it is the same global religious movement that is being traced in these two places, but it is also because there are similarities as well as differences in the histories and experiences lived out in these regions. Such convergences allow for greater homogeneity of global movements generally; evangelicalism is no exception.

Further details of my research methodology, including who I interviewed, the churches I studied, and how I selected these two countries can be found in Appendices I and II.

MAP OF THE BOOK

The book is divided into three sections. The first section lays the groundwork for the book's argument. Chapter 1 defines the term "evangelical" and provides an overview of the different schools of thought currently used to explain Global

Christianity. Chapter 2 introduces the country contexts of El Salvador and South Africa. This is followed by the second section, which addresses the different kinds of religious social forces that are acting upon NCEs. Chapter 3 examines global religious social forces and the people in NCEs who interface most directly with them. Chapter 4 looks at local religious social forces, particularly local entrepreneurs. The final section of the book examines the new characteristics that have emerged in NCEs. Chapter 5 considers the new social contours and global reach of NCEs. Special emphasis is placed on the new evangelical social hierarchy, the increasing size and complexity of their organizations, and the newfound ability to export religion across borders. Chapter 6 examines new strategies of public engagement in NCEs. These include higher levels of social ministries and new strategies of political engagement. The Conclusion reviews the argument put forward in the book and considers basic principles that may be relevant for other global religious phenomenon.

I

A New Way of Thinking about a Global Faith

On Sunday mornings, people all over the world wake up, have breakfast, and go to their local church. When they get there, they learn that many aspects of their church aren't very local. On any given Sunday, they might find out about short-term mission opportunities, speakers visiting from other countries, or international humanitarian aid projects. The people in the pews next to them might have recently migrated from a different country. Conversely, letters might be read from former members of the congregation who have crossed borders to live in a new place. The pastor might discuss relationships the church has with sister congregations in far-off lands, transnational denominational projects, or other visions the church has to affect the world with the gospel. In short, simply by going to church, people see the international dimensions of local congregations.

It is thus quite easy to find evidence for the notion of global, rather than geographically bound, faith communities. But even the most basic questions about how global faith communities work show the complexities that lurk just below the surface. One might ask, for example, who is in a given global faith community, and how is this decided? Or how do members of global faith communities relate to one another across borders? One might even ask: How do changes in one corner of the globe affect members in another part of the world? Scholars considering such questions are engaged in lively debates as they seek to properly portray the big picture of global faith communities.

Efforts to analyze global Christian communities have resulted in a colorful array of competing terms and dueling frameworks. The most commonly used terms in these debates are Christianity, Pentecostalism, and evangelicalism. While authors tend to focus on one or the other of these terms, their collective efforts represent a single body of literature. Still, how these categories are broken down must be explained – I begin the chapter with that task. I then lay out the conceptualizations of Christianity that are currently the most useful. I close the chapter by introducing my own framework for analyzing global Christianity, which is built around the concept of *religious social forces.*

GLOBAL CHRISTIANS, PENTECOSTALS, OR EVANGELICALS – WHAT'S THE DIFFERENCE?

Three terms are often used to describe the religious movement of interest in this book: Christianity, Pentecostalism, and evangelicalism. Of these, Christianity is by far the largest group and the one that needs the least introduction. The term encompasses all major strands of the faith, be they based in Constantinople, Rome, Geneva, Salt Lake City, or elsewhere. A Jesus Movement hippie in Los Angeles, for example, may not seem to have much in common with a sharply dressed Presbyterian in Seoul, or a Russian Orthodox priest in Moscow. But all three would fall into the category of Christianity. Lines can blur when one encounters a Muslim follower of Jesus or other cases in which people may have a foot in more than one world religion. But for the most part, Christianity, though exceedingly wide and possibly including more than 2 billion people, is a distinct and self-contained entity.[1]

Two great schisms in the early church created the three historic branches of Christianity. The Great Schism of 1054 formally divided the Catholic Church, based in Rome, from the Eastern Orthodox Church, based in Constantinople. Over time, these two seats of eastern and western Christianity developed different Christian cultures. The second major schism was the Protestant Reformation, formally initiated by Martin Luther in 1517. Protestantism would itself prove to be inherently schismatic as different denominations spun off in a multitude of directions. But despite its infighting and heterogeneity, Protestantism continues to be a useful and dominant category of Western Christianity.

---

[1] Christianity, Pentecostalism, and evangelicalism are not, in this case, theological terms. Rather, they are social categories whose memberships are determined by sociological criteria. Theology can certainly influence the boundaries and behaviors of social groups and networks. I acknowledge this reality and include beliefs in the definitions of specific groups. Ultimately, however, I am more interested in evaluating the results of how religious groups react, fracture, and regroup than in examining a faith community's theology.

Using these terms to signify categories or social groups is also a departure from efforts to use self-identification to determine religious affiliation. A person cannot simply claim to be a member of a faith community and it is so. It is not a new phenomenon for public figures to affiliate themselves with a religion to capitalize on political or other advantages that could be gained by membership. These self-affiliations are sometimes made in spite of a lack of relational or institutional ties to the religious group in question. The approach used here is more community oriented: it requires that people identify with a religious group *and* that other members of the group agree to this identity-based claim. Individuals do not, ultimately, have the final say about whether they belong to a certain group. Rather, membership is negotiated both by those who seek entrance and by the existing members of the community.

Finally, some scholars are now pointing to a "fourth wave" of Christianity (Tennent 2010). Churches with no direct lineage to Rome, Constantinople, or the Reformation now dot the Global South and East. Many African Independent Churches, the house church movement in Asia, and independent Pentecostal denominations in Latin America are part of this fourth wave.

Evangelicalism and Pentecostalism have their roots in Protestantism but spill into the three other categories of Christianity. A person might, for example, define himself or (more likely) herself as a Catholic evangelical Pentecostal, or a Catholic charismatic, which has a close relationship with both Pentecostalism and evangelicalism. Similar statements could be made by adherents of Eastern Orthodoxy or by a member of a Chinese underground church. Such developments signal that evangelicalism and Pentecostalism are not entirely confined by millennia-old boundaries within Christendom, and in fact have made some progress in eroding them.

The differences between Pentecostalism and evangelicalism are complex. As mentioned in the Introduction, the origins of global Pentecostalism are several, and the expressions of Pentecostalism are diverse (Anderson 2004). It has roots in the Wesleyan revivals in England during the nineteenth century. The Pentecostal fires passed through the United States near the turn of the twentieth century, specifically Azusa Street in Los Angeles, before they spun out all over the globe, partly on the wings of U.S. cultural radiation (Chesnut 1997; Martin 2002). Although Pentecostalism voyaged through U.S. territory and has tarried there for more than 100 years, it is neither originally nor primarily an American story; it is an international phenomenon.

Pentecostal growth has been well documented. A widely accepted estimate puts the number of Pentecostals worldwide at 500 million (Pew Forum 2006), and their most explosive rates of growth are found in Africa, Asia, and Latin America. In Latin America, for instance, the Pew Forum (2011) charts the growth of Pentecostals to have gone from 12.6 million adherents in 1970 to 156.9 million in 2005. In Africa, the overall Christian population grew from 30 million in 1945 to an estimated 380 million in 2005 (Carpenter 2005). All of these numbers must be taken with caution, and the most careful scholars speak only in general terms. But all agree that the growth of the movement has been massive and global.

Deciding who is and who is not a Pentecostal is tricky, partly because its "defining" characteristics have migrated into other Christian traditions and partly because it is constantly growing, experimenting, and reinventing itself. A "second blessing," or an encounter with the Holy Spirit that takes place after an initial conversion experience, is a central component of most definitions of what it means to be Pentecostal. Pentecostalism is almost always a subset of Christianity, and perhaps the fastest-growing one over the last century, but it sometimes rubs up against even the bounds of Christendom. David Martin states that "[Pentecostalism] is a repertoire of religious explorations controlled, though sometimes barely, within a Christian frame and apt for adaptation in myriad indigenous contexts" (2002, 6). The extraordinary flexibility of Pentecostalism is a chief reason it spreads so easily, but it also lends the movement to having sharp divides within.

Evangelical identity, on the other hand, is more conscientiously and directly affiliated with the Reformation. Evangelicals fancy themselves to have a more direct link to Luther, Calvin, Wesley, and in some corners even St. Augustine than non-evangelical Pentecostals or, for that matter, liberal Protestants. In non-Western contexts, evangelical identity is also in general more concerned about issues of orthodoxy than Pentecostal identity. Put differently, whereas Pentecostalism has a perceived historical newness about it, evangelicalism is more rooted in the Western expression of the Christian faith. It must, however, be immediately pointed out that, while these observations hold in a general sense, individuals, congregations, and denominations can (and do) maintain both identities simultaneously. Thus, while distinct, the two terms are far from mutually exclusive.

Certain characteristics and institutions provide the still nimble and adaptable evangelical faith with a global coherence. David Bebbington's definition (1989) of evangelicalism – which is centered on four principles: an emphasis on conversion or a need for change in one's life, an active bent toward sharing the gospel, a high regard for the Bible, and an emphasis on Christ's atoning work on the cross – continues to be the most appropriate within the international context. Such beliefs are carried and reinforced by hallmark global evangelical networks, including the Lausanne Movement, which Billy Graham helped found, and the World Evangelical Alliance. Today, many Pentecostals fit Bebbington's definition and circulate in these networks.

I use the terms evangelical and Pentecostal as nouns to signify existing religious communities. The terms can also be used adjectivally. In fact, it is only within the past few decades that an evangelical community has been constructed in many African countries. Previously, it would have been more accurate to suggest that this or that mission group had an evangelical orientation, but its primary identity remained denominational – Baptists or Anglicans, for example – with the term "evangelical" serving as a descriptive detail. Today, there is a stronger sense of a cross-denominational evangelical community, although smaller groups continue to hold onto their own identities.

So who are the Pentecostals and evangelicals in El Salvador and South Africa? Pentecostals predominate in these two religious milieus, just as they do in most new centers of evangelicalism (NCEs). But the term *evangelicalism* is more useful in understanding faith communities. In South Africa, this is because a critical split exists within Pentecostalism between evangelical Pentecostals and the Pentecostal African Independent Churches (AICs). The latter groups maintain similar worship practices to the former groups, but they deviate enough on fundamental doctrines and maintain such cultural separation that neither group considers the other to be part of the same faith community. The evangelical community, on the other hand, unites evangelical Pentecostals and non-Pentecostal evangelicals.

Differences remain and infighting exists, but the bickering is mutually understood to be "insider bickering," or conflict within a single faith community. Thus, an evangelical Anglican in South Africa deploys the full weight of his religious rhetoric against Neo-Pentecostal prosperity teachings and yet immediately, although a bit glumly, concedes that he and they are co-religionists. Conversely, a member of the Apostolic Faith Mission (AFM), which has its origins in the Azusa Street revivals, speaks of the need to evangelize members of the Zion Christian Church (ZCC), one of the AICs, or the Zulu-dominated Shembe movement. This is a clear indication she does not consider such AICs as brothers and sisters in the faith (in spite of the fact that the ZCC was part of the AFM until it broke away in the early twentieth century).[2]

The split between Pentecostals is a critical social reality that is sometimes glossed over by scholars of global evangelicalism. Jean Comaroff most eloquently explains the relationship of most AICs to evangelicals: "Zionism is part of a second global culture; a culture, lying in the shadow of the first, whose distinct but similar symbolic orders are the imaginative constructions of the resistant periphery of the world system" (Comaroff 1985, 254). In this book, I argue that NCEs are being constructed mostly by local actors, but they are embedded in global relationships and they are part of a global community. This stands in contrast to Zionism and other AICs in South Africa that are far less infiltrated by outside cultures and meaning systems. In other words, evangelicalism is in conversation with, rather than in the shadow of, the global culture to which Comaroff refers. This is perhaps the best way of understanding that AICs and evangelicals, although both are largely Pentecostal, are not part of the same faith community.

There are further complexities to the South African evangelical community. While the boundaries between evangelicalism and AICs in South Africa are defined, the boundaries between evangelicals and main-line or more progressive Protestants, the third Christian group, are porous. This is because mainline Protestantism tends to be more conservative both socially and theologically than its counterparts in the Northern Hemisphere, thus a higher ratio of their churches tends to be evangelical in South Africa. In addition to a blurry outer boundary, the fissures within the evangelical community, such as the example of the Anglican and the prosperity adherents just mentioned, complicate the notion of a single, multidenominational faith community.

It is nonetheless possible to find a broad consensus among evangelical leaders concerning who is in their ranks and who is not. The membership lists of evangelical umbrella organizations are also telling and often include

---

[2] Respected scholar of South African religion Anthony Balcomb (2001) offers a reasonable difference of opinion when he argues that AICs are evangelical. Still, in Balcomb's (2007) more recent work on evangelicals, he chooses to exclude the AICs from his analysis. Although his stated reason for doing so is simply for organizational convenience, the decision signals an implicit recognition of distinctions between the two faith communities.

branches within traditional Protestant denominations whose "confessing" or evangelical component grew during the charismatic renewal of the 1960s and 1970s. The Anglican and the Dutch Reformed families of churches are prime examples, along with Lutherans, Methodists, Presbyterians, and to a small degree, Catholics. Evangelicalism also includes classical Pentecostal denominations such as the Assemblies of God, Apostolic Faith Mission, Church of God (Tennessee), Church of the Nazarene, Four Square Gospel Church, and other smaller denominations. To these must be added the International Fellowship of Christian Churches and newer independent, Neo-Pentecostal churches and church-planting movements, including the Vineyard, New Covenant Ministries, New Frontiers, Foundation Ministries, and New Harvest Ministries, some of which report dizzying growth rates. In all, South African evangelicals also make up more than a quarter of their country's population (Teichert 2005).[3]

Religious identity in El Salvador is less complex. There, Catholicism is the dominant religion, and almost everyone who identifies with a Protestant denomination falls within the evangelical community. The only notable exceptions to this are the small, non-evangelical Lutheran community, the Luz del Mundo sect, and a very small Mormon presence. Salvadoran evangelicalism thus includes the traditional[4] Pentecostal denominations, such as the Assemblies of God, Church of God, United Pentecostal Church, Apostles & Prophets, and Prince of Peace. It also includes traditional non-Pentecostal denominations such as the Central American Mission, several strains of Baptist churches, and the Seventh Day Adventists. A high percentage of Salvadoran evangelicals now attend newer independent churches and denominations, including Elim, the "Friends of Israel" Bible Baptist Tabernacle (In El Salvador, this church is commonly referred to as *Tabernaculo Bautista*, or Baptist Tabernacle, which is how I refer to it in this book), Camp of God, and the International Center of Praise (La CIA). Many other small groups and independent churches appear in El Salvador's evangelical community, but this list captures today's largest and most important players. The growing Catholic charismatic population is a complicating factor in this description. They have more in common with evangelicals than traditional Catholics, but their identity remains Catholic, not evangelical. In all, evangelicals make up at least 25 percent of the population of El Salvador, and possibly 30 percent or more (IUDOP 2009; Johnson 2014).[5]

---

[3] These numbers are based on 2001 Statistics SA Census data. Regrettably, the 2011 Statistics SA Census dropped the religious question, so no newer data is available (Hendriks 2014).

[4] They are referred to as *traditional* because they have early roots in the country.

[5] An explanation of the sources that I use to determine the size of the evangelical populations in El Salvador and South Africa is needed, particularly concerning why they appear to be valid and how I use them. In El Salvador, the most recent comprehensive study was done by the University Institute for Public Opinion (IUDOP). This institute is housed at the University of Central America (UCA), a respected Catholic University in San Salvador (the same university where six Jesuits were killed by government forces in 1989). The study, conducted in 2009, is cited by academics who study religion in El Salvador, the U.S. Department of State (2010), and (non-evangelical) national

MAPPING THE NEW CENTERS OF EVANGELICALISM

If El Salvador and South Africa represent evangelicalism's new centers, then where are the other centers? How does evangelicalism map out at the global level? The short answer is that NCEs are scattered throughout the Global South and East. Countries such as South Korea, Nigeria, Kenya, and Brazil are particularly important. But there are other countries and regions in which evangelicalism is also thriving. Map 1.1 shows *a sample* of the most important NCEs. It is not intended in any way to be comprehensive – many nations with large evangelical populations are not highlighted.

The map also confines itself to places in which evangelical populations comprise a significant percentage of overall national populations. It does not reveal the high concentrations of evangelicals that exist within smaller regions of larger countries. In northeast India, for example, Christians (most or all of whom are evangelical) in the states of Nagaland and Mizoram exceed 80 percent of the total population (India National Census 2011). Evangelicalism's overall presence in India, however, remains small with respect to the national

politicians in El Salvador. The poll indicates that evangelicals make up 38 percent of the Salvadoran population. IUDOP defines evangelicalism in much the same way that I do.

I also rely on the World Christian Database (WCD) for the Salvadoran statistics. This database was created and is maintained by Todd Johnson. I need to make two points about this database. First, I accessed the database most recently in 2014, and I followed the citation instructions listed on the front web page of the database. But it appears that all data are based on 2010 numbers. Second, Hsu et al. (2008) argue that the WCD is likely to be the most reliable source for statistics about global Christianity and that their data are generally consistent with other sources, including the World Values Survey, the Pew Assessment Project, the CIA Fact Book, and the U.S. Department of State. They also note, however, that one of the main criticisms scholars have for the WCD is its categorization of religious populations. This is also the point of disagreement that I have with the WCD. Its category of evangelical is quite restrictive and appears to exclude all Pentecostals. As I have just explained in the text, that is not how the term evangelical is used in El Salvador (or elsewhere in Latin America or Africa), and it is not what I mean when I use it in this book. Evangelicalism in El Salvador includes all non-Catholics except for a few main-line denominations and other sects. This definition corresponds to the sum of the WCD categories for evangelicals and "renewalists," the latter of which is a category that includes classical Pentecostals, charismatics, and neocharismatics. In the WCD, this accounts for 37 percent of the population in El Salvador, indicating strong agreement between IUDOP numbers and WCD numbers.

For the South Africa numbers, I rely on Karl Teichert's work (2005). He defines evangelicalism in much the same way that I define the term. Teichert provides strong evidence to support his statistics, relying primarily on denominational membership. The study I use is now a bit dated, and based on trends before 2005 as well as less scientific observations, it is very likely that the numbers have increased since then. I know of no other competing or more current calculations, aside from the WCD.

I do not, however, rely on the WCD for the South African statistics. It appears to use the same restrictive understanding of the term evangelical as it does with the El Salvador statistics. However, the renewalist category appears to contain all African Independent Churches. It therefore cannot be used in the same way that I use it in the El Salvador case (doing so would vastly inflate the number of evangelicals in the country). The fallout of this is that the definitions of its terms and the categories it provides make it incompatible with the present study.

MAP 1.1 The Centers of Evangelicalism

population, although in places like Bangalore, it is growing quickly. Emerging evangelical communities can also be found in parts of West Malaysia and certain parts of Indonesia. No one knows how large the house church movement in China has grown, but that too is an area of evangelical growth. These developments reveal some of the difficulties in tracking evangelicalism around the world.

Because counting evangelicals is such a tricky business, the ratios presented here should be held lightly; there is greater consensus that whatever the specific numbers, these are the areas where evangelicalism is thriving. I use input from the World Christian database (Johnson 2014), the International Religious Freedom Report (U.S. Department of State 2011), data gathered from local polling efforts, reports from international leaders in NCEs, and my own personal experience of several country contexts to arrive at these estimates. The estimates I provide are both greater and smaller than estimates that others provide. I have been conservative in my estimates. The bubbles correspond to evangelical population sizes. Each NCE has a connected but different story of emergence, and the timelines of their development can vary by as much as two or three decades.

NCEs share the globe with their preexisting Western Centers of Evangelicalism (WCEs), which are also noted in the map. The numbers of evangelicals in WCEs are still significant, and it should be emphasized that the rise of new centers does not imply the death of the old centers. Scholars debate whether evangelical ranks are shrinking or growing in the West, but both camps agree that a modicum of stability exists. Even in established Western contexts, estimates of evangelical populations vary widely. Provisionally, one can speak of about 25 percent of North America's population being evangelical and about 10 percent of Britain's population falling into that category.

The demographic presentation of global evangelicalism reveals the emergence and evolution of NCEs to be the most important current development in the movement. Evangelicalism's balance of power still lies with the West, but a global evangelical leadership cadre is emerging. It is composed of leaders from around the globe who are deeply enmeshed in transnational networks, culturally savvy, and living in today's global cities. This group, or rather this series of overlapping groups, contains many members from NCEs and could be the movement's most important locus of influence in the coming years.

CONCEPTUALIZING GLOBAL EVANGELICALISM

Six concepts in the literature on global Christianity are important to this study. They emerge from a bewildering array of arguments, some better than others, about this complex global phenomenon. The different terms introduced at the beginning of the chapter – Christianity, Pentecostalism, and evangelicalism – allow for scholars to focus on slightly different aspects of the overall movement. Often, scholars choose to contribute using a case study of a single country or region. This has had the effect of breaking the literature into Latin American studies, African studies, and so on. As the following pages indicate, strong differences among evangelicals do exist across regions. However, studies that span these boundaries, providing they do so with sensitivity and sophistication, can be particularly useful.

Lamin Sanneh's (2003) distinction between global and world Christianities provides a useful heuristic for organizing the six concepts. Sanneh considers World Christianity to be indigenously rooted Christian groups, such as AICs and other local faith initiatives. Sanneh then uses the term global Christianity to refer to Christian groups that have a stronger Western heritage and influence. I subtly shift the meaning of Sanneh's categories to indicate literature that addresses macro elements of this international community on the one hand and local level or grassroots activities within the movement on the other. A couple of the concepts have relevance to macro and micro developments such as David Martin's work, which is explained in the section titled "Modernity and Modernization in the Global South." But for the most part, the scholarship stays on one side or the other. I begin with Global Christianity.

Global Christianity

America's Imperial Expansion
The growth of evangelicalism in the 1970s and 1980s occurred within the bipolar world system and often in the hot spots of the Cold War. A school of thought in the 1980s and 1990s thus interpreted evangelicalism as a cultural tool in the hands of America's political and economic interests. This perspective took religion and its cultural implications seriously. In fact, there was some alarm about evangelical intentions and activities. However, authors in this school of thought also usually subjugated religion to other forms of power and perceived religious actors to have a covert political, economic, and even military agenda.

Two books that took this position stand out in their quality and impact. The first is David Stoll's (1990) *Is Latin America Turning Protestant?* Stoll explores the role of evangelicals in American political, military, and economic involvement in Latin America toward the end of the Cold War. He argues for a distinction between local religious actors and their North American counterparts, suggesting that there were two different projects being undertaken. On the one hand, a local Latin American Pentecostal movement was spreading because it had a coherent cultural logic and provided existential answers for people caught in intense political conflict. On the other hand, the religious right in the United States, especially during the Reagan era, made intentional and aggressive efforts to combine political and religious agendas in the region. Although distinct, the two groups were connected. Evangelistic crusades spearheaded by North American actors, such as Pat Robertson, were explicitly aimed at providing people with an alternative to communism and liberation theology. Local actors were heavily involved in carrying out these crusades.

Stoll focused primarily on North American actors' mix of politics and religion. Major evangelical NGOs, such as World Vision and World Relief, were suspected of working with the CIA and/or the U.S. State Department. In this account, there were efforts of collusion between evangelicals and authoritarian leaders across the region. The Pentecostal message was presented as an ideological alternative to liberation theology, with the hope that it would have a pacifying effect on the oppressed who adopted it. Rios Montt, Guatemala's brutal evangelical military dictator, is highlighted in this account. Stoll notes that Montt had the prayers and blessings of many of his evangelical brethren throughout the United States and in Latin America.

In *Exporting the American Gospel: Global Christian Fundamentalism*, Steve Brouwer, Paul Gifford, and Susan Rose (1996) also employ a hermeneutic of suspicion but shift the focus from a political to an economic critique. The authors also reclassify most global evangelicals and Pentecostals as Fundamentalists. Using case studies from Africa, Asia, and Latin America, they argue that, as American business and media culture spread worldwide, American Fundamentalism is undergoing a universalizing process that is "intertwined with the homogenizing influences of consumerism, mass communication, and production in ways that are compatible with the creation of an international market culture" (3). In this schematic, international actors and indigenous churches are active participants in spreading the religion, but the religious product for sale is, nonetheless, made in America. The global Fundamentalist movement is also dangerous: it prospers under political authoritarianism, it develops rhetoric based around notions of spiritual warfare, and "it may have the potential to create more conflict internationally [than Islamic fundamentalism], for it can avail itself of all the advantages and power generated by a western-dominated economic system and its invasive message of consumption" (9).

Both pieces of scholarship show deep concern that host societies will be damaged by the growing Pentecostal/Fundamentalist influence. Stoll, however, complicates his analysis by noting in 1990 that Protestantism in Latin America was "an open-ended proposition." He observed that, "as churches incorporate more and more of the poor, they may be forced to deal with the economic and social crisis fueling their growth" (xix). Although the politics of the region have changed drastically since Stoll penned those words, the social activities to which Donald Miller and Tetsunao Yamamori (2007) have alerted readers, and which will be discussed shortly, make Stoll's words appear prophetic.

New Faces

Meanwhile, a body of literature has been developing that portrays a very different understanding of Christianity's global dynamics. Other leading scholars of global Christianity (Bediako 1995; Carpenter 2005; Jenkins 2002, 2006; Robert 2000; Sanneh 1983, 2003; Shaw 2012; Walls 1996) document the radical changes Christianity underwent in the twentieth century. Against expectations, the demographic locus of Christianity shifted away from the West: Christianity surged in Africa, Asia, and Latin America just as colonial powers receded. It seems counterintuitive that a religion should flourish while the imperial structures that introduced it were crumbling. To resolve this puzzle, scholars successfully show that neither Christianity's present nor its past indicate that it is an exclusively Western religion.

Scholars attack the assumption that Christianity is purely Western using several arguments. First, Christianity may have journeyed West in the millennia following Christ's birth, but it also in the early years journeyed East and South. Christian communities resulting from these developments in the first century AD continue to exist, such as the Coptic Church of Egypt and the Saint Thomas Church in India. Second, scholars show the limitations of Christianity's spread during the colonial period. Jenkins (2002), who has emerged as the scholar principally associated with this framework, argues that it was in fact the direct presence of Westerners that held colonial Christianity's growth in check. Meddling Westerners had to leave Christianity in the hands of local leaders for it to blossom. As local leaders gained control, Christianity became much more indigenized and non-Western. Third, the current tensions that exist between Western and non-Western components of Christianity reveal the independent nature of non-Western Christians. Jenkins particularly focuses on interactions within the Anglican Communion, stating that current frictions are the result of vast differences in social values, expressions of the faith, and readings of the Bible. The differences have caused churches in the Global South to militantly plot against Western counterparts – further evidence of the lack of supposed Western cultural hegemony. In sum, the argument in this school of thought shows the non-Western origins of Christianity in the Global South, it shows the relative ineffectiveness of Western missionaries and of colonial activities in spreading the faith, and it shows the deep differences that exist between Christianities that exist in different cultures.

Secularization in the West, independence from the West by non-Western churches, and the sheer size of Christian communities in the Global South are developments that have re-centered the locus of global Christianity. Jenkins (2002) controversially projects, for example, that by 2050, only about a fifth of the world's Christians will be non-Hispanic whites. He and other authors note that even today the typical Christian should not be considered a white male living in an American suburb but rather a woman living in a Brazilian favela or an itinerant pastor in Nigeria. In short, Jenkins posits that Southern Christianity, rooted in Africa, Asia, and Latin America, is largely leaving a withered, Western Christianity behind.

Jenkins and others acknowledge that Westerners had a role to play in Christianity's global spread. Clearly, the Catholic Church of Latin America is the result of Iberian empires. Likewise, most evangelicals in Latin America trace their roots to U.S. missionary activities. In Africa and Asia, the passage of the Christian message from Western actors may not have been the only ways Christian communities there originated, but diffusion of Western Christianity has been critically important.

Still, these authors argue that once the message was conferred, the religion took on a life of its own. Jenkins states: "While missionaries began the process of Christianization, they had little control over how or where that path might lead. As we trace the spread of Christianity across Africa and Asia from the 19th century onward, we see the role of grassroots means of diffusing beliefs, through migrants and travelers, across social and family networks .... Sometimes missionaries themselves were appalled at the radically different and radical forms that the Christian message took ..." (2006, 20). Western actors, according to this view, have a limited role in non-Western Christian contexts.

Global Connectedness

The most recent major interpretation of global Christianity focuses on transnational religious connections and global flows. In this "Global Connectedness" framework, scholars contend that high levels of interaction exist among Christians across the globe. They do not think of this multilateral connectedness as an even playing field. Rather, it is mapped onto an international political economy that is anchored and extensively influenced by North American actors. Actors in other parts of the world maintain their autonomy and exhibit agency. Nonetheless, greater resources of all kinds enable North Americans to unevenly influence the identity and trajectory of the global movement.

The scholars formulating this framework, most notably Robert Wuthnow and Mark Noll, acknowledge the remarkable religious activity occurring in Africa, Asia, Latin America, and elsewhere. They argue, though, that North American Christianity continues to play a significant role in these developments. Wuthnow (2009) shows that the robust North American Christian community currently generates faith-based NGOs, overseas missionary efforts, congregational activities, and faith-influenced foreign policy initiatives. The result is that American Christianity is more globally connected today than at any time in history. Embedded in these organizational structures are transnational people flows that include migration, short-term missions, and business and tourist travel. Historian Mark Noll (2009) corroborates this position by arguing that today's global Christianity bears the mark of American influence, albeit in ways that facilitate independent initiatives of local actors. According to Noll, Christianity in the Global South has adopted an organizational model of religion that originated in nineteenth-century America, and which is characterized by voluntarism and self-directed strategies of organization. Through missionaries and other forces of dispersion, the American model of religious social organization was eventually adopted by most Christian communities around the globe. The confluence of these religious developments with a particular set of social, economic, and political conditions is aiding the explosion of Christianity in the Global South. Neither scholar claims a hegemonic role for the United States in global Christianity, but Wuthnow, especially, marshals impressive amounts of empirical data showing how deeply involved U.S. religious actors are in the global movement.

Recent developments in transnational theory provide the backdrop for Wuthnow's argument. Rather than concentrating on issues of identity, deterritorialized space, or global citizenship, Wuthnow contributes to the literature that treats transnationalism as *flows* of people, goods, information, and other resources across national boundaries (Freeman 2006; Hannerz 1996; Kellner 2002; Steger 2003; United Nations 2005). Although Peggy Levitt, perhaps the most important scholar in the field of religious transnationalism, often focuses on identity (Levitt 1998, 2001, 2004), her concept of social remittances, or "the ideas, practices, social capital, and identities that migrants send back into their communities or origin" (Levitt 2007, 23) further illuminates Wuthnow's argument.

The sheer volume of transnational activity in contemporary society makes Wuthnow's case compelling. Wuthnow uses his own research as well as government and other academic sources to show movement across a number of sectors. The religious implications of migration, for instance, are profound, given that as many as 214 million people around the globe are not living in their countries of origin (UNFPA 2013). The number of U.S. missionaries or Christian workers in other countries also continues to rise: the World Christian Database (Johnson 2014) reports that there are as many as 126,650 people who fit this category. Conversely, the number of foreign-born religious professionals inside the United States has also spiked; just one example is that 16 percent of all current U.S. priests were born elsewhere. The short-term mission phenomenon, which has exploded in recent decades, is even more staggering: 1.6 million adults go on these trips every year; it is likely that the number of short-termers under the age of 18 is even higher (Wuthnow 2009). To these statistics are added the ever-increasing flow of business and tourist travelers; these people often look to engage in religious communities and activities even as they travel. Given this set of data, it becomes more difficult to consider religious developments in one part of the world as completely distinct from religious developments in other parts of the world.

World Christianity

Modernity and Modernization in the Global South

The question of religion's role and link to modernity (and secularization) is as old as the discipline of sociology. Marx, Durkheim, and Weber all weighed in on these issues. Fittingly, the question has been important to global evangelicalism literature since its inception, and David Martin has had the most dominant voice in this discussion.

In *Tongues of Fire*, Martin (1990) argued that Pentecostalism signaled and constituted the cultural advance of the Anglo version of modernity. This advance amounted to a multifaceted cultural revolution in Latin America. First, according to Martin, Pentecostalism helps people escape from (usually oppressive) premodern social systems, be that an oppressive religious hierarchy, such as formal structures of the Catholic Church, or from the elders of a gerontocratic tribal society. As converts exit these relationships, they enter into more horizontal and voluntaristic forms of relating to one another. Second, Pentecostalism introduces beliefs and values that increase productivity. This belief system has led Pentecostals everywhere to a more ascetic lifestyle, leaving vices behind that can block productive participation in the economy and in society. Third, Martin argued that Pentecostal congregations are highly participatory. They thus foster skills in public speaking and social organization that are transferrable to other social venues. Church members become more able to participate in, and further develop, a healthy civil society. Finally, Pentecostal beliefs and organizational patterns prioritize individual choice, high levels of mobility, fraternal association, and the nuclear family. Based on these observations, Martin claims that "it is reasonable to view evangelicalism as offering an induction into modernity" (Martin 1990, 108).

Martin applied and adopted this Latin American–based theory to the global Pentecostal movement in *Pentecostalism: The World Their Parish* (2002). Martin paints Pentecostalism as a many-centered movement, with points of origin that span the globe. Still, the American Pentecostal story is globally the most important; American Pentecostalism emerged during the country's modernization process in the nineteenth century. At that time, "there emerged a potent variant capable of stomping alongside modernization world-wide. It met life-threatening and feckless disorder with personal discipline and collective ecstasy" (Martin 2002, 5). Within this framework, Pentecostalism gained steam across the Global South and East, finding social niches in each society where it made the most cultural sense. Such niches included the respectable poor in Latin America, the new middle classes and those making their way in the great megacities in Asia, the young and upwardly mobile in Africa, and minority ethnic groups almost everywhere.

Pentecostalism has proven to be tremendously elastic around the world, integrating itself into existing culture such that it does not make sense to call it a religious import. Rather, Pentecostalism has served as a way in which antecedent forms of culture could be "brought together in an unbroken continuum opening on to modernity. People can dance their way through the rebirths of a great transition, bringing the whole person to bear rather than a split-off segment of the rational self. The past is carried forward even as a line is drawn under it ..." (Martin 2002, 7). The elasticity of the religion is increased by its escape from ecclesiastical hierarchies linked to territory, its dependence on choice rather than hereditary belonging, its lay participation and enthusiasm, and its splintering and fractiousness. Such characteristics ensure that Pentecostalism does not manifest itself as a religious import, but it nonetheless provides a passageway out of traditional society and into something new.

Life Improvement Theory
A major strand of the literature on global evangelicalism falls under what I call the Life Improvement Theory. It argues, in sum, that evangelicalism improves the lives of its members in the here and now. It does so by helping converts escape

oppressive vertical relationships, prohibiting vices that drain personal and family resources, strengthening primary plausibility structures such as the family, empowering women, and helping believers overcome psychosomatic stress caused by the horrors of war and civil conflict (Berger 1991; Brusco 1986; Chesnut 1997; Godsell 1991; Gomez & Vasquez 2001; Hexham & Poewe 1997; Martin 1990, 2002; Smith 1999; Steele 2011; Steigenga & Smilde 1999).

David Smilde and Paul Gifford have made important contributions to this school of thought. Smilde (2007) examined evangelicals in Venezuela. His primary interest was in understanding if and how people might choose to believe the tenets of evangelical faith *because* they see positive life outcomes of evangelical lifestyles. Rather than being unintended consequences, as conventional wisdom in the field has it, Smilde observed that improvements evangelicalism brings are the reasons that conversions occur. Or, in the words of one of Smilde's subjects, the "spiritual and economic fruits" are better than the other options in the Latin American religious marketplace.

The way this works is that evangelicalism represents a form of *imaginative rationality*, or a set of concepts that enable "people [to] get things done in this world" (13). The meanings that are carried by the evangelical faith help its adherents proactively address the most significant challenges in their lives, be that drug or alcohol addiction, marital strife, unemployment, or crime and violence. Given the proven utility of evangelicalism, Smilde confronts the obvious question: "Why wouldn't everyone choose to convert?" He argues that not everyone has access to evangelicalism – it is available to people based on the beliefs of the people around them. In other words, conversion occurs along existing networks: what people "can imagine and when they can imagine it largely depends on their relational context" (14).

Paul Gifford's (2004) study takes place in Accra, Ghana, one of the hotbeds of African Pentecostalism. Gifford examined the supply side of religion, analyzing the messages emitted from the five most important new megachurches in Accra. He found that, while churches may provide any number of positive externalities for their members, the primary reason people are drawn to them is that they provide answers to their "existential problems and especially to their most pressing existential problem, economic survival" (Gifford 2004, ix). The churches Gifford studied taught regularly on issues of success and wealth. One of Gifford's subjects, Mensah Otabil, tied the acquisition of wealth to hard work, but Gifford shows that most of the other "superstars" of the new Pentecostal megachurches preach that wealth is either bestowed or acquired through other means, usually supernatural. In providing this analysis, Gifford provides nuance and clarity to the prosperity gospel component of the evangelical community in Accra. Even with this nuance, Gifford argues that Pentecostalism's emphasis on faith's ability to lead to economic gain remains pervasive.

Smilde and Gifford analyze two very different contexts that are divided by distance, language, and culture. They also employ very different research methodologies. They nonetheless posed, in essence, the same question: why is evangelicalism so popular? Their answers were also related: they report that the unintended consequences of faith have in fact become the intended consequences of faith. People become evangelicals because they believe it will provide other-worldly assistance for this-worldly problems. An important point of distinction between these two authors is that Smilde's work assumes that the core of the literature making up the Life Improvement Theory is more or less right: evangelicalism does improve lives. Gifford is more skeptical: he limits his argument to recognizing the *claims* of Pentecostals to improve economic life. He views the evidence that Pentecostalism actually does so as quite thin. Together, these two authors do note an important turn: in conflict-ridden societies, such as the ones Stoll examined, the general consensus was that evangelicalism provided hope in the world to come for those caught in hopeless cycles of poverty and violence. The Pentecostals that Smilde and Gifford have analyzed in economically unstable but relatively peaceful contexts are seemingly just as attracted to the faith.

Local Social and Political Engagement
The type and nature of local evangelical social and political activities are shaped by the processes that forge the movement's identity. Why people become evangelicals, how they think about their faith, where they stand in relation to international actors, and their social location within their national contexts all play into evangelicalism's social and political aspirations and strategies. To date, it seems that variation between actors is the best way to describe evangelical activity in these spheres. Still, there are some developments worth noting.

A growing body of literature (Miller & Yamamori 2007; Street 2013) argues that a "progressive Pentecostalism" is increasingly active across the Global South. Miller and Yamamori, the most influential voices in this school of thought, define progressive Pentecostals as people "who claim to be inspired by the Holy Spirit and the life of Jesus and seek to holistically address the spiritual, physical, and social needs of people in their community" (2007, 2). They point to evidence gathered around the world that Pentecostals are increasingly interested in providing ministries to the poor and the downtrodden. Indeed, Pentecostals see such activities as central to their faith. In Miller and Yamamori's words, Progressive Pentecostals "view their responsibility toward social problems within their community as a mandate from God" (34). The resulting ministries are many: examples include prison outreach, programs for street children, and various addiction and substance abuse programs. Miller and Yamamori make it clear that not all Pentecostals are doing this kind of work, but the trend has grown steadily in recent years, and its continued rise is likely in years to come.

In the political arena, Rios Montt, the aforementioned former president of Guatemala, became the unfortunate poster child for evangelical politics the world over. Although his most memorable activities occurred in the early 1980s, Montt remains one of the most recognizable names associated with evangelical politics in the Global South. Much has changed since that time, both in politics and global evangelicalism.

A major recent effort to capture more contemporary activities is the *Evangelical Christianity and Democracy in the Global South* project – a four-volume series based on seventeen national case studies from Latin America, Africa, and Asia. Academics living in the regions were invited to write the case studies. Timothy Shah served as the series editor, while Paul Freston edited the Latin American volume (2008) and Terence Ranger edited the African volume (2008). The volumes use clear empirical data to demonstrate that evangelical political initiatives run in multiple directions. Some evangelicals promote authoritarian leaders while others protest against such leaders, often doing so concurrently and in the same country. Likewise, evangelical political parties have been found across the political spectrum, but all such parties have failed at the ballot box. In fact, argue the authors, evangelical institutions are by nature fissiparous and fragmented, making the movement too weak to either create a coherent agenda or influence policy at the state level. For these reasons, in Freston's words, the movement is not capable of realizing either the "messianic hopes" or the "apocalyptic fears" (Latin America volume, 32) of some of its earlier observers.

The volume's authors do support the idea that evangelicalism's voluntaristic congregations serve as "schools of democracy" (Latin America volume, xiii), providing members with skills that are transferrable to civic and political life. Where national contexts permit (and in several African cases, cultures of violence and repression do not), evangelicals so equipped are increasing their participation in host societies. Felipe Vasquez Palacios, author of the Mexican case study, finds evangelicals involved in human rights organizations, ecological groups, and many other civil and political organizations. Of course, participation can also be intended for personal gain; the chapter on Nicaragua highlights the activities of an evangelical leader nicknamed "Pastor Bribe." Such varied observations serve to confirm the complex and ambiguous nature of evangelicalism's political engagement.

Analysis of Global and World Christianity Frameworks

It is worth weighing these frameworks against one another. In doing so, basic points of agreement quickly become evident. All frameworks point to an evangelical/Pentecostal form of Christianity that is sweeping across much of the non-Western world. All acknowledge that the West has had a role to play in this expansion. Most show that cultural change and adaptation must occur as the movement spreads. Many surmise that the movement carries potential for collective action in spheres other than religion.

There are also competing elements and different foci to these accounts. Different questions that are addressed include: Why and how does evangelicalism grow and spread? What is its role in ushering in the modern world? How does

Christianity hang together globally? How does the history of its growth correspond with political and economic developments? How does the global movement
influence the political and economic spheres? Different questions lead authors to
different conclusions, which are not always contradictory.

Sometimes, however, they are. In the Global Christianity category, both the
American Imperial Expansion and the Global Connectedness frameworks share
important assumptions about the nature of the international political economy
and the corollary positions of religious actors: U.S. religious actors can produce
religion more powerfully than those situated elsewhere. This position stands in
contrast to the New Faces framework, which insists on independent contemporary developments in the non-Western world, and sees increasing pressure on the
West to accept positions taken elsewhere. But there are also fissures between the
American Imperial Expansion and Global Connectedness frameworks.
Globalization is conceptualized very differently, and the former asserts relationships between religion, politics, and economics that the latter does not explore.
Not all of these interpretations can be equally correct, but they all add to our
understanding of Christianity's global identity and dynamics.

In the World Christianity category, deeper levels of consensus run across the
three groups. All perceive some level of interaction between evangelicals and
modernity, although the degree and the type of relationship vary. Martin himself
is a strong proponent of the life improvement theory, perhaps more so than the
authors highlighted in that section. There is also broad agreement about the
empirical statements concerning evangelical involvement in social and political
activities. Differences exist in how evangelical motives are analyzed by authors
in the three camps, as well as in how to interpret specific country cases. Still,
broad levels of agreement are maintained in spite of differences about particular
issues and details.

INTRODUCING THE RELIGIOUS SOCIAL FORCES FRAMEWORK

In spite of the richness and depth of current scholarly discourse about global
Christianity, pressing questions remain unanswered. It is widely acknowledged
that the global Christian movement changes rapidly (e.g., Bornstein 2005;
Gifford 2004; Martin 2002). Such changes are important because they affect
how local and global components of a faith community intersect, determine the
types of social and political strategies a faith community uses, and shape the way
the movement produces culture. As evangelical faith communities become more
prominent actors in societies around the world, a greater understanding of these
kinds of dynamics becomes increasingly valuable.

Not many explanations about how global Christianity changes have been
offered. Where social change is included in analyses of global Christianity, the
focus tends to be on economic or political causes of change that act upon
the movement. These forces can be powerful. The following chapter highlights
the interactions among the religious, political, and economic spheres in

El Salvador and South Africa. It is simply impossible to fully grasp the nature of a faith community without understanding something of its social, political, and economic environment.

But there are also limits to the amount of change that can be created by external factors. Global movements, including evangelicalism, exhibit trends that are movement-wide. Such trends can be seen in very different societies around the world, a fact that runs counter to the idea that political or economic contexts can control the trajectories of religious communities. Parallel developments in the evangelical communities of the Central African Republic, Singapore, and Colombia, to take three examples, might be partly explained by the social homogeneity that globalization can provide, but even this argument seems stretched in the face of differing levels of participation in the global community and the fact that even globalization's reach becomes weak in certain corners of the world.

The argument I present in this book is that religious sources of change are far more immediate causes of key transformations occurring within the NCEs than are agents of change located in other social spheres. I make this argument by introducing the concept of *religious social forces*. As explained in the Introduction, *religious social forces* are ones in which religious symbols, resources, actors, or organizations are in motion and are setting other (in this case, religious) symbols, resources, actors, or organizations in motion. This new analytic framework intersects with most of the alternatives just outlined, and the influence of several scholars, especially Wuthnow and Martin, should be evident. But the religious social forces framework also pushes beyond existing schools of thought to address new sets of questions (What are the drivers and trajectories of change in NCEs?), to take new data into account, and to synthesize issues in new ways.

Five basic principles serve as axes around which the religious social forces framework revolves: First, local actors are building NCEs. Second, in line with the Global Connectedness framework, religious forces emitted from the West greatly influence NCEs. Third, as local actors build social institutions and organizations, they organically synthesize local and global resources. Fourth, consistent with basic theories of social empowerment and sustainable development, local actors create more sustainable organizations and institutions than outside actors, however sympathetic the latter might be. Fifth, global religious forces can be imperial, but they can also be sources of empowerment. They thus play an important role in the rise of the NCEs, just as transnational activities are critical in the economic rise of China, India, and the other BRICS. I return to these principles in the book's Conclusion.

A central dilemma in this discussion is how individuals in NCEs express agency and have ownership of their own religious movement in the face of the tremendous power of global religious forces. A primary image within this story is that of the local entrepreneur who takes stock of the local and global religious resources within reach and then pulls them together in new ways. The term entrepreneur, however, can be ideologically charged, and people can perceive the word's definition differently based on their positions along the ideological spectrum. I am using the term *entrepreneur* in its most technical sense, which will be explained in more detail in Chapter 4. I am also interested in showing that a social entrepreneurship can emerge from evangelicalism that benefits entire societies, even as some evangelicals practice a more self-interested form of entrepreneurship that often serves as a detriment to others.

The products of these creative activities reflect the local and international symbols, relationships, and other ingredients that entrepreneurs forge together. Pastor Mario, for instance, merges local and "foreign" symbols when he develops Sunday School curriculum. The resulting curriculum reflects his own somewhat unique reading of the Bible even as it features references to authors from the United States and across the globe. Pastor Sonono, in another example, merges local social structures with transnational religious connections to nurture the creation of a megachurch in a South African township. He generates local authority, legitimation, and respect by displaying charisma in the township, and he demonstrates the cross-cultural adeptness necessary to develop valuable relationships with pastors in Detroit, Indianapolis, and elsewhere. In a third example, the super-church Elim illustrates how homegrown organizations integrate international organizations' programs and messages into their own congregational environment. Elim is a purely Central American creation that has no formal ties to any Western denomination. But it partners with Compassion International in several impoverished communities and plasters Focus on the Family posters on its church bulletin boards. Such examples illustrate the myriad ways in which innovators mesh local and global religious forces together and, in doing so, contribute to the construction of NCEs.

In the midst of constant innovation by local actors, it remains true that not all organizations in NCEs are homegrown. Many U.S.-based ministries and NGOs open country offices in these regions. It is true that these transplants hire in-country personnel to staff and lead the national offices, allowing such organizations to be mapped onto local social structures. In the Salvadoran context, where families form the underlying structure of society, one particular family network has held director positions in several of the most important international evangelical NGOs, including World Vision and Campus Crusade for Christ. But even so, there are limits to local ownership and initiative. Homogeneity between El Salvador and South Africa can be striking, especially as it relates to the organizational universes that evangelicals create in these two countries (churches, NGOs, and media outlets predominate in both places) and the way that these types of organizations are structured. It is this kind of tension, the push and pull of local individual agency versus global religious forces, and the trajectories that NCEs are consequently set on, that the following chapters explore more fully.

2

Historical Sketches of El Salvador and South Africa

The new centers of global evangelicalism do not exist in a vacuum. They are part of larger national and regional contexts. The success or failure of many evangelical initiatives depends on the economies and political climates in which they exist. To understand why faith communities, including evangelical ones, look and act the way they do, their local contexts must be examined.

The intersection that new centers of evangelicalism (NCEs) have with other social, political, and economic entities also determines their contributions to the national moral order. How people think society *ought* to function, the values that people have, and the centers of power and influence within society are all components of a moral order. The growth of NCEs in recent decades means that they can play an increasing role in shaping the moral order of their national contexts, even as their national contexts continue to shape them.

Thus, the task of this chapter is to sketch the economic, political, and social histories of El Salvador and South Africa while paying attention to the global forces at work in shaping these national environments. Such an analysis allows deeper insight into the forces guiding social change within evangelical communities. It also clarifies the role of evangelicals within these two countries.

CONTEMPORARY EL SALVADOR

More than 6 million Salvadorans squeeze into a country about the size of Massachusetts. El Salvador's ethnic composition has become increasingly homogeneous as time has passed, although some of the municipalities near Guatemala still maintain an indigenous culture and population. People of African origin do live in Central America, but very few ever migrated to the western side of the isthmus where El Salvador is located. For this reason, a *mestizo* ethnicity predominates and is broken only in the upper classes. Among the ruling elites, an Arab merchant community grows more powerful over time (ex-president Tony Saca is of Palestinian descent), and a few elite families maintain strictly European identities.

Politics

In 1992, El Salvador's civil war, which began in 1980, ended with the signing of the peace accords. But the potential for renewed conflict hovered over the country at least until the date of the first postwar elections in 1994. The political keys to genuine peace rested on civilian control over the military and on legitimate democratic space in which the Farabundo Marti National Liberation Front (FMLN), the armed guerrilla group that was transitioning into a political party, felt it could participate fairly. False steps were taken on both fronts, but enough forward progress was made to hold the 1994 elections. The National Republic Alliance (ARENA),[1] the party of the Salvadoran establishment, won the presidency in a process that was far from perfect. But the elections crossed a threshold of fair play that allowed all sides to recognize their legitimacy and to accept the results. Meanwhile, the military's ominous presence began to recede. By the late 1990s, the military had been deserted by its former allies and had become a political nonfactor despite many earlier predictions of a different trajectory for it. A peaceful transition to democracy had thus been imperfectly but completely achieved (Juhn 1998; Williams & Walter 1997; Wood 2000).

Today, ARENA and the FMLN are the two dominant parties in a multiparty system. ARENA was founded by Roberto D'Aubuisson, the same person who formed many of the death squads during the war (Williams & Walter 1997; Wood 2000). From its origins on the far right, ARENA has swung toward the center. Although it would still qualify as a strongly conservative party in most political systems, it has become moderate in the sense that it now advocates political openness to international actors, especially the United States, and a move away from the agro-export economy that long characterized the country. In ARENA's journey away from the hard right, it parted company with a group of wealthy landowners, who then formed the Party of National Conciliation (PCN). The PCN favors less international interference in El Salvador and (de facto, given the party constituency) a stronger voice for the traditional agricultural oligarchy.

The FMLN has been moving toward the center of the political spectrum as well, and in the process it has taken over political space previously inhabited by several small center-left political parties. The most notable of these is the Christian Democratic Party (PDC), the party of the late Napoleon Duarte, who served as El Salvador's president in the 1980s. Within the FMLN, various

---

[1] All parties are commonly referred to by their acronyms in El Salvador.

younger members have emerged as leaders of the party, who did not hold leadership positions during the Salvadoran civil war. Some such leaders are trying to establish a slightly different agenda for the FMLN and are attempting to do so by instituting different political strategies. These younger FMLN members have been the engine behind the more centrist activities of the FMLN – and in the process have alienated some of the long-time activists within the party.

The shifts within ARENA and the FMLN have caused feisty battles within each party. Ex-president Tony Saca broke with ARENA after the 2009 elections and made an unsuccessful bid to regain the presidency in 2014 with a coalition of small centrist parties, although Saca has historically been strongly conservative (Thale 2014). The FMLN has dealt with strong internal divisions since its inception, the most important of which has been the difference between ortho-dox or hard-line members and those who are more moderately left of center. They have not, however, suffered a major split.

These dynamics notwithstanding, the relative institutional strength of El Salvador's political parties and of its political system compares favorably to those of other countries in Latin America. The FMLN won the presidency for the first time in 2009, with moderate former journalist Mauricio Funes as its candidate. In 2014, the party put forward Salvador Sanchez Ceren, a hard-liner who was a commander for the guerrillas in the civil war. Ceren defeated ARENA's candidate, Norman Quijano, in the runoff elections by winning 50.11 percent of the vote to Quijano's 49.89 percent. The FMLN also controls the majority of the mayoral positions in the country, including San Salvador. But ARENA remains strong, as it held the presidency from 1994 to 2008 and continues to be a credible threat to win future elections.

Economy

Perhaps the most positive aspect of El Salvador's economy is that it maintains a modicum of stability. Economic growth hovered around 2 percent from 2003 to 2008 (Economic Intelligence Unit 2011a) and then consistently fell below this mark starting in 2009, after the global economic downturn (Trading Economics 2014a). During its rule, ARENA adhered closely to neoliberal trade policies, as evidenced by its ratification of the Central American Free Trade Agreement (CAFTA) in March 2006 and its dollarization of the economy in 2001. The Funes regime did not greatly modify these policies. The strongest sectors of the Salvadoran economy are finance and commerce. The recent global lending crisis has had little to no effect on El Salvador's banks, making their strength partic-ularly evident (Economic Intelligence Unit 2008a). Within the commerce sector, construction and retail have done especially well, a trend directly related to the remittances sent from Salvadorans in the United States to friends and family members in El Salvador. Remittance income rose to a record $3.97 billion in 2013 (Reserve Bank of El Salvador 2014) and is by far the most important economic dynamic in the country. The remittance issue will be addressed again in the following pages.[2]

Social Concerns

El Salvador's social concerns revolve around three very stark and interrelated problems: inequality, poverty, and crime. Even after a class-driven war, El Salvador continues to experience deep inequality. Its Gini coefficient, which is an oft-used measure of national income inequality, ranks El Salvador the 18th most unequal out of 104 countries (CIA World Factbook 2011). At the highest level of society, there exist powerful groups that control various economic sectors and make them monopolies or oligopolies. The senior leaders of ARENA play an integral role in brokering these powerful economic interests (Kevin Sanderson, personal interview, 2006). Although El Salvador's mythical fourteen families,[3] and the very real oligarchy, were displaced by the war (Wood 2000), great resources and power are still concentrated in the hands of a few super elites. Below this small group of players are different levels of upper class, upper middle class, and middle class actors. The richest 20 percent of the country holds more than 51 percent of the country's income share (Index Mundi 2012). This top fifth of the population is itself stratified and is composed of people with more moderate (although sometimes still significant) business interests, the professional class, and some members of the government.

Looking up at these middle and upper classes is an estimated 37.8 percent of the population that lives below the poverty line (World Bank 2009). In 2011, the legal minimum wage in El Salvador was $192.10/month for retail workers, $166.82/month for apparel assembly workers, and $89.86/month for agricultural workers (Minimum-Wage.org 2012). The National Labor Committee at Columbia University (2005) considers that "relative poverty" still afflicts Salvadorans who make up to $287.67/month. It has further estimated that the lowest living wage in El Salvador should be $421.00/month, which indicates that for many who are fully employed, a job does not imply that they have the

---

[2] Those familiar with El Salvador's history will note that its agricultural sector has not yet been mentioned. Former president Alfredo Cristiani (1989–1994) re-ordered the country's economic priorities to move away from the agro-export model in favor of the finance industry. As he did so, he made agricultural inputs more difficult to access. Those who have controlled ARENA since Cristiani's term ended have maintained this economic agenda. But El Salvador does continue to export crops such as coffee, sugar, cotton, and a small but growing number of non-traditional crops. There are also some maritime interests as well as a small textile industry (Economic Intelligence Unit 2008a).

[3] When talking of the era before the war, most people familiar with El Salvador's history will reference the "fourteen families" who owned the country. This refers to the very real fact that the coffee-growing elite was made up of interlocking families who owned most of the country. These families formed the oligarchy. However, precisely how many families should be considered part of this oligarchy would be a subject of endless debate.

ability to make ends meet. In 2010, the national unemployment rate stood at 7.2 percent (CIA World Factbook 2011), but the underemployment rate could be as high as 35 percent. Activity in the informal economy, as well as remittances, must be kept in mind. Still, a large swath of Salvadoran society continues to face the daily challenges of grinding poverty.

El Salvador's significant rates of crime and violent crime are connected to issues of poverty and inequality, but they are also facilitated by the post-conflict nature of Salvadoran society and a heavy gang presence. This post-conflict period has been nearly as violent as the war itself: about 75,000 Salvadorans died during the war (1980–1992); since then, roughly 60,000 homicides have occurred in the country (Holland 2013). In 2011, an average of more than ten homicides occurred per day in a country with slightly more than 6 million inhabitants (Holland 2013). El Salvador ranks among the most violent nations in the world – surpassed only by Honduras for 2010 global homicide rates (UNODC 2012). Alisha Holland states that "the most notable feature of crime in El Salvador, like much of Central America, is that it faces high levels of gang violence, not simply diffuse street crime. Official estimates variably link anywhere between 20% and 50% of all homicides with gang activity" (Holland 2008, 4). In 2012, Father Antonio Rodriguez, a Catholic priest, helped to broker a cease-fire between the two main gangs, and the official murder rates dropped precipitously in the following months (*Economist* 2013a). But crimes such as extortion and armed robbery remain high (*Economist* 2014). Some local residents looked suspiciously at the official dip in murders that was being reported; they did not feel a strong increase in their own personal security.

It is impossible to take a simple stroll through the working-class neighborhoods of San Salvador without noticing gang presence in some form, whether it is gang signs spray-painted on the sides of buildings or gang members themselves congregating on street corners. The constant presence of violent crime and gang activity shapes the lives of Salvadorans in myriad ways – and, as we shall see, helps to shape the social dynamics surrounding Salvadoran evangelicalism.

Religion

Despite, or perhaps because of, these issues, El Salvador remains a very religious country. The two main religious groups are Catholics and evangelicals, and most evangelicals are Pentecostals. Traditional Protestant denominations that have their historical roots in Europe make up a third religious category in El Salvador, but it is quite small even when compared with other Latin American countries. A Lutheran denomination of about seventy congregations is its largest component.

The Catholic Church maintains a dominant position within Salvadoran society. However, dynamic changes within the institution are occurring as it attempts to stem the flow of people out its doors. These changes include the incorporation of praise songs and door-to-door evangelism, which are both imitations of evangelical strategies. There is also a strong Catholic charismatic presence in the country.

Frances Hagopian (2009) states that 59 percent of the country still self-identifies as Catholic. Although that is lower than other Latin American countries such as Mexico (74 percent) or Brazil (70 percent), the percentage of Salvadoran Catholics who practice their religion at least once a week is quite high (61.1 percent). Multiplying these two variables together leads Hagopian to argue that El Salvaodor's Catholic Church continues to enjoy a relatively high level of religious hegemony in the midst of growing regional religious pluralism.

The Catholic Church does not, however, have a high capacity to mobilize its base to pursue the Catholic social or political agenda. The national Catholic leadership continues to reflect the ideals of the progressive, and martyred, Archbishop Oscar Romero. About a fifth of the Salvadoran Catholic constituency remains radically progressive. But most Salvadoran Catholics are strongly conservative: the World Values Survey shows that of the ten Latin American countries surveyed, El Salvadoran Catholics are the most opposed to homosexuality, abortion, divorce, and euthanasia. On homosexuality and divorce, their opposition was "twice or more as high as that of Argentines" (Hagopian 2009, 288). Hagopian sums up El Salvador's place in the Latin American Catholic Church continuum by stating that "on both moral and socio-economic issues, [the most conservative electorates] are located in Peru and El Salvador, though both have a leftist constituency" (Hagopian 2009, 295).

Evangelicalism, the country's other main religious category, first emerged among El Salvador's poor. Since then, the movement has expanded into all socioeconomic levels of society. In the early 1990s, Coleman, Aguilar, Sandoval, and Steigenga (1993) reported that evangelicals made up 12 percent of the population and were at that time the poorest, most illiterate religious group in the country. A few years later, Williams (1997) estimated evangelicalism's presence to have grown to between 15 and 20 percent. Today the most reliable sources believe it has increased to more than 35 percent (IUDOP 2009; Johnson 2014). All evangelical denominations have grown but none as much as the Assemblies of God (AG), which now has an estimated 300,000 members (Johnson 2014). Two other major evangelical forces are megachurches. One is the Baptist Tabernacle: Friends of Israel, a locally founded congregation of about 15,000 that has spawned 370 daughter churches. The Baptist Tabernacle network has a self-estimated 75,000 adult members and 50,000 children who attend. The second new evangelical power is Elim, which was founded in 1977 and is now one of the ten largest churches in the world. More than 110,000 people regularly attend its weekly small group network. The *poder de convocatoria*, or the ability to gather the Salvadoran evangelical masses, lies exclusively with the heads of the AG, the Baptist Tabernacle, and Elim. This makes them the three most influential people in the movement.[4]

---

[4] The statistics for the AG, the Baptist Tabernacle, and Elim were self-reported by interviewees or found in church-produced literature. Each year all denominations must report their membership to

Evangelicalism has also climbed the social ladder, most noticeably by growing rapidly in the country's business class. The few churches that existed in the business classes of El Salvador twenty years ago have all exhibited steady growth, and a number of independent Pentecostal churches have also sprung up in the more affluent neighborhoods. Evangelical ministry organizations on university campuses in El Salvador have been a critical contributor to growth in this area. They funnel university students into evangelical churches and create a university-educated national evangelical leadership. While the wealthiest circles within El Salvador have thus far resisted evangelical advances, some evangelicals are now targeting members of the country's most powerful families for conversion.

The current political, economic, social, and religious conditions of El Salvador represent a moral order that is still shifting and taking root. The nature of this moral order and the way in which the different sectors of society affect one another can only be understood through an examination of the country's historical context.

HISTORICAL EL SALVADOR

The Traditional Moral Order

Three traditional pillars of society were gradually established in El Salvador: the Catholic Church, the oligarchic elite, and the military regime. The first, the Catholic Church, historically propagated a culture of monistic corporatism, which Christian Smith describes as being "grounded in the pre-Enlightenment, pre-scientific-revolution, pre-capitalist ... monolithically Catholic, and structurally semi-feudal world of the Iberian Peninsula" (Smith 1994, 120–121). Monistic corporatism proposed that human fulfillment could be found in a community ordered by a central authority, whose task it was to construct the common good. Collective harmony was prized over a system of checks and balances, and the state was expected to organize the community in a system of caste and class (Smith 1994).

Beginning in the nineteenth century, a rift emerged in Latin American societies that ran along classically conservative and liberal political lines. Conservatives drew on corporate monism as the philosophical grist for their religious, political, and economic outlook. The Catholic Church was a major force for the conservative side, and it was populated by some of the region's richest and most established families. With ideals such as order, protectionism, and the stability of traditional institutions (Woodward 1999), conservatives hoped to re-create an Iberian society in which the Catholic Church had "a religious monopoly through the formal exclusion of other sects, a close alliance with the state ... and a vast

the government, and these are the numbers that they submit. There are likely many more people who attend AG churches who are not formal members, including high numbers of children.

amount of property and wealth" (Bushnell & Macauley 1994, 14). Catholic paternalism also carried with it a culture of active engagement in helping the unfortunate and providing education for the poor. This led to the construction of hospitals, schools, orphanages, and other social institutions. Indeed, such activities represent a central plank of corporatist culture (Grace Goodell, personal correspondence, 2008).

For their part, liberals were under the sway of the Enlightenment as embodied by the French and American revolutions. They championed "elective and representative offices, relaxation of commercial restrictions, a conscious effort to stimulate production and to develop intellectual as well as economic resources,[5] and the emergence of incipient political parties" (Woodward 1999, 83). There was also a strong anti-clerical component to Latin American liberalism. However, it is important to note that, especially in El Salvador, where liberals uniquely gained the upper hand in the mid- to latter nineteenth century and never really relinquished it, liberals could be found among the clergy themselves. In other words, the struggle between liberal and conservative ideals was waged both inside and outside the Catholic Church. And it was a struggle that the liberals won. Within this context, a traditional and very controllable Salvadoran Catholic Church emerged. Church officials provided religious legitimacy to incoming presidents, regardless of the morality of their paths to power, and maintained their silence when the state employed repressive tactics against its own citizens (Cardenal 1990). Even with the Church situated thusly, society maintained a deeply Catholic identity and tended to be very religious, especially when compared to South American countries whose cultures were more European.

Coffee's intrusion into the country in the 1870s and 1880s brought in the second pillar of twentieth-century Salvadoran society: a tightly knit, landed, coffee-growing oligarchy. Coffee's original home was in the highlands where other crops could not grow, and so it existed alongside plantations that produced items sold in the Salvadoran market, such as fruit, maize, beans, and cattle (Anderson 1992; Williams 1994). This created a balance within the economy of goods to be exported and goods that could be consumed domestically.

Soon, though, vested interests were seduced by coffee's ability to serve as a cash crop. When they sought to expand its cultivation in the last decades of the

---

[5] The point here is not to contrast liberal efforts to develop such resources against a fictitious inactivity by the Catholic Church in these areas. The point is rather that liberals drew from a different fount as they developed intellectual and economic capacities. The Catholic Church's schools tended to outperform the liberal movement's public schools and made room for poor children. This was especially so among the educational efforts of the Salesian and Franciscan orders (Goodell 2008). Bosco University, named after the Salesian order's founder, John Bosco, stands out prominently in the popular residential districts of northern San Salvador, and the University of Central America is a Jesuit institution in the capital that sets El Salvador's educational standard for many disciplines.

nineteenth century, land in tiny El Salvador became for the first time a deeply conflicted issue. Its first manifestations were in the western side of the country, where the altitude is higher and the ground is particularly fertile for coffee. But large tracts were being held by indigenous populations. To place the land in the hands of coffee-growing *Ladinos* (people of European descent), military and government leaders created radical land reform laws, which were then used as legal justification for the forced removal or subjugation of the indigenous populations. Unsurprisingly, this move was met with significant indigenous resistance and continued uprisings. But the military and police forces ultimately prevailed in their efforts to extend coffee's territory (Williams 1994).

Labor as well as land is needed for coffee production, and the Ladinos employed the indigenous populations they had just displaced. Newly landless, the indigenous were in need of employment, but they were also still prone to uprisings. It was thus that class, ethnicity, and cultural differences added to the tensions over land and permanently damaged relations between the two groups. Farms were sabotaged, and labor contracts were routinely violated in the 1880s. Coffee growers continued to use police and military forces to retaliate and to ensure that coffee workers, whether they were living in modest accommodations within haciendas or coming in as migrant workers from outside the coffee zones, were both economically productive and politically passive (Williams & Walter 1997). The conflictive relations built among coffee, power, land, Ladinos, and indigenous populations that would last for more than a century had thus been established.[6]

---

[6] The following paragraph picks up the story of Salvadoran politics after 1931, but a description of the earlier political environment is also useful. The Central American Region declared its independence from Spain in 1821. When Mexico followed suit later that same year, the six former colonies joined the Mexican Empire. Mexico subsequently reinvented itself as a republic in 1823 and allowed the Central American states to decide whether to remain in the union. Only Chiapas stayed, and Costa Rica, El Salvador, Honduras, Guatemala, and Nicaragua joined to form the Federal Republic of Central America (Booth 1991). The federation, however, lasted only a couple decades, as tensions grew among the former colonies and power changed hands by the sword (Anderson 1992). When in 1838 Honduras pulled out and the federation collapsed, each of the five states began to craft independent histories and identities. Although fully autonomous, El Salvador still did not have the ability to govern itself effectively. In a twenty-year period beginning in 1841, the presidency changed hands a remarkable forty-two times (Lindo-Fuentes, Ching, & Lara-Martinez 2007). It was not until after the twentieth century commenced that power was peacefully passed from one leader to another (Williams & Walter 1997).

Civilian politicians occupied the presidency from 1911 to 1931. The country's oligarchy had by that time coalesced (Wood 2000), and it was not surprising that the presidency should fall into the hands of a specific family. The Melendez-Quinonez dynasty lasted from 1914 to 1927. The use of force did not disappear during this civilian period of rule, as coercion during polling procedures was routine fare. When the Melendez-Quinonez families did not have a suitable candidate for the 1927 elections, they directed a collaborator, Romero Bosque, into office. Bosque, however, had truly democratic tendencies: he tried to reform the political process while in office and sought to let the public select his successor. Such attributes contributed to the military's decision to intervene (Anderson 1992; Lindo-Fuentes et al. 2007).

A military coup in December 1931 put into place the third pillar of twentieth-century Salvadoran society: a military-run state. National instability had been created by the 1929 stock market crash and the accompanying plunge in the international price of coffee. The coup represented a relatively bloodless attempt to restore order, but the peace was short lived. In January 1932, peasants stormed at least six different city centers in the coffee-growing regions. They destroyed the assets of the wealthiest Salvadorans, killed more than 100 people, and held the towns for up to a day before troops from San Salvador dislodged them. The regime's response is now known simply as *la matanza*: "the massacre." Perhaps 8,000–10,000 people were killed in reprisal (Anderson 1992).[7] An American missionary living in the region, Roy MacNaught observed the proceedings from his home and wrote: "It appears they have decided to exterminate the Indians" (Tilley 2005, 137).[8]

This event remains a scar on the Salvadoran psyche, but it also solidified the moral order of the twentieth century. Elites never seriously questioned military governance after this event, and the military continued to police the privately held coffee farms and labor right up until the civil war of the 1980s. Labor unions became illegal while military and paramilitary networks in the countryside expanded to some 40,000 members by 1960. The Commission on Truth for El Salvador summed up the arrangement by stating that "a kind of complicity developed between businessmen and landowners, who entered into a close relationship with the army and intelligence and security forces. The aim was to ferret out alleged subversives among the civilian population in order to defend the country against the threat of an alleged foreign conspiracy" (Wood 2000, 34). Such elite strategies and political developments followed general Latin American trends during that period.

The Moral Order Begins to Fray

Although social change would not be effected until the civil war of the 1980s, its seeds can be found in developments of the 1960s within the Catholic Church. Internationally, the Second Vatican Council (1962–1965) was followed by the Medellín Conference of Latin American Bishops (CELAM) in 1968, which formally introduced more progressive Catholic thought to the region.[9] These conferences were not impulsively staged by a fast-changing Catholic Church.

[7] Anderson is the most authoritative voice on this estimate but also represents the low end of the scale. More scholars weigh in at about 30,000 casualties (Lindo-Fuentes et al. 2007; Perez Brignoli 1995).

[8] MacNaught, among the first evangelical missionaries in the country, came to work among the Pipiles in El Salvador. Enemies of missionary efforts in El Salvador used the occasion to accuse those Pipiles who had converted to evangelicalism of being communists and assassinated many of them. MacNaught's own life was also threatened (Comisión Nacional del Centenario 1996). Tilley (2005) argues that MacNaught sought to maintain neutrality in the conflict, not wishing to be killed by the communists or the military. She does, however, mention the personal pain MacNaught experienced when his personal assistant and others who had converted were killed during the massacre.

[9] Gill (1998) questions the importance of the conferences themselves and points to increased religious pluralism as the reason Catholic clergy were moving toward liberation theology. In El

Rather, they were a manifestation of long developing trends that were initiated by parish priests and orders within the Catholic Church that had always been oriented toward the poor. But such conferences as Vatican II and Medellín brought the long running, informal, and grassroots sentiments into the formal discourse of the Catholic Church. In El Salvador, the "National Pastoral Week" in July 1970 brought together the archbishop, two auxiliary bishops, and more than 100 priests. They came to teach their followers the doctrine of liberation theology and to show them how to form base communities, or self-reliant, smaller groups that could come together to pray, worship, or engage in political action (Peterson 1997). In 1972, a group of Jesuits arrived in El Salvador to refine and enforce these efforts.

Simply put, the idea behind liberation theology is that parishioners can be agents of social change and that God wants them to change repressive structures (Berryman 1984). Because of political and economic trends, repression and poverty increased among the lower classes in the 1970s (Booth 1991). This affected the process of *reflexión* as experienced in the Christian base communities and made it easier to funnel people from Bible studies into organizations designed for political action.

Many social scientists who study liberation theology argue that it radically reorients the individual from passive behavior and a fatalistic world view to activism and a belief that one can shape the world in which he or she lives (Berryman 1984; Cardenal 1990; Peterson 1997; Smith 1991, 1994). This view is reinforced by the short-term events in El Salvador during the late 1960s and 1970s. Berryman (1984) is certainly right when he states that popular organizations grew out of pastoral work in the rural areas.

But it is worth remembering that this was not the first peasant revolution in El Salvador (Kincaid 1993). The perception that the Salvadoran world view was fatalistic, and that the Salvadoran poor were thus passive before the arrival of liberation theology, must be tempered with the reality that the state found it necessary to militarize the coffee zones decades earlier, that monistic corporatism had been subdued by liberalism for more than a century, that the country's archbishop[10] had been accused of being a communist in the 1940s – evidence that he was not just a puppet of the elite (Cardenal 1990) – and that the syncretistic elements present in the rural areas may or may not have supported a more fatalistic outlook. In the Salvadoran context, it seems the more realistic claim is that liberation theology provided institutional legitimacy and the ability to articulate

Salvador, this would be surprising because evangelical growth accelerated long after the decisive moves within the Salvadoran Catholic Church had already been made.

[10] Archbishop Oscar Romero became an internationally recognized martyr in the Salvadoran conflict. The Archbishop who preceded Romero was Monseigneur Luis Chávez y Gonzalez. He served as Archbishop of San Salvador for thirty-eight years, from 1938 to 1977. There were some conservative elements to Chavez y Gonzalez's thinking. However, he supported the spread of liberation theology in El Salvador and in fact presided over the most important years of its expansion. He also wrote some important pastoral letters advocating social justice.

feelings of injustice that already existed, and which at times had been acted upon. Just as importantly, the progressive sectors of the church provided the critical resources necessary for mobilization, including effective leaders and organizational structures. This assessment is in line with Roger Lancaster's (1988) view that people will always do what they can to resist oppression and that religion often offers tools for this resistance.[11]

Fueled in part by religious actors, political tensions escalated throughout the 1970s, and civil war formally broke out in 1980. The war itself was an extremely complex event. The primary activity swirled around six different sets of actors: the elites, the military, the Salvadoran government, the U.S. government, the Farabundo Marti National Liberation Front (FMLN), and the Catholic Church. The groups allied or pitted themselves against one another during various stages and in different spheres of the conflict.[12] The Salvadoran civil war was both a logical progression of the country's longstanding tensions and one of many theaters in which the Cold War was played out. As such, it had the power to fundamentally reorient the country's identity and structural constitution, moving El Salvador from a tightly controlled territory to a nation that essentially exists across state borders. In many ways, El Salvador emerged from the war as an authentically transnational state.

It was also shortly before and during the civil war that the evangelical presence in El Salvador first became discernible.[13] The turbulence of the war

[11] In the introduction to his seminal work on coffee in Central America, Robert Williams (1994) recounts his first trip through the region in the early 1970s, when he was struck by the variation of attitudes and culture among the different countries. Given such variation, it is quite possible that a passivity associated with corporate monism has stronger explanatory power in other parts of Central America.

[12] El Salvador's civil war was a horrible and bloody affair. Roughly 75,000 people lost their lives. More than 85 percent of the serious acts of violence analyzed by the Truth Commission for El Salvador (1993), organized by the United Nations, were initiated by Salvadoran state agents. The military's strategy of waging a low-intensity war resulted in large numbers of civilian deaths. U.S. government funding for military activities made them complicit in many of these deaths. Several massacres were carried out in the countryside, among the more infamous of which occurred in and around a town called El Mozote in the remote department of Morazan, where about 1,000 people were killed (Binford 1996). In January 2012, the Funes administration issued a public apology for the massacre on behalf of the state. In all, the Salvadoran army "massacred thousands of *campesinos* in guerrilla zones in a deliberate strategy to terrorize the population and eliminate sources of supply and information for the guerrillas" (Popkin 2000, 47). The environment was such that assassinations, kidnappings, and various other types of human rights violations became routine.

[13] The history of Salvadoran evangelicalism up to 1980 has been adequately covered by Philip Williams (1997). He describes the entrance of traditional and Pentecostal churches into the country in the late nineteenth and early twentieth centuries. He also charts the growth and ultimate predominance of the Pentecostal sector while noting the continuing importance of the Central American Mission and some Baptist denominations. Among Pentecostals, the largest denominations were the Assemblies of God and the Church of God. But all of these groups remained quite small up through the 1970s, when together they represented approximately 3 percent of the population.

hastened evangelical growth because it served as the pyre for the old moral order. Evangelical churches rushed into the unsettled environment and provided a message of transcendence in a troubled world as well as a secure and more egalitarian set of social relationships. These wartime evangelicals were almost exclusively poor. In fact, Coleman et al. (1993) found that when compared with practicing Catholics, non-practicing Catholics, and religiously non-affiliated Salvadorans, Protestants ranked last in mean income and median income, displayed the lowest percentage of respondents in the high-end income category, and were the least educated. This is consistent with what Lancaster (1988) found in neighboring Nicaragua. Because evangelicals in El Salvador still did not represent more than a tenth of the population and because of their social status, they had little to no effect on the war itself. This comes as no surprise to scholars of Latin American religion; David Smilde (1998, 288) sums up the view of Latin American Pentecostal scholars nicely:

... new identities, expectations, and social formations are distanced from overt political action, argue these scholars, not because of some inherent incompatibility (between Pentecostalism and politics), but because of Pentecostals' social marginalization (Burdick 1993), the practical impossibility of success (Levine and Stoll 1997), and the danger of political action in Latin America (Stoll 1990; Martin 1990).

Although still marginalized, the evangelical movement had clearly arrived in El Salvador and would have to be recognized in future chapters of the country's history.

Recasting Salvadoran Society

At the end of the war in 1992, peace and democratic consolidation were the highest priorities on the national agenda, but massive migration during and after the war was (and continues to be) the primary shaper of El Salvador's identity. The war forced roughly 1 million people to flee the country (Lungo Ucles 1996), and emigration has remained heavy since then. An estimated 3.2 million Salvadorans live outside the country, with more than 2 million of those in the United States. This accounts for a remarkable 30 percent of the Salvadoran population; the magnitude of this demographic shift has dramatically altered the country's social, economic, and political structures.

The alteration has been such that some scholars refer to El Salvador as "perhaps the perfect example of transnationalism," or the way nation states are no longer constrained by geographical boundaries (Yelvington 2004, ix). The Salvadoran case is an empirical example of how social, political, and economic systems adapt to a transnational way of life (Pederson 2013). Such adaptations help to ensure that emigrants remain connected to those they leave behind and that a steady migration flow will continue indefinitely. While the original spurs for migration were war and violence, today young Salvadorans flow through these (still treacherous) cross-border constructions motivated by economic need but also by economic opportunity, adventure, and the chance to be seen as heroes in their villages of origin (Coutin 2007). They often join the Salvadoran communities in Los Angeles (which is the second largest Salvadoran city, after San Salvador); Washington, DC; San Francisco; or New York (Baker-Cristales 2004; Pederson 2013). Because of U.S. migration policy, Salvadorans who come illegally are now also being pushed into new destinations that include Kentucky, Virginia, the Carolinas, and other traditionally "non-immigrant" states (Massey 2007). But not all Salvadorans who come are poor or illegal, and some who did come while they were poor have moved into the middle class. The composition of the Los Angeles–based Salvadoran community roughly corresponds to the ratios of rich, middle class, and poor in El Salvador (Baker-Cristales 2004).

Back in El Salvador, people who live in Department 15 – an imaginary department that covers all territory beyond the country's fourteen departments or provinces – are considered to be very much a part of the Salvadoran community. Cultural narratives have emerged through songs, poems, visual art, and other forms of popular discourse that both confirm and help to construct an identity of a single nation that is now spatially located in numerous other countries (Rodriguez 2005).

Among the strongest civil institutions that hold this identity together are churches. The normal migrant experience now allows travelers to stay within existing social networks as they cross territorial borders. Family networks are most important in the process, but religious networks also play a critical role, and often family and religious networks are one and the same (Levitt 2007). In the Salvadoran transnational experience, Catholic and evangelical churches played a particularly important role in migration from the outset because of their response to the wartime migration wave. Not only did Catholic and mainline churches serve as sanctuaries, but a Baptist denomination led the struggle for Salvadorans to gain Temporary Protected Status (TPS) in the U.S. District Court for the Northern District of California case *American Baptist Churches v. Thornburgh* (Menjivar 2003; Smith 1996). Links are also maintained by U.S.-based Salvadoran civic and business associations and other community-oriented groups (Baker-Cristales 2004; Coutin 2007; Mahler 1995). The tremendous and troubling strength of transnational Salvadoran gangs and other more clandestine networks must also be noted (Brenneman 2012; Gomez & Vasquez 2001; Reisman 2006). But ultimately, family and congregations create and sustain transnational linkages far more frequently than any other social institutions.

El Salvador's social networks have facilitated transnational economic flows. Remittances to El Salvador rose from an estimated $75 million in 1980 to $3.97 billion in 2013 (Central Reserve Bank of El Salvador 2014). They now account for the equivalent of about 17 percent of the country's GDP, and UNDP surveys show that an estimated 21.3 percent of all families in El Salvador receive remittances (United Nations Development Programme 2005). As early as the mid-1990s, remittances had outstripped all other Salvadoran exports *combined.*[14]

Salvadoran economic structures have adapted to remittances and to a larger strategy of regional integration. Part of this strategy included the dollarization of the national economy in 2001, a politically hazardous move by then-president Flores, but one motivated in no small part by its ability to reduce transaction costs associated with sending remittances (Quispe-Agnoli & Whisler 2006). Remittances and the existence of a large Salvadoran migrant community in the United States also certainly played a role in El Salvador's rapid ratification of CAFTA in March 2006. Policy makers now depend on remittances to stabilize the economy and to provide a buffer when structural adjustments either fail or take time to create their intended effects.

Such macroeconomic policies reveal the extent to which remittances have reshaped El Salvador's private sector. Because of economic and political forces that took shape in the 1970s, the agro-export model upon which El Salvador was originally built became moribund (Wood 2000). In its place, a remittance-based economy has arisen in which the most important sectors of the business community compete to capture the domestic consumption of remittance dollars. Many observers have thus noted the resulting consumer orientation of Salvadoran society, especially in the nation's capital.[15]

El Salvador's political structures are also adjusting to the country's transnational realities. In the 1990s, the Salvadoran government tried to usher the emigrants and their contributions to society into a formally recognized position.[16] President Calderon Sol (1994–1999) successfully lobbied the Clinton administration for legal recognition of undocumented workers in the United States. To create a united front, ex-ambassador to the United States, Cristina Sol,

---

[14] The question of remittance classification and ownership is also an interesting one. They are claimed by both sending and receiving nations; it shows up on the balance of payments of El Salvador's budget as both a product that has been exported (labor) and a gift that has been imported. Meanwhile, the United States (laughably) claimed remittances as part of its aid package to El Salvador after the 2001 earthquakes (Hernandez & Coutin 2006). Such questions reveal that while some scholars have described the initial impulse for migration and others have shown how remittances are part of a long-term family economic strategy, much confusion continues to swirl around this relatively recent social phenomenon.

[15] The popular conception of the economy in El Salvador is that nothing of moment is produced in-country. Rather, El Salvador is simply and only a country that consumes. Such perceptions are reinforced by the numerous major malls and shopping plazas that have sprung up since 2002. Experience tells residents that remittances come to El Salvador, foster consumption, and when the money is spent, it ends up in the hands of powerful economic elites in the country or back in the United States. "Es un gran ciclo" (It is a big cycle), I was told repeatedly, in both interviews and in ethnographic work. Although the economic realities are (slightly) more complex, the popular perception is that El Salvador has become a "remittance republic," close cousin to the "banana republic."

[16] Previously the government has been either hostile or indifferent to emigrants, as many were enemies or potential enemies of the regime who had become political refugees. Migration dynamics were thus played out under the radar and without support from the state.

made frequent visits to Salvadoran hometown associations that were formed in the United States by migrants. In the early 1990s, these overtures were strained because the government, controlled by ARENA, represented the very people who many of the migrants had been trying to escape. But the new transnational reality brought government and grassroots interests into line, as both sides recognized the need for an alliance in seeking legal security for keeping Salvadorans in the United States (Coutin 2007).

In addition to diplomatic work, the Salvadoran government created the General Directorate of Attention to the Community Living Abroad (DGACE), which is intended to promote migratory stability, family reunification, local development as it is connected to remittances, economic integration, and the promotion of a (transnational) national identity (DGACE 2007). The Francisco Flores administration (1999–2004) also required "all government ministries to report on their efforts in relation to Salvadorans in the exterior, developed a website with more than five hundred pages of information for and about Salvadorans in the exterior, devised a competition to award matching funds to support hometown associations' development projects, and in 2004 created a ministry post devoted to the community in the exterior" (Coutin 2007, 74). Subsequent administrations have continued Flores's initiatives.

Salvadoran community associations in the United States have also become active at the polls. A business association in Los Angeles supports municipal candidates through endorsements and campaign contributions. These kinds of activities may open up the major political parties to more transnational influence in the future. Baker-Cristales (2004) reported that at the time of her research, both ARENA and the FMLN had maintained a fairly territorial focus. However, Tony Saca made multiple, politically motivated trips to Los Angeles toward the end of his presidency, and Mauricio Funes visited Los Angeles, Miami, and Washington, DC during his term in office. National political actors now clearly see the need to network with El Salvador's diasporic communities.

In sum, El Salvador's new transnational identity continues to be negotiated. The influence of Salvadorans in the United States is likely to increase, at least in the short term. El Salvador's political and economic structures have largely been reoriented to reflect such changes. Religion will continue to provide civil structures that are critical to a transnational way of life. The evangelical community in El Salvador will continue to be active in starting new churches in the United States and elsewhere. How this will affect the Salvadoran evangelical community over the long term remains to be seen.

SOUTH AFRICA

If El Salvador is relatively homogenous in its ethnic mix, South Africa's population of 50 million is celebrated for its diversity. The country proudly proclaims eleven official languages. According to Statistics South Africa's mid-year estimates in 2011, the population is 79.5 percent black African, 9.0 percent white, 9.0 percent Coloured,[17] and 2.5 percent Indian or Asian. These demographic categories are holdovers from the apartheid regime but are still used in South Africa today. The black population is constituted by numerous tribes; among the more important are the Xhosa, Zulu, Venda, and Basotho. The Afrikaners, who are descendants of Dutch colonizers, and the English are the primary white groups. However, several other European nations and a Jewish population are also present. The Indians in South Africa were first brought to the country to serve as slaves beginning in the seventeenth century and were joined for similar reasons by a strong Malay population. Some Chinese and Taiwanese have immigrated more recently. Ethnic ties in South Africa thus stretch up into Africa and across other continents.

Politics

Excitement was in the air when South Africa emerged from apartheid in 1994. The latter moments of its struggle for democracy were played out on the world stage, and Nelson Mandela became one of the great figures of the twentieth century. The country's new leaders immediately went to work crafting a new order and laying the foundations for consolidating the young democracy. South African journalist Allister Sparks (2003) provided a litany of the new South Africa's achievements in its first decade: the entrenchment of a democratic constitution, a constitutional court, the scrapping of all the old race laws, the advancement of women in many areas of life, the (nominal) integration of 30,000 public schools, a dramatic rise in the literacy rate of the young, and the new and prominent role of South Africa in the international community. The early period of democracy was indeed a time of significant social progress.

Political control now rests with the African National Congress (ANC) and its tripartite alliance with the South African Communist Party (SACP) and the Congress of South African Trade Unions (COSATU). In fact, one of the few structural concerns for South Africa's democracy is that the ANC now effectively governs the country as a single-party state.[18] Most of South Africa's political intrigue thus occurs within the ANC, a fact that is almost daily put on public display. The 2007 battle for the ANC presidency revealed a major fissure in the party. Thabo Mbeki, a highly educated, aloof incumbent, had become the representative of a classically liberal, pro-capitalist, globally oriented new black elite. He was defeated by Jacob Zuma, a charismatic populist whose formal education did not go beyond grade school and with whom the masses identified. Other fissures plagued Zuma's subsequent presidency. Zuma's team clashed with the powerful ANC Youth League and was unable to restore harmony

---

[17] "Coloured" refers to people of mixed race descent in South Africa.

[18] One party that has visions of becoming a legitimate opposition party is the Democratic Alliance (DA). Presently, though, it has no real bite and contents itself with nipping at the ANC's heels in such a way that the ANC may or may not pay any attention.

between the ANC and the SACP and between the ANC and the trade unions. It had been expected that Zuma's victory over Mbeki would shore up these relationships. Although the ANC's dominance over other South African political parties is still unquestioned, commentators increasingly believe that this will not always be the case (*Economist* 2013b). Still, Zuma was reelected as the president of South Africa in 2014.

The country's current political realities are the product of a history that dates back to the colonial period. The Dutch became the first European power to establish a colony in the region. Initially, they came in 1652 to establish a trading post and populated the areas of Cape Town and Stellenbosch over the next several decades. Many of the early immigrants were Huguenots, who were responsible for much of the intellectual activity. Indeed, many of the leading colonial families were Huguenots, according to early scholar Bartle Frere (1889). The Dutch were able to develop their colony without interference by other European powers until the end of the eighteenth century, importing slaves via the Dutch East India Company to help them in this task (Frere 1889). At the end of the century, however, the British established themselves for the first time in South Africa. British troops came first to thwart Napoleon Bonaparte's designs on the region, but the British soon recognized the benefits of British rule along the Cape. By 1815, the English had established sovereignty over the Cape and over the Afrikaners[19] who had been living there for well over a century.

Unrelated to the Dutch and English incursions, seismic shifts among southern Africa's indigenous tribes occurred in the early nineteenth century. Shaka became king of the Zulus in roughly 1815. A warrior by trade, Shaka used innovative warfare strategies to unite and mobilize as many as 300 formerly independent chiefdoms into the Zulu Kingdom. As he expanded his empire, Shaka displaced or conquered numerous neighboring pastoral tribes. This set off a chain of events that is now referred to as *Mfecane* or *Difaqane*, where war among multiple tribes enveloped the western and central regions of South Africa from roughly 1815 to 1840. The widespread destruction and loss of life caused by these wars led to the Mfecane becoming one of the pivotal events in the history of southern Africa. The decline of the Zulu Kingdom after Shaka's assassination, the weakening of the other tribal powers through the Mfecane, and the increasing European interest in the area helped to make European colonialists the region's most powerful actors (Deflem 1999; Hamilton 1992).

The Afrikaners, however, were increasingly unhappy with the English intrusion into their colony. In addition to the loss of independence, Afrikaner culture clashed with certain Enlightenment values the British brought with them, such as the equality of all races. To escape British control, a group of Afrikaners began what is known as the "Great Trek" in 1835. They traveled north, into the

---

[19] Over time, the Dutch who had migrated to South Africa developed an identity distinct from their mother country. South African descendants of Dutch immigrants are thus referred to as Afrikaners or as Boers.

wilderness of Africa and away from the Cape Colony. It was a journey and a ritual that still affects their identity and geographic location within the country. The Trekkers settled in pastoral lands that had just been cleared in part by the Mfecane, in the general region of what is now Johannesburg. The Afrikaners' wilderness experience allowed them to transform into a pastoral community and to become, in many ways, essentially tribal (Harrison 1981).

Afrikaner life in the Cape was largely structured by their congregational life and religious beliefs. But Irving Hexham and Karla Poewe (1997) argue that the Trekkers, in an important sense, left the church in the Cape. That is, leaders of the established church in the Cape forbade the Great Trek and considered it to be a rebellion. Those who left did not officially renounce their faith in the process, but they were only in the most marginal sense accompanied by the institutionalized church. This left them open to developing a religion that closely fit their surroundings. Many beliefs and practices of the black African tribes surrounding them seeped into their own world view, including the formation of small clans, the practice of witchcraft, and the development of skills such as telepathy. One could surmise that a religious spirit more closely attached to ethnic identity than the historic Christianity of Europe might relate to later Boer religious justification for apartheid (Wood 2011). As early as 1839, an American missionary wrote that Afrikaners were in dire need of evangelization.[20] Subsequently, the Dutch Reformed Church made some moves to address this behavior, but use of witchdoctors by the Boers persisted into the twentieth century (Elphick & Davenport 1997).

It would only be a matter of decades before the British followed the Afrikaners into the African bush. Vast mineral mines were found in Kimberly in 1867, and gold was found in Johannesburg in 1886. Both areas had been claimed and inhabited by Afrikaners, but the precarious task of building a colonial empire induced the British to aggressively seek these resources (Richardson & Van-Helten 1984; Van-Helten 1982). The Afrikaners, of course, had little sympathy for the needs of the British Empire. The clash of interests and the personal ambition of Cecil Rhodes resulted in the Boer Wars of 1880–1881 and 1899–1902. These wars were gruesome[21] and, to the black African, not entirely sensible.[22]

---

[20] The religious indigenization of the Trekkers should not be overstated. Nurnberger (1990) lays out four ways in which the Bible continued to shape their cosmos: 1) spiritual sustenance: biblical faith supplied the overall system of meaning and a system of values and norms; 2) identity formation: Trekkers depended on the Bible for its clues concerning its self-interpretation and the interpretation of its historic experience, merging concepts of Israel and the church; 3) educational medium: the Bible was often the only book the family possessed, and it linked them to their European heritage; and 4) the use of biblical presuppositions to legitimate Boer social, economic, and political institutions.

[21] A popular British strategy was to keep Afrikaner women in what amounted to prison camps. This served to de-motivate and cut off important support for Afrikaner soldiers. About 500,000 British troops were fighting against less than 50,000 Afrikaners. The war was nonetheless bitter to the end. A quote from a captain of the British unit captures the social implications of the war: "We can't exterminate the Dutch or seriously reduce their numbers. We can however do enough

A new political arrangement was forged in the aftermath of the British victory. This was a moment in which liberal ideals of the British Empire could have created political openings for people of all colors. Instead, the British brokered an exclusive peace agreement with the Afrikaners. Anthony Marx (1998) quotes at length both the revisions Afrikaners' General Jan Smuts made to the peace treaty and the words of Lord Alfred Milner, Britain's leader in southern Africa, to show that the Afrikaners, driven by a nationalist sentiment, which was fortified both by religion and the war experience, would not enter a more inclusive agreement. Because the Afrikaners remained the primary threat to stability for the British, British decision makers essentially sold out black African allies by agreeing to terms dictated by the Afrikaners (Marx 1998).

After the Boer Wars, Lord Milner oversaw the development of structures that continue to shape South Africa's political economy today. A Lockean, Milner believed that the rule of law was the key to providing a secure environment in which people could compete in a free market and thus improve their lot in life. The Anglo liberal-capitalist model he instituted thus sought to gather the disparate African tribes and cultures into a single unified state. Having already broken the principal resisters to this project (the Afrikaners), Milner then induced the other pastorally based African tribes to acquiesce in this arrangement, and modernization began. Milner and his cabinet, or "kindergarten," consisting of highly educated recruits from Britain, set about to create bureaucratic and taxation structures, as well as an "efficient civil service, police force, and judicial system. These became the foundation for South Africa's unified system of government. The kindergarten framed the legislative backbone upon which modernization, capitalist industrialization, and urbanization was built" (Louw 2004, 11).

An orderly state thus emerged under British rule that was based on liberal enlightenment principles, but it was also an inherently racially stratified social system. Such stratification predated even the Boer Wars. George Fredrickson notes that the "two key elements of apartheid – a white monopoly on political power and the designation of separate living areas or 'homelands' – were set out in preindustrial frontier polities still struggling with independent African nations on their borders" (1997, 46). In the first half of the twentieth century, when the British controlled South Africa and before apartheid was instituted, black Africans were not allowed to vote. Only a few were integrated into the colonial education system. Rather, blacks found employment in the mines, as domestic servants, or in the labor-intensive agricultural industry. From a cultural

---

to make hatred of England and thirst for revenge the first duty of every Dutchman" (Cassidy 1989, 58).

[22] When standing on one of the battlefields of the Boer War, a black African commented to me that many white men had died in this place fighting for land that belonged to neither side. The comment provided even more nobility to the war than it deserves, as it implies that it was a "white-on-white" war. The reality was that both sides employed black Africans to their own ends; Marx (1998) estimates that 50,000 non-white Africans were involved in the war efforts.

perspective, black and white South Africans remained worlds apart. It was not too great a jump, then, from this arrangement into apartheid.

The apartheid system grew out of a move toward Afrikaner nationalism that was led by Boer intellectuals and spurred on by the unpleasant Afrikaner experience with British imperialism. The movement was already afoot in the 1930s when theologians, such as Nico Diederichs, built a political theology from Dutch Calvinist theologian Abraham Kuyper's work that justified, and in many ways mandated, the separation of different nations into different geographical spheres.[23] With Kuyper as an intellectual antecedent and German schools of thought also heavily influential (Cassidy 1989), there was a profound distinction in theory between the Lockean English model and the apartheid model proposed by the Broederbond[24] and the rest of the National Party leadership. Concurrently, the working class Afrikaners intensely felt that the English had imposed upon them the status of second class citizenship. They were forced to compete with black labor for jobs, which kept wages quite low, and which were further lowered by the English practice of bringing in migrant workers. Beyond the problem of wages, migrant workers presented yet another preoccupation for Afrikaners: they were worried that whites would be numerically swamped and a black African state would become inevitable. Thus, at its heart, "apartheid represented a radical nationalist program for ending Anglo hegemony and reconfiguring the racial-capitalist socioeconomic order" (Louw 2004, 33).

In theory, apartheid's proposition was to break down the single state that Milner had established and recapture the independence of the various nations that had been drawn into the South African political economy. Geographical separation would allow African tribes to become self-governing, and South Africa would shrink and become exclusively white. In particular, for Afrikaners, the move made sense because it would allow them to avoid the black rule that would come with a majoritarian democracy, and it would keep them from being reconquered by the British; since 60 percent of whites were Afrikaners, they would be able to enjoy a majority rule in a white democratic state (Louw 2004). In practice, however, the apartheid system failed miserably.[25] Even though considerable resources were dedicated to this massive social

---

[23] It should be clear that it is Diederichs's work, not Kuyper's, that mandated the separation of different nations. Some current scholars believe that Kuyper's original work was twisted by the apartheid theologians (Freston 2001). The Abraham Kuyper Center's web page certainly agrees with this analysis and provides some justification for the few times where Kuyper's work does explicitly appear to be racist.

[24] The *Broederbond* is technically an Afrikaans term meaning "league of Afrikaner brothers." It was founded in 1918 and became a secret society whose primary goal was to further the interests of Afrikaner nationalism.

[25] This depends, of course on what one considers the true goals of apartheid. Some contend that the primary goal of apartheid was to lift working class Afrikaners out of their fight for employment opportunities with blacks and into a higher social class. If this was the driving force behind apartheid policy, then the scheme was quite successful (John Stone, personal correspondence, 2008).

engineering enterprise, the end result was a single state characterized by an overt
and legally instituted form of racism.

Apartheid lasted from 1948 to 1994, during which time the various heads of
state exhibited different levels of commitment to a full implementation of the
apartheid project. Prime Minister Hendrik Verwoerd (1958–1966), referred
to as the "architect of apartheid," was the most radical in his efforts to implement the system of apartheid (Stone 2002). The ANC and other black political
parties were banned under his leadership. Verwoerd was assassinated on the
floor of congress in 1966 (Miller 1993), and John Vorster (1966–1978), his
successor, charted a slightly more moderate course. By the early 1980s, Prime
Minister P. W. Botha (1978–1989) recognized that apartheid would never be
implemented and began to seek other political options to ensure Afrikaner
independence (Louw 2004).

Botha's pragmatic outlook was affected by the growing resistance to apartheid both domestically and internationally. While resistance made apartheid
harder to implement, it also caused the apartheid regime to become more
militarized, and increasingly greater authority and autonomy was accorded to
the state's security apparatus. This in turn resulted in more and more human
rights violations (Louw 2004). In fact, the mid-1980s witnessed violence that
was previously unprecedented in the conflict (Cassidy 1989; Tutu 1999).[26]
Statistics on casualties during this time vary, but social unrest became such
that foreign investment was rapidly withdrawn from the country, thus crippling
the economy (Wood 2000). Many observers at this point believed that South
Africa was headed toward full-scale civil war, although a few scholars were able
to imagine strategies that would result in the successful dismantling of the
apartheid regime (Adam & Moodley 1986; Berger & Godsell 1988).

Like El Salvador, events in South Africa were heavily influenced by the Cold
War. Members of the National Party, and in fact most white South Africans,
believed that they were fighting against communism as they fought against the
armed wing of the ANC. This restricted the options of negotiating with the
ANC for National Party leaders and kept some measure of support for the
government coming from Anglos in the country as well as from the government
in the United States. However, when the Berlin Wall fell in 1989, the new Prime
Minister F. W. De Klerk gained more room to open a dialogue with ANC
leaders, and the Anglo-American preference for apartheid largely evaporated

---

[26] The atrocities of the apartheid era are far too long to be recounted here. Unjust legislation included
the 1950 Group Areas Act, the 1953 Bantu Education Act, and the 1956 Mines and Work Act.
Such legislation undergirded activities like forced resettlements in the 1960s, 1970s, and 1980s.
The Sharpeville massacre in 1969, the Soweto uprising in 1976, the assassination of Steve Biko,
the incarceration of many ANC leaders, and numerous other smaller and more personal events,
such as the murder of the Cradock Four, torturing political prisoners, the very existence of
Robben Island, and the routine oppression in many townships (especially in the 1980s) all created
a moral outrage that cannot be fully vetted in this text. It has, however, been captured by other
authors, including Tutu (1999).

(John Stone, personal correspondence, 2008). In 1990, Nelson Mandela was released from prison, and the ban on political parties such as the ANC, SACP, and the Pan Africanist Congress (PAC) was lifted. This marked the formal beginning of the dismantling of the apartheid system, a process that was fraught with multiple political dangers, any of which could have derailed efforts for peace. Indeed, the death tolls resulting from violence from 1990 to 1994 significantly exceeded the numbers of even the mid-1980s. The following statement from the Final Report of the Truth and Reconciliation Commission provides some idea of the scale of political violence that was endured as well as the power dynamics involved.

Of 9,043 statements received on killings, over half of these (5,695) occurred during the 1990 to 1994 period. These figures give an indication of violations recorded by the Commission during the negotiations process. They represent a pattern of violation, rather than an accurate reflection of levels of violence and human rights abuses. Sources other than the Commission have reported that, from the start of the negotiations in mid-1990 to the election in April 1994, some 14,000 South Africans died in politically related incidents. While Commission figures for reported violations in the earlier part of its mandate period are underrepresented in part because of the passage of time, they are under-reported in this later period because the abuses are still fresh in people's memories and closely linked into current distribution of power. (Truth and Reconciliation Commission 1998, 584)

But due to a coalescence of political and economic interests of the primary players involved, as well as intense background negotiations (some by evangelicals), extraordinary political acumen by key players, and a series of rather fortuitous turns, the process culminated not in full-scale war but in free and fair, if somewhat chaotic, democratic elections in 1994 (Sparks 2003). International media and political actors widely referred to this positive outcome as a miracle.

Such a claim makes more sense when it is remembered that the politics of South Africa have always been soaked in religion and spirituality. Spiritual authority is critical for political leaders in the African context (Ellis & Haar 2004). Accessing the spirit world through witchcraft, praying to ancestors, and the highly important symbolism of blood are just a few of the indigenous religious ideas that have shaped political action in the past and continue to do so today. But it was Christianity that provided a theological justification for apartheid and helped to pattern race relations in South Africa (De Gruchy 1990). Christian beliefs, institutions, and actors were also instrumental in South Africa's democratic transition (Amstutz 2005). The South African Council of Churches was deeply involved in "the struggle." Some denominations, like the Methodists, allowed member churches to bring black and white congregations together in the midst of apartheid. Perhaps most importantly, there were many religious leaders such as Archbishop Desmond Tutu who played important roles throughout. Some of these were evangelicals, such as Michael Cassidy, who co-chaired the National Initiative for Reconciliation in the 1980s with Tutu, and

Frank Chikane, a Pentecostal minister who spoke out against the apartheid regime and who served as a member of Mbeki's cabinet. The entire enterprise of the Truth and Reconciliation Commission was based on Christian theological principles and led by religious leaders. In short, the political history just outlined was profoundly shaped and steered by religion, a reality that has been more fully elucidated by other scholars (see Comaroff 1985; Elphick & Davenport 1997).

Economics

Two decades removed from apartheid, it is now possible to understand the continuity of South Africa's economy throughout the twentieth century. The management of the economy has changed from regime to regime. When regimes changed, different ethnic groups became favored, but important continuities survived through British, Boer, and now ANC governance. These include a formal economy that is not expansive enough to include all of South Africa's citizens, a prominent migrant labor force, and economic structures built around the exportation of minerals.

There have long been essentially two economies in South Africa. One is not particularly different from other First World economies; the other is driven by desperation and informal economic activity. Under Mbeki, South Africa's president from 1999 to 2009, neoliberal economic policies were the norm. The Zuma presidency, for the most part, maintained these policies. GDP grew at a rate above 5 percent from 2005 to 2008 (Economic Intelligence Unit 2011b) but did not go above 3.5 percent from 2009 to 2012 (Trading Economics 2014b). High prices on the world market for metal, significant new mining ventures, and the major infrastructural upgrades that were made for the 2010 World Cup, which South Africa hosted, have buoyed the first economy and have modestly expanded it to include a few more South African citizens. Some apartheid-era townships, like Soweto, now contain comfortable and even affluent neighborhoods. This indicates a growing black middle class (Schlemmer 2005), the development of which has long been high on the national agenda.

But such gains have been more than offset by rampantly growing squatter camps that surround all of the country's major cities. South Africa's inequality since 1994 has at least held steady if not increased, and the country's Gini coefficient currently ranks it the second most unequal out of 104 countries surveyed (CIA World Factbook 2011). About 37 percent of working-age people are jobless (*Economist* 2013b). South Africa's largest squatter camp, Khayelitsha, runs along the highway between Cape Town and Stellenbosch in a seemingly endless and densely populated maze of makeshift housing. Frustration is mounting in these large pockets of poverty, and whispers of a second revolution have been growing.

Like the political context, present economic dilemmas are better understood when their historical development is known. In the 1880s, about the time coffee was being planted in El Salvador, gold was found in the Witwatersrand of South Africa. The gold presented an irresistible temptation for the British to further penetrate Afrikaner territory, as they had already come up to Kimberly in the 1860s when diamonds were found. Thus, British commercial interests arrived in Johannesburg and began to create the necessary structures for a successful large scale mining project.

Capital, labor, and transportation systems were the primary components needed for this undertaking. The English and their closest European allies provided capital and owned the mines. Africans provided the necessary unskilled labor. Lord Milner, who relocated to Johannesburg after the Boer Wars, helped to bring migrant laborers from Mozambique, Lesotho, Swaziland, Botswana, and Malawi. According to Louw, "this migrant labor system underpinned racial capitalism throughout the twentieth century" (Louw 2004, 11). Semi-skilled labor was also needed, and people flocked from Europe to fill these posts, boosting the number of white settlers in South Africa far beyond that of the typical British colony (Marais 2001). Finally, South Africa's transportation systems were rapidly expanded and upgraded so that they could import supplies and export gold (Louw 2004). Johannesburg quickly became, and continues to be, the primary economic hub on the continent.

The scale of mining in South Africa overwhelmed all other economic activity in the country. It grew so expansively and so rapidly that by the late 1890s, just a little over a decade after gold was discovered, South Africa was producing a quarter of the world's output of gold (Van-Helten 1982). There had been relatively little economic or infrastructure development in the colony previous to the mineral finds, and pastoral and agricultural activities had dominated economic life. Most of the industries that were to develop after the discovery of gold were secondary to mining and dependent on mining activities.

The Afrikaners did not change the basic structures of the British economy when they introduced the apartheid system in 1948. In fact, the Afrikaner vision for the economy was never fully articulated (the National Party, which was the Afrikaner party, did not expect to win the 1948 elections and was not fully ready to implement apartheid at that point). But during apartheid the economy became more sophisticated through industrial growth and the introduction of diversified manufacturing (which was actually cultivated under Milner) and financial sectors. While intended to strengthen an economy run by the Boers, such economic expansion also "provided crucial new elements in the overthrow of white supremacy: the gathering strength of organized labor, the powerful tactics of consumer boycotts, and the expanding, politically conscious, urban proletariat, so often associated with demands for social change" (Stone 2002, 116). Stone notes the way in which South Africa developed an integrated economy, a development that ran counter to the stated political goals of apartheid. But the integrated economy maintained very distinct tiers: the many migrant and non-migrant mine workers barely managed to get by on their extremely low wages while the few elite grew stronger and richer.

In the past two decades, the South African economy has become even more complex. Technological advances and the end of economic isolation in the apartheid era have sped innovation under the ANC government. As the population has grown, increased division of labor has occurred, and greater economic diversity has resulted. New economic sectors, especially white collar areas such as computers or finance, have made the overall economy less dependent on the mines and heavy industry. This is reflected by the fact that mining now accounts for only 5.4 percent of South Africa's GDP (Economic Intelligence Unit 2008b).

And yet the basic economic template still exists. Although mining's percentage of GDP is modest, minerals continue to make up about 50 percent of the country's exports (Economic Intelligence Unit 2008b). Gold continues to play a central role, and platinum's importance is growing in national economic policy and strategy. Some have justifiably argued that South Africa underwent a revolution but did not change (Goodman 1999). Stability during regime change was indeed a priority, as every effort was made to avoid full-scale war. Thus, especially in the first two years of his presidency, Mandela sought to avoid a counter-insurgency movement from white conservatives, many of whom were armed (Sparks 2003). Mandela emphasized the messages of reconciliation and the new rainbow nation. He followed economic policies that would calm the nerves of the business sector and keep "white flight" to somewhat manageable levels. A relationship developed between the ANC leadership and corporate moguls, which began in secret meetings in Angola in 1986. During the Mandela administration, a process commonly called Nedlac (the National Economic Development and Labour Council) formally brought representatives of trade unions, business, and the state together within a structure that effectively pressured all sides to make compromises for the national interest (Louw 2004).

In this way, the system of two nations and two economies within South Africa has been preserved. After a slow start, ANC-instituted neoliberal economic policies have bolstered the position of the "first economy," but they have at least maintained if not widened the gap between it and the "second economy." Pressure is becoming more intense to expand the circle of "winners" in the overall economy. Some blacks are integrating themselves into the middle and upper classes, but many more are being left behind. Zuma, like his predecessor Mbeki, strove to maintain a unified black national ethos through cultural projects, but such efforts have been undermined by the fundamental economic cleavage in society and the fact that delivery of social services for the poor, including core services such as health care and education, is one of the ANC's glaring weak spots (*Economist* 2012a, 2012b). These problems have plagued the ANC since it took office in 1994.

Migration

Today, there are two distinct migration patterns: mostly white emigration from South Africa to Western countries and mostly black immigration from the rest of the African continent into South Africa. Emigration, also known in South Africa as "white flight" or "the brain drain," was one of the ANC's major concerns as it came to power. In 1994, 10,235 people left South Africa, and about 8,000 to 9,000 per year continued to leave for the rest of the decade (Hussein 2003). The South African Network of Skills Abroad estimated that between 1989 and 1997 a total of 233,000 South Africans emigrated permanently (Oucho 2006). It is believed that, in 2003, the number of emigrants was 16,000, up by as much as 50 percent over the previous year. In 2009 *Newsweek* reported that the South African government does not keep reliable emigration statistics but that whites continued to leave the country in large numbers (Johnson 2009). As they have flowed out of South Africa, white South Africans have created enclaves in Australia, New Zealand, the United Kingdom, and elsewhere. These enclaves include scientists, medical professionals, lawyers, businesspeople, and others. Migration of black professionals from African countries into South Africa has somewhat eased the problems created by the loss of skilled labor. This kind of movement has occurred in lower volumes than anticipated, but changes in South African immigration law could create greater flows in the future. This may, however, ultimately create greater inequalities between South Africa and its weaker neighbors (Crush et al. 2006; Oucho 2006).

Migration into South Africa by poor, unskilled workers is morphing as it increases. No one knows how many migrants are in South Africa,[27] but the 2001 census reported that South Africa's foreign-born population was 3 to 5 percent of the total of 48 million (Schlemmer 2006), and although a national total was not given, a province-by-province analysis yielded roughly similar statistics in 2011 (Statistics South Africa 2011). Within the Milnerist system, regional migration has long been cyclical, and male workers have regularly returned home to their families in other southern African countries. To wit, 41 percent of Botswanans and 54 percent of Mozambiquans claim their parents at one point worked in South Africa (Crush, Williams, & Peberdy 2005). But an important change in southern African migratory patterns is that cyclical migration appears to be *decreasing* even as overall migration is increasing. There are now different global and economic forces generating migratory patterns (Oucho 2006). The assumption of the South African government is that migrants are now coming with the intent to stay. It is difficult to know where migrants are coming from, but it is safe to say that two prominent groups are Nigerians and Zimbabweans. Women are also coming with greater regularity. Finally, those who come are creating economic chains back to their countries of origin. They are drawn by the markets that South Africa's cities provide, sell their wares in the market, and often send the profits back home. These newcomers are often visible simply because they are

---

[27] One scholar of South African migration states, "clearly, there is no reliable base on which to enumerate in a precise manner the demographics of the migrant foreign populations in South Africa," (Bouillon 2001, 20). Less academic sources, such as NationMaster.com, estimated that in 2011 there were about 1.1 million immigrants in South Africa.

on the city streets and because they are competing with South African black nationals for jobs. Immigrants are often winning these competitions (Crush & McDonald 2000), thus adding to feelings of xenophobia that are part of South African culture. A 2006 survey showed South Africa to be more against immigration than any other country in the world (Crush et al. 2006).

In May 2008, the xenophobic feelings were enflamed by immigration in South Africa and displayed for the world to see: violence broke out between South Africans and immigrants. At least fifty-nine people were killed and more than 50,000 were displaced (Seria 2008). The atrocious scene, in which mostly immigrant victims were lit on fire by attackers, could be seen on television screens across the world. Many acts of violence were carried out in Johannesburg townships, and the government was forced to respond by constructing refugee camps to remove immigrants from their aggressors. This was an embarrassment to the nation's reputation and a black eye as it prepared for the 2010 World Cup.

Religion

Christianity is by far the dominant religion in South Africa today, accounting for roughly 80 percent of the national population (Johnson 2014). The other major religions are Hinduism (the majority religion among Indians), Islam (most adherents are Indians or Malays), and Judaism. Indigenous beliefs are still held by many Africans, and practices such as worship of ancestors and blood sacrifices are still common. But these beliefs and practices are usually merged with other religions and so do not appear to be significant when a census is taken.

Among Christians, there are as many as 830 unique church groups operating in South Africa (Hendriks 2006). There are a number of different ways to group this vast array of denominations. Teichert (2005) uses the categories of main-line denominations, evangelicals, African Independent Churches (AICs), and the census to argue that there are roughly 11.5 million main-line Christians, 12 million evangelical Christians, and about 13 million members of African Independent Churches. Using a different classification system, Jurgens Hendriks (2006) argues that there are more than 14 million members of main-line churches, about 2.6 million members of charismatic/Pentecostal churches, 4.3 million members of "other churches," and 14.5 million members of the AICs. Counting anything in a context like South Africa is a speculative business.[28] Nevertheless, these estimates provide a general idea of the Christian landscape in South Africa.

---

[28] There were classification errors in the 2001 Statistics South Africa survey data, which both Hendriks and Teichert analyzed. Two examples include 215,000 whites were classified as members of AICs, when in all probability should have been classified as Pentecostals, and more than 1.4 million responses were incorrectly coded under Other Apostolic Churches, more than 1 million of whom should have been coded as members of the Apostolic Faith Mission and almost 400,000 of whom should have been coded as the Dutch Reformed Church (Teichert 2005; Hendriks 2006). Still, the 2001 census provided a general idea of the

Statistics for some of the most important individual denominations seem more dependable, if only because similar numbers or trends are reported year after year. In the main-line category, the families of Dutch Reformed and Methodist denominations as well as the Catholic Church have the greatest memberships, representing roughly 3.2 million members, 3.3 million members, and 3.18 million members, respectively. Numerically speaking, a second tier of main-line churches includes the Anglicans (1.7 million), the Lutherans (1.2 million), and the Presbyterians (800,000) (Hendriks 2006). Some of the larger and more established evangelical groups include the Apostolic Faith Mission (1.53 million), the Assemblies of God (600,000), the International Federation of Christian Churches (IFCC) (400,000), and the Full Gospel Church of God (343,000) (Teichert 2005). There are also newer church-planting movements that, by many accounts, are growing at dizzying rates, but for which no reliable data exist. These include the New Covenant Ministries International, New Frontiers, and Foundation Ministries.

The final group, the African Independent Churches, is credited with helping to redefine global Christianity (Jenkins 2002, 2006). There is a heavy mix of Christianity and African culture in the AICs, all of which have a Pentecostal orientation. By far, the largest AIC is the Zion Christian Church (ZCC), which has 5 million members (Hendriks 2006). The ZCC's roots are found in the Apostolic Faith Mission (AFM). Engenas Lkganyane, once a member of the AFM, founded the ZCC in 1925 (Anderson & Pillay 1997). Another influential AIC movement is commonly referred to as the Shembe movement, after its founder, the late Isaiah Shembe. The movement is particularly strong among the Zulus, but no reliable membership statistics are available. This is in large part due to the many divisions within the movement. It is worth repeating, though, that overall the AICs are numerically the most important sector of South African Christianity.

CONCLUSION

El Salvador and South Africa have very different histories, cultural contexts, and social foundations. The Spanish, British and Dutch were all European imperialists, yet they had very different visions of colonial life and rule. As they arrived in El Salvador and South Africa, respectively, they encountered vastly different local people groups. The differences of both the colonial powers and the local cultures persist in different ways even today. They are complemented by the two countries' different types of natural resources, distinct avenues of commerce, and variations in the kind of things their economies produce. The political systems and civil institutions of El Salvador and South Africa also have different starting points and have evolved in different ways. All of these

South African religious landscape. Regrettably, the 2011 census did not ask the religion question, so newer numbers are not currently available (Hendriks 2014).

distinctions have a great impact on where religion is located and how it is practiced within these two different societies.

And yet for all their differences, the historical trajectories of El Salvador and South Africa have recently converged. Both have moved out of oppressive political systems and into authentic democratic regimes. Before the transitions, El Salvador and South Africa were either intentionally closed to outside influences or shunned by the global community. Both, however, have taken dramatic steps to open their countries to the full impact of globalization. As a result, El Salvador and South Africa both have strong ties to the West, even as they choose different moments and issues to demonstrate their independence from the West.

El Salvador and South Africa have also opened themselves up to global culture. Movie theaters that feature the latest Hollywood creations are part and parcel of both countries' urban culture. Bob Marley T-shirts can be found in the most remote villages of Central America and Southern Africa, and sports stars from Europe and the United States smile down from billboards along Salvadoran and South African highways. Western entertainment industries are thriving, not just in these two countries, but throughout the Global South and East.

Opening to outside religious influence is part of the greater exposure to global culture in South Africa and El Salvador. Religious groups, though, have become locally owned and rooted. This allows them to be simultaneously expressions of their national context and of a global religious movement. To the extent that evangelical communities are expressions of their national contexts, they begin to differ from one another. The two communities in this study differ in their outlook on key international issues (Salvadoran evangelicals strongly support Israel; black South African evangelical leaders remember the ties the Israeli government had to the apartheid regime), their stresses on specific evangelical practices (Latin Americans focus on healing; Africans are more attuned to visions), and their agendas (Salvadorans are bent on sending missionaries overseas; black evangelical identity is deeply intertwined with nation-building processes in the new South Africa). These differences show the impact that the political and economic spheres can have on religious actors.

Whereas some studies stop at the discovery of the economic and political forces that shape religious communities, this study acknowledges their presence but notes that religious forces are also creating change in NCEs. Religion creates convergence and variation in local evangelical expressions, sometimes working with economic and political forces, and sometimes working against them. The following chapters show how religious forces create this kind of change and argue that they are even more powerful than the (still important) economic and political factors considered in this chapter.

3

Encountering Transnational Religious Social Forces

> The solutions to Africa's problems will not land in a jumbo jet at Jo'burg's International airport.
>
> – *South African evangelical leader*

Untold volumes of transnational religious flows enter the new centers of global evangelicalism every day. They often arrive from points West, and most frequently from the United States. America's dominant position in the international political economy allows its religious actors to export their products nearly everywhere. Most scholars of global Christianity acknowledge this basic reality (e.g., Martin 2002; Stoll 1990; Wuthnow 2009; Yang & Ebaugh 2001), even if they provide different interpretations of what this means for the movement and the world.

Wuthnow's (2009) account of transnational flows emanating from the United States is particularly compelling. He traces the different kinds of organizations that religious actors have used over the years to send missionaries and goods across borders. His story begins with the denominational boards of the nineteenth century, which were used to send out America's very first missionaries. By the dawn of the twentieth century, independent agencies that operated outside of denominational structures had come into vogue, as they could draw on a diverse constituency for resources and were not beholden to denominational agendas. But World War II changed the way Americans thought about missions, and faith-based nongovernmental organizations (NGOs) were created to help Army veterans and other Americans link their faith with efforts to address the poverty they had encountered overseas. The size of the NGO industry exploded in the 1980s and 1990s, but several of the largest and most established faith-based NGOs date their founding back to the post–World War II time period. Finally, local congregations have more recently taken a direct role in engaging internationally. No longer content to delegate international outreach to "professionals," local pastors and their congregants are creating church-to-church partnerships, sending short-term mission teams, and using other techniques to insert themselves into transnational and transcultural activities. All four of these organizational techniques – denominations, independent agencies, NGOs, and U.S. congregations – are still being used and are responsible for channeling high volumes of religious goods, services, people, and communication outside the United States' borders.

The origin of transnational religious flows has thus been established, but the rather straightforward fact that transnational flows have to *land* somewhere has not been sufficiently analyzed. These flows do, after all, contain tangible items. Usually, *someone* has to receive them. And frequently, they have to be distributed through specific *channels*. In this chapter, I identify the groups most often on the receiving end. I describe their faith identity, the way they have organized their communities and social networks, and how they are both shaped and empowered by the transnational flows in their midst.

Three important observations emerge from the chapter's analysis. First, there is a transnational evangelical professional class that is strategically located to capture or serve as a gateway for many transnational religious flows. It is knit together in part by networks and institutions that were introduced by international actors and which continue to have transnational links. The professional evangelical class or community has an increasingly strategic location, both globally and locally. Second, as central as these educated urban and suburban transnational receptors are, there are important transnational streams that bypass them, including streams contained in transnational migration, church-to-church partnerships, and global mass media. Finally, the transnational religious forces that these social structures and flows constitute are influencing social change within new centers of evangelicalism (NCEs). This influence is significant, and it is pushing these communities, as well as the global evangelical movement, in very specific directions.

GLOBAL CITIES AND THE EVANGELICAL PROFESSIONAL CLASS

Global Cities

"Global cities" have emerged around the world on every continent (Sassen 2000, 2012). Sao Paulo, Lagos, Manila, Mumbai, and numerous other metropolises have developed strong communications and transportation systems that link them to the rest of the world. The financial districts in many global cities are highly developed, and they are closely watched in New York and London. Multinational corporations base their headquarters there, and exotic shopping centers cater to international and domestic clientele. English is often the *lingua franca* in global cities, but offices are managed and run by Brazilians, Nigerians, Filipinos, or Indians, as the case may be. These professionals are increasingly better educated, globally savvy, and actively engaged in transnational relationships, both business and personal.

San Salvador, Johannesburg, Cape Town, and Durban have all emerged as global cities. Although wrenching poverty is a prominent characteristic of these urban centers, the commercial sectors have the capacity to carry on business activities in a First World manner. Organizations seeking efficiency choose to locate their offices in this sector. These include government offices, universities, banks, department stores, major technology vendors, and industrial headquarters. They also include embassies, offices for multilateral organizations like the United Nations, regional development banks, and many international NGOs (INGOs). In the midst of these crowded sectors, there are also surprising numbers of transnational evangelical organizations. They are diverse and include INGOs, megachurches, denominational headquarters, ministry organizations, and media outlets. Their ubiquitous presence is difficult to overstate, especially in NCEs, and is perhaps best captured by providing a brief tour through parts of San Salvador and Johannesburg, highlighting the topography of the evangelical community.

San Salvador's Metro Centro is a natural starting point for such a venture. It is one of the largest malls in Central America, and just across the street is the Hotel Intercontinental, with its international business clientele. From there, a number of prominent evangelical institutions are easily accessible. ENLACE, a rapidly growing local NGO dedicated to helping local churches fight poverty, is an easy five minute walk down *Boulevard de los Heroes*. In 2013, a very large billboard celebrating the fiftieth anniversary of the Christian school system started by Assemblies of God (AG) missionary Juan Bueno was also visible from the mall. Just a block north is the quiet office and abode of an independent Mennonite organization. Farther down the road and a few turns later is Operation Blessing, whose offices are in the shadow of the National University. At this point, there are several main arteries that lead east, to San Salvador's more affluent residential neighborhoods. Depending on the route chosen, travelers are in easy striking distance of dozens of other evangelical organizations, churches, and schools. One might pass by Christian Reformed World Mission's offices, the large building that World Vision inhabits, the sparkling new offices that Compassion International has just built, or the denominational headquarters for the Assemblies of God. If Escalon, the most affluent neighborhood in the country, is the destination, the road will lead past the Evangelical University of El Salvador, which was jointly started by the Assemblies of God, the Central American Mission, and a Baptist denomination.

Johannesburg's landscape is equally littered with transnationally oriented evangelical entities. The Westgate Shopping Centre, located on the western side of Johannesburg, is again a good place to start. The national offices of the Baptist Union are an easy drive from there, and the African regional headquarters for the Church of the Nazarene are also not far off. Walk Thru the Bible's offices are just a bit farther north; the offices for the Evangelical Association of South Africa require taking the road east, into downtown Johannesburg. The Business Place, a faith-based jobs training organization run by former World Relief employees, is in the heart of the city. Just a bit north is Rosebank Union, the church with which Ndaba Mazabane the vice chairman of the World Evangelical Alliance is affiliated. If the northwest suburbs are the destination, one would encounter a number of Christian media outlets and ministry organizations along the way. Once there, the sprawling campus of Rhema, a megachurch, sits at a key intersection in the upscale suburb of Randburg and is one of the most prominent landmarks in the area. As it dominates the Randburg landscape, it also depends on the infrastructure that makes Johannesburg a global city to reach its program objectives.

These quick descriptions are just samples of the total layout of the two cities. They show how important evangelicals believe it is to have a presence in global cities, and likewise how prominent international evangelical organizations are in these contexts. They also reveal the easy way in which organizational strategies and the institutional ethos of evangelicals meld into the consumer orientation and technologically astute culture found in such contexts (Martin 2002).

The Evangelical Professional Class

Consistent with the normal *modus operandi* of global cities, transnational evangelical organizations are managed and staffed primarily by people who are from their respective countries. Such staffing strategies require an evangelical professional class, which not only exists in most NCEs but is in the midst of dynamic and rapid growth. As noted in the Introduction, evangelicals have not always felt welcome or been attracted to middle and upper echelons of society. But an upward surge in NCEs has been under way for the better part of two decades, and evangelicals can now be found managing transnational organizations and populating the offices of other business and government organizations.

The evangelical professional class plays a number of important roles within evangelicalism. First, this is where the leadership of national evangelical communities can be found. Individuals within this class tend to have more training, more resources, more legitimacy, and more strategic networks than other evangelicals. They often speak for evangelicals in broader public forums. Second, evangelicals in the professional class are increasingly important in the coalescing structures of global evangelicalism. As non-Western leaders are provided greater space in global evangelical conferences, these new voices inevitably are drawn from the evangelical professional class within NCEs. Finally, the evangelical professional class serves as a gateway to other communities within NCEs. Their language and cross-cultural skills, usually developed within the context of global cities, enable them to more easily relate to evangelicals from other countries. Their knowledge of their own national contexts allows them to channel or rechannel transnational flows to more remote locations and to serve as an interlocutor for senders and recipients of those flows.

Examining different components of the transnationalized lives of the evangelical professional class will help to underscore these points. Their family and clan structures have, for example, been transnationalized. In El Salvador, people from all walks of life have family members who have departed the country. The difference for many in the professional classes is the relative ease with which they make these journeys legally and the diversity of places that family members go. For example, Alberto Escamilla, who owns a niche construction company, has four siblings living in different places throughout the United States. His oldest daughter lives in New York and was studying fashion design at the time of the interview. Dynamics are similar, although not as prolific, in South Africa. Tendai Musikavanhu, a financial investor and entrepreneur in Johannesburg, is originally from Zimbabwe and still has many relatives there. He also has family ties in the United Kingdom.

Members of the evangelical professional class usually have a college education or more, and they have often gone overseas to study. Dr. Noko Frans Kekana, for example, has degrees from universities in Texas and in the Netherlands. He is now a consultant for South Africa's Department of Labor and teaches classes at Rhema's Bible College. Tharsis Solomon, a Salvadoran involved in both ministry and business, received his bachelor's degree from the University of Illinois. Other colleges and universities that respondents attended included Duke University, Columbia University, Oral Roberts University, University of Oxford, Regent University, and John Brown University, to name just a few. In the case of both Kekana and Solomon, the friendships they developed with fellow classmates have been sustained over the years and across borders, and they have attempted to maintain their status as active alumni of their respective institutions.

Professional networks almost universally cross boundaries for those who live and work in global cities. Again, evangelicals have become ingrained in this new form of social organization. Evangelicals who work for multinational corporations, such as Anglo American, General Electric, JP Morgan, and Maytag, are seamlessly integrated into transnational business models. Evangelicals who have started their own companies or who work for local businesses also regularly source goods, services, and personnel internationally. For example, Luis Valiente, the founder of a Salvadoran company that produces natural health products, contracts technical consultants from Cuba and Austria. These colleagues come to El Salvador to help him develop new product lines, and he also visits their offices in the Caribbean and in central Europe. David Molapo, the owner of a telecommunications company in South Africa, has business contacts in Dubai, Europe, and elsewhere. When he travels, he often takes a personal assistant, who at the time of the interview was an American from Mississippi. Such connections are critical to the very definition of a global city; evangelicals have taken their place at the table in these fast paced international environments.

Faith, Values, and Identity in the Evangelical Professional Class

Some scholars who have studied evangelicalism and Pentecostalism have wondered if there would be a secularizing trend within the movement as their leaders "bettered themselves, relaxed their rigor, and went to school" (Martin 2002, 2). As the movement has grown and surged upward, it has clearly picked up members that do not adhere to the strict norms and beliefs that have characterized the movement. But those leaders at the center of the movement show that it is entirely possible to become integrated into the global society and economy and to construct and maintain a traditional evangelical and Pentecostal faith identity. Although different nuances emerge, this is just as true on Latin American soil as it is in Africa.

For instance, in El Salvador, members of the faith community pay surprisingly close attention to the etymological roots of the term "evangelical" when considering what it means to be a member of this community. The literal translation of the *evangelio* is "Good News," and many respondents were able to identify that the word comes from the Greek term *euangelion*. The term was important to them – they defined themselves as carriers of the gospel of salvation (the Good News) to the world. The central figure within that story is Jesus Christ; evangelicals argue that salvation comes when a person enters into a relationship with him. Jose Chevez, an elder at the megachurch Elim and a banker, stated simply that "the ideal [for evangelicals] would be for every human being to have an encounter with Jesus Christ." Others noted variously that people are saved by the blood of Christ, they are born again into a relationship with Christ, and that without Christ, they would be lost. In short, the Good News of Jesus Christ is the dominant and uncontested narrative of the Salvadoran evangelical professional class.

There is also in the Salvadoran professional class a strong orientation toward defining evangelicals through actions. They share the Good News, they preach and teach, they make a conscious decision to convert, they go to church, and they are discipled or mentored. For example, Juan Pablo Ventura, a senior member of World Vision, stated that he fasts on occasion, and he also attends all-night prayer vigils. Aversion to alcohol, tobacco, and extramarital sex is also still an important sphere of activity, or restraint thereof, for evangelical identity. In interviews, this ascetic behavior was linked to the fact that many respondents perceived themselves as Jesus's ambassadors in the world, as being good witnesses, and as being salt and light in the world. Respondents were also painfully aware of their inability as a group to live up to that responsibility. But such actions nonetheless constituted what evangelical professionals thought it *should* mean to be an evangelical in El Salvador. These aspirations formulate the ideal type.

In South Africa, evangelical professionals also described what it means to be an evangelical by highlighting a relationship with Jesus. But accompanying beliefs, such as an emphasis on conversion and the preeminence of Scripture, are articulated more clearly by South African evangelicals than by their Salvadoran counterparts. South African respondents considered a relationship with Christ to include "walking in the heart of the Lord," as well as believing that Jesus is who he claims to be (i.e., the only way to the Father and the Son of

God) and being born again. Meshak Van Wyk, a coloured[1] pastor who is involved in a fledgling South African political party, stated that Christ "had one purpose, and that was to reconcile men and women back to Christ, back to God." Even though the terms "evangelical" or "Good News" are not as widely used as they are in El Salvador, the importance of sharing the gospel is still central. Indeed, the very purpose of an evangelical's life, according to Thuso Siziba, a Church of God pastor, is to reach out to others with the gospel.

Other action components of the faith in South Africa overlap considerably with its manifestation in El Salvador's professional class. Concerns about maintaining holiness and purity, a desire to be God's ambassadors, and the importance of making disciples can all be found in South Africa. The one notable difference is the greater attention to spiritual interactions in daily life. For instance, Portia, a Johannesburg-based lawyer, recounted a conversation she had with God about the timeline of one of her cases. Already overworked and sleep deprived, Portia reported God telling her that the case would be delayed and that she should sleep rather than prepare for it. The next day the judge announced that he would not hear the case until certain papers were in order, thus validating God's words to Portia. These kinds of experiences are reported frequently. Other South African professionals recounted visions they had, the times when they were operating in the "realm of the spirit," and the miraculous healings that had saved them from various maladies, including demon possession. This spiritual dynamic is part of the Salvadoran evangelical ethos; numerous professional Salvadorans also reported hearing God's voice, observing and experiencing miracles, and being concerned about evil spiritual forces. Still, spiritual interaction is more deeply interwoven into the everyday conversation of South Africans, and it is a deeper part of their discussions of faith.

What it means to be evangelical in the Salvadoran and South African professional class thus holds to Bebbington's definition of evangelicalism as activism, biblicism, crucentrism, and conversionism, which was introduced in Chapter 1 (Bebbington 1989, 2). Latin American and African cultures intersect with evangelicalism in different ways. This can be seen in distinctive components of their faith identity and lifestyle choices, which will become more evident in following chapters. But in both cultural contexts, evangelicals maintain a fidelity to traditional notions of their faith as they climb the social ladder. Salvadoran and South African professional evangelicals participate vigorously in the modern world, even as they maintain deep and active religious lives.

Knitting Together the Evangelical Professional Class

While evangelicals integrate themselves into mainstream global economic and social structures, they are also building the institutions and networks necessary

---

[1] "Coloured" is a term that was created in the apartheid era but is still used in everyday parlance in South Africa. It refers to people of mixed race descent.

to maintain their distinctive faith community in a transnational context. The most important social institutions in this regard are leading local churches and two kinds of evangelical networks: ones that are designed to connect transnational evangelical leaders in the same country and ones that are intended to link evangelical leaders together across national borders. The former provide the ties necessary for national faith communities to operate effectively. The latter provide links that give structural coherence to the global evangelical community. Such social structures keep evangelicals in NCEs connected locally and internationally, and they also often serve as channels for transnational flows.

Churches

Local churches in the transnational sectors of society bring together leaders from multiple sectors of business and ministry. They are nestled in affluent neighborhoods, and their facilities are often filled with state-of-the-art technology and communication systems. The largest churches, like Rhema, have spacious auditoriums, huge screens for audiovisual presentations, and vast parking lots. Most have a highly professional staff that is charged with developing sophisticated ministries and programs. These characteristics enable such churches to be actively involved in multiple and overlapping transnational networks and to regularly host international denominational leaders, evangelists, musicians, and short-term mission teams.

The national leaders of transnational evangelical organizations typically worship in these kinds of venues. They do so with committed evangelicals in other vocations, as well as churchgoers who are not as committed to evangelical beliefs and codes of conduct. These churches often maintain a low bar of entry and invite all to come; this creates a continuum of congregants ranging from the highly committed to those who may be in a more experimental phase of their religious lives. Those who are highly committed, including those leading evangelical organizations, attend church activities as much as three to four times a week. They may come for an early morning breakfast before the business day begins, stop there after work for prayer meetings or Bible studies, or dedicate entire weekends to one of the church's service or ministry projects.

Iglesia Josué, a church in San Salvador's affluent neighborhood of Escalon, provides a case in point. As one of the country's leading churches, it counts among its members those who have served the Evangelical Alliance (two as its president), World Vision (director of WV's regional office), Compassion International (director, ex-director), Samaritan's Purse (director of Evangelistic Outreach), Operation Blessing/700 Club (ex-director), AGLOW (director), Full Gospel Businessman's Association (president), and Orphan Helpers (director). Local Pentecostal or evangelical organizations have also been founded or managed by Josué members. These include the owner of the leading Christian bookstore chain in El Salvador; the president of MIES, a Salvadoran missionary sending agency; and another local ministry with transnational connections called Asociación Amiga (ex-director). These leaders congregate with other kinds of transnational professionals in other sectors, including a former national director of El Salvador's police force, an alternate member of El Salvador's Supreme Court, and a manager in a transnational pharmaceutical company, to name just a few. These actors come together regularly for worship on Sunday mornings. They also attend small groups together, send their children to the K-12 Christian school that Josué runs, and volunteer in Josué's various outreach programs. As members of the same church community, evangelical leaders have the opportunity to develop strong bonds with one another.

In-Country Evangelical Networks

National leaders of evangelical churches, organizations, and ministries are particularly important in understanding the reception of evangelical transnational flows in NCEs. They make decisions about what transnational networks their organizations will pursue and how they will direct flows to and through their organizations. As was just illustrated, local churches help to connect these kinds of actors. Leaders are also more intentionally connected through formal religious networks that bring evangelical organizations and their leaders into conversation with one another.

It is more difficult to create meaningful interactions among evangelical leaders than it may appear. The organizational nature of evangelicalism does lend itself to networking types of social organization (Berryman 1999; Martin 1990, 2002), and there are tremendous advantages to this: networks can provide community cohesion and create space for personal initiative. But the voluntary nature of networks provides very little accountability among members and little to no leverage that might be necessary to enforce participation. Thus, if members feel threatened or co-opted by others in the network, or if they feel as though network participation does not help their own organizations, they simply stop participating. Typical evangelical networks thus have a few dedicated members at the center and a larger periphery who desire association but not active involvement. This type of social organization is very common throughout NCEs (as well as OCEs).

In spite of such significant limitations, networks remain the signature way that evangelicals knit their communities together. The most important networks find their locus of activity within the evangelical professional class. They allow information and resources to flow between leaders, and they connect participants to activities and actors beyond their normal scope of activity.

The most prominent networks that knit together national evangelical leaders in NCEs are the national chapters of the World Evangelical Alliance (WEA). The WEA is the oldest and broadest global evangelical network, founded in Britain in 1846. Its headquarters are now in Canada, but Washington, DC is also an important hub of activity. The WEA has chapters in 126 countries which are organized into continental and regional groupings. WEA chapters in Latin America are aggregated into the Forum of Latin American Evangelical Dialogue; the parallel structure in Africa is the Association of Evangelical Alliances in Africa.

Each national chapter has been started for different reasons and at different times. The genesis of El Salvador's Evangelical Alliance stemmed precisely from the need for a group of evangelicals that could receive transnational flows. In 1986 an earthquake killed 1,500 people and left 100,000 homeless around the capital city. Evangelicals in the United States wanted to channel emergency aid through local churches but needed some sort of organizing body that could legally accept the donations and then distribute them to the appropriate congregations. CONESAL (Salvadoran Evangelical Association), which changed its name to the Evangelical Alliance in 2004, was created to serve this purpose. Campus Crusade's offices served as its first headquarters, and CCC Director Adonai Leiva was one of the alliance's early presidents. This was El Salvador's first evangelical, pan-denominational network.

When the period of disaster response ended, the Evangelical Alliance was compelled to rework its identity. According to Leiva, it was at that point "quite simply a place where friendships can be made (una fraternidad)." As such it did not invest much in its institutional capacity, and even the position of the president remained (and remains) unsalaried. Still, the simple process of some evangelical leaders meeting about once a month generated stronger relationships among attendees, and in the 1990s two events increased its legitimacy in the larger community. First, leaders decided to celebrate 100 years of an evangelical presence in El Salvador by writing a book on the community's history. Committees were formed that included leaders, pastors, and missionaries. They came from groups such as the AG, the Central American Mission, the Baptists, the United Pentecostal church, World Vision, the 700 Club, and the Christian University of the Assemblies of God. Leiva presided over the project. Second, the Alliance facilitated the March for Jesus campaigns during the mid-1990s. This annual event originated in the United Kingdom and quickly spread around the world, with vigorous participation throughout Latin America. According to Alejandro Amaya, who was then the president of the Alliance, the marches were intended to be "a one day expression of faith in Jesus Christ," and in El Salvador all evangelicals in the country were invited to march down the center of the nation's capital. Amaya stated that the first year there were 40,000 to 60,000 participants and as many as 200,000 in the following years, which very roughly represented about a quarter of the evangelical population. The Alliance's legitimacy was deepened through these two events, but there was still no effort to build the Alliance's institutional capacity.

A lull occurred in the Alliance's activities beginning in the late 1990s because of a dispute about appropriate leadership. Jorge Martinez, a politician who had formed a Pentecostal political party to run for president in 1994, had been elected president of the Alliance. Many felt, however, that the leader should be a pastor, not a politician, and thus curtailed their participation.

In 2004, a new leadership group brought another burst of effort for evangelical unity. President Juan Manuel Martinez, the bishop of a neo-Pentecostal network of churches called Campamento de Dios, and Vice President Terri

Benner Dominguez, owner of the country's largest Christian book distributor, led this effort. They surveyed the network's members to find out what they were looking for from the Evangelical Alliance. World Vision sponsored a three-day seminar for the Alliance's board members, which today include Mario Vega, the head pastor of Elim, and Jorge Mira, the director of TBN's local television affiliate in El Salvador. A strategic plan was developed, and according to Martinez, "we declared that our vision is to serve the church and prepare it to be able to transform the Salvadoran society in justice, peace and happiness, so that it will be a society that dignifies the family and that lives in good relationship with Jesus Christ and with the creation." Operationally, they chose to focus on three areas: social concerns, advocacy before the government, and ecclesial engagement, such as prayer, evangelism, and pastoral training.

There are currently about seventy members of El Salvador's Evangelical Alliance. Denominations, pastor associations, churches, parachurch organizations, and individuals can all register. Denominational members include the Central American Mission, the Church of God, the Association of Baptist Churches, and the Campamento de Dios. Pastor associations from different cities and towns around the country are officially members, as are evangelical organizations such as Campus Crusade, Compassion International, and World Vision. The Central American Mission (CAM) likely represents the highest number of people with about 20,000 baptized members in the denomination. Elim is significantly larger than CAM, but it is not organizationally represented in the Alliance. Rather, Vega has a personal membership in the Alliance.

Meetings of the Alliance are fairly casual and are intended to build relationships among its participants. Usually, it is a breakfast meeting in a centrally located church. After breakfast, attendees enter into a brief time of prayer and worship, followed by a devotional. Then, announcements are made that might be of concern to the entire evangelical community, such as a citywide evangelistic campaign by an international evangelist or an international event like the Global Day of Prayer. If there is something in the country that might warrant an official stance by the evangelical community, this is also discussed. The meetings are cordial. Attendance varies from meeting to meeting, but they usually attract about 30 to 40 pastors, denominational leaders, and organization heads.

There are, though, very significant actors in the evangelical community who have not joined the Alliance and who do not attend the meetings. The two most important absentees are the AG (the largest Salvadoran denomination with roughly 300,000 members) and Baptist Tabernacle (perhaps the third largest evangelical group in the country, also very conservatively estimated at 75,000 adults and 50,000 children). Bolaños, head of the AG, stated that "We as AG do not participate in any of the networks or the alliances, because in the past we had more than one difficulty, so to avoid this we are staying on the sidelines and this allows us to have much better relations with all of the evangelical churches in the country." Bolaños did not elaborate on the kinds of difficulties they experienced, but one leader surmised that the AG soured on the Alliance during Jorge

Martinez's tenure. It is worth noting, however, that several key individual members of the Alliance attend AG churches, and individual AG pastors are also affiliated with the Alliance.

The Evangelical Alliance of South Africa (TEASA) has a different history and links transnational actors together in different ways. During the apartheid era, a white-run Evangelical Fellowship of South Africa (EFSA) served as an umbrella group for the evangelical community. On the whole, evangelicals of both races were obedient to the apartheid authorities and sought to claim neutrality in the civil conflict. But as violence increased in the 1980s, neutrality became impossible. A group of black pastors in Soweto emerged who felt that some sort of resistance was necessary. They did not feel that their voices were being represented in EFSA in spite of their strong evangelical identity, so they formed a new group in 1986 called Concerned Evangelicals.

The group elected Moss Nthla to be their general secretary. Nthla was initially motivated to move into professional ministry partly because apartheid policies denied him entry into the chemical engineering program at a South African university. He subsequently started a left-of-center student group to engage evangelicals in the struggle against apartheid. On the formation of Concerned Evangelicals, Nthla stated:

I found some pastors there thinking and talking and discussing the theme of what does it mean to be a Christian in South Africa in the context of apartheid? . . . It almost seemed as if to be a Christian you had to be pacifist, to not be concerned about what was going on around you and so on. And somehow instinctively, these black pastors knew that wasn't the only option. It was certainly the option that the white evangelical leadership said was the only evangelical response to apartheid. And so this was the beginning of the revolt against that perspective of the white community.

For a decade, EFSA and Concerned Evangelicals coexisted but had little interaction. Nthla stated that "we had these little groupings of evangelical persuasion, but not working together." However, once the 1994 elections were held, there was little logic in keeping the two groups separate. A white evangelical leader who had partnered with Desmond Tutu to run the National Initiative for Reconciliation (NIR), Michael Cassidy, had good relations with Nthla and with EFSA President Hugh Whetmore. Cassidy thus called the two groups together, and they agreed to consolidate into one body under the title of TEASA. The formal union took place in 1995; Nthla was asked to serve as general secretary and Cassidy as one of two vice presidents.

TEASA's successful organizational integration of evangelical umbrella institutions did not lead to a real unification of the black and white evangelical communities. Race remains a significant boundary within the evangelical community. TEASA is led by those who are strongly interested in closing that gap, but they have not found TEASA to be an extremely effective instrument in achieving those ends.

In spite of this, the network's membership has climbed steadily. Denominations are the primary form of membership in TEASA, although mission agencies can also participate – a contrast to the more diverse enrollment in El Salvador – and denominational leaders make up the TEASA board. By 2004 more than thirty denominations had claimed membership, including the recent addition of the Dutch Reformed Church, with its more than 1 million members. TEASA's representational claims have also been bolstered by the increases in membership experienced by most member denominations since TEASA's founding, including the Apostolic Faith Mission, the Foursquare Gospel Church, the Free Methodist Church, and the Baptist Union of South Africa. Through both the addition of denominations and denominational growth, official membership in TEASA denominations went from 3.2 million in 1994 to 4.7 million in 2004 (Teichert 2005).[2]

In sum, the Evangelical Alliances are leadership networks. They are often initiated by major events within their countries, and they map themselves onto their national social contexts. Although their ability to pursue united agendas is limited, their simple existence helps to link together some of the national evangelical community's most important actors.

Border-Crossing Evangelical Networks

While the Evangelical Alliances link leaders together within El Salvador and South Africa, other networks develop ties between evangelicals across borders. The World Evangelical Association is one of these. It has an international leadership board and attempts modest efforts of coordination between country chapters. Chapter presidents attend regional events on occasion. Some programs are made available to all national chapters that are interested. And occasionally the WEA will represent all evangelicals globally, as it has done when advocating for the Millennium Development Goals in various venues, including the United Nations headquarters in New York.

A second important global evangelical network has coalesced around the Lausanne Congresses that are held every seven to ten years. Delegates from 198 countries descended on Cape Town in October 2010 to participate in the conference. Six representatives came from El Salvador, including two who participated in this study, and much of the South African evangelical community was called upon to help host this event. In 2012, Michael Cassidy was asked to become the honorary chairman of the entire Lausanne movement, replacing the late John Stott. Back in Cape Town, various committees were formed, each of which was composed of delegates from different parts of the globe. These

---

[2] These numbers by no means include the entirety of South African evangelicals. Nthla candidly admits this and estimates the total number of evangelicals in the country to be about 10 million; Teichert (2005) believes it to be as high as 14 million. In either case, less than half of all evangelicals are represented by TEASA.

committees were created to continue the initiatives introduced at the congress. Lausanne is perhaps the most resource intensive and highest profile effort to draw global evangelical leaders into relationships with one another and to build a common vision among them.

Younger, non-Western global networks also link evangelicals together. The Cell Church Missions Network (CCMN), for example, was begun in 1997 by Hong Kong–based megachurch pastor Ben Wong. The CCMN is an example of emerging South–South evangelical networks; Elim pastor Mario Vega is part of this network. He helps to coordinate the Latin American chapter of this network and serves on the CCMN's World Advisory Committee. In 2007, 230 pastors from across Latin America came to attend the CCMN Latin American conference, which was hosted by Elim. The goal of the conference, according to Vega, was to "connect with other cell churches that are interested in joining forces for missions." Other examples of younger networks crossing borders include an Argentine-based network called Rivers of Life that links different actors in El Salvador, Panama, Houston, and elsewhere. A church in Australia, called Hillsong, has developed an extensive network that runs through Europe, South Africa, and other locations around the world. These types of networks tend to run outside of traditional denominational structures and can be issue specific.

Global networks like the WEA, the Lausanne Congress, and the CCMN have the net effect of more tightly linking evangelicals in the professional class across borders. This is especially so when major networks work closely with each other, which is currently the case with the WEA and the Lausanne movement. The relationships created by these networks are critical for directing flows of information, people, and resources. They are also critical in coordinating movement-wide action at the global level – an aspiration that is not yet entirely possible for this fissiparous movement and, due to its organizational structure, may never be possible. But coordinated efforts by members of the professional classes who participate in such networks are becoming an increasingly important reality.

Gateways to Other Social Sectors

Not all transnational networks intend to coordinate the professional class. Many instead view interaction with the professional class as a necessary means to reach their expressed goals of operating either throughout the country or within the poorest sectors of society. Organizational forms most prone to this mindset are denominations, pseudodenominational networks, and NGOs.

Denominations are not new, nor are the transnational connections they create. But they have grown consistently stronger and more numerous over time. Denominations channel missionaries, money, programs, literature, and ideas across borders. The Assemblies of God (AG), for instance, has more than 50 million members located in 192 countries around the world (Miller & Yamamori 2007). The AG has an organizational hierarchy: the international

AG headquarters in Springfield, Missouri, is at the top; regional or national executive committees, which are most often located in global cities such as San Salvador and Durban, report to Springfield. National leadership and U.S. missionaries often sit together on these executive committees. Together they consider any number of issues, including how best to distribute transnational denominational flows throughout the country.

AG resource flows and transnational relationships are used differently in different countries. In El Salvador, transnational flows of personnel, capital, and legitimacy were instrumental in creating an AG elementary and secondary school system that now has around forty schools across the country. Most of these are located in rural or poor urban settings, although a few also serve the professional class. Although an American missionary, John Bueno, was the catalyst for the school system, it is now managed by Salvadorans; its national office is in one of the capital city's more affluent neighborhoods. Those leading the school system continue to use transnational flows as they expand their network and improve the quality of existing schools. As they do so, they remain in close contact with actors in Springfield, Missouri.

In South Africa, a recent focus for the AG has been reunification. The denomination fractured during the apartheid years. Progressive black AG leaders such as Nicholas Bhengu and white AG churches had little to do with each other, and their complicated histories were not entirely linked. In the new dispensation, however, these and other affiliated denominations were gradually united. South African leader Colin LaFoy, who sits on national presidential religious advisory committees, was the driving force behind unification efforts. But actors from the AG headquarters in Missouri came at critical junctures to lend legitimacy to LaFoy's efforts, and the AG remains strategically interested in expanding their presence in every sphere and strata of South African society.

In both El Salvador and South Africa, partnership between international actors and members of the evangelical professional class is critical to the AG's efforts to operate in other sectors of society. The same can be said for almost all global or Western-based evangelical denominations and church associations. Evangelical denominations have wide variation in their overall organizational strategies: the AG's episcopal polity can, for example, be contrasted with the congregational polity of the Baptists and other low church groups. Megachurch associations are very active in El Salvador and South Africa and have even more distinctive networking efforts. The most prominent megachurches engaged in such activities are the Willow Creek Association, based out of Bill Hybels' Willow Creek Community church near Chicago, and the Saddleback Church in Lake Forest, California, led by Rick Warren. In fact, these kinds of associations overlap preexisting denominational structures. But almost all denominations and church associations seek capable national leaders to oversee or to be active partners in their congregational and ministerial strategies.

International NGOs also call on the evangelical professional class to help them access other sectors of society. The landscape of NGO country offices in capital cities is the domain of educated, capable, and reasonably well paid leaders. But the goal of World Vision, World Relief, Compassion International, and other NGOs is not to establish beautiful offices in cosmopolitan centers. Rather, most of their programming targets the poorest areas of the countries in which they are operating. World Vision El Salvador, for example, runs programs among villages along the Honduran border that have been repopulated by wartime refugees. It uses funds from private donations in the United States as well as grants from USAID to carry out these programs. The office in San Salvador is responsible for all accounting and most program management even in sites as remote as these. In another example, Youth for Christ South Africa does, among other things, literacy and feeding programs in public schools that serve the poorest 20 percent of South African society. International funds are often blended with donations from within South Africa to carry out these programs. Here again, all accountability and programming responsibilities ultimately fall to their Johannesburg-based national office. Within the reverse commodity chain of NGO activity, national offices have become an increasingly influential middle man in the process, and some have even gained legal autonomy (Lindenberg & Bryant 2001) from their U.S. parent organizations.

In sum, the evangelical transnational professional class is a vibrant and strategically located part of global evangelicalism. It maintains a strong evangelical identity even as it operates in the epicenters of globalization and modernization. It creates and manages churches and networks that channel transnational flows, just as these transnational structures help to organize the evangelical professional class. Flows that are sent specifically to the professional class and flows that hope to use the transnational class as a point of entry into their respective countries help those in the professional class to extend their influence at home and around the world.

POWER DYNAMICS AND TRANSNATIONAL FLOWS

This book emphasizes the way transnational religious resources empower actors in NCEs. However, those who send such resources have power and influence on those who receive them, even if the desire for power is not the impetus for religious flows, and even if the senders are not fully aware of the power they exercise.

Such dynamics are part and parcel of the era of globalization. The current global system is responsible for the rise of a transnational business class in many countries of the Global South and East. It also allows and enables members of civil society to engage in cross-border activities and relationships. That is to say, the existence of transnational religious flows and the existence of a "receiving class" have emerged together within a liberalized global political economy.

The underlying structures of the international political economy constantly shift. This fact is a reminder that the growth of economies in the Global South and East is bound to shift the global balance of power and, consequently, the location of power in global communities of faith. Those who live in the strongest economies and have access to the greatest number of resources are in a position of advantage. Currently, these fundamental realities allow Christians in the United States to maximize their influence in places further afield and to remain safely independent of issues and events affecting evangelicals in other parts of the globe. To put the matter another way, if transnational flows to NCEs were abruptly cut off, NCEs would be dealt a serious blow. On the other hand, if the transnational classes in the Global South and East were to cease functioning, most local religious communities in the Global North would not feel significant, immediate repercussions. (It would, however, disrupt global elements of the evangelical community and wreak absolute havoc on economies the world over.) These hypothetical situations help reveal where power resides, at least for now, between the sending communities in the Global North and the receiving communities in other parts of the globe.

NCEs in countries that have not opened their borders to international flows have different experiences. Evangelicals in places like China or parts of the Arab world still have *some* access to global resources, but the volume of transnational religious flows is much lower than in countries that have liberalized their political economies. They are thus not as empowered by having international resources available, but they are also less susceptible to uneven power dynamics that accompany flows. They have had to rely more heavily on local religious resources to build their communities.

For countries that have more open societies, there is another complicating trend within transnational evangelical flows. Data collected for the *Atlas of Global Christianity*, edited by Todd Johnson and Kenneth Ross (2009), shows evangelical flows from most Western countries outside the United States to be in slight decline, whereas U.S. evangelical flows remain robust. Even if U.S. flows are merely growing faster than other non-Western countries, which is a safer claim as not all scholars are in agreement on this point, flows from the United States would make up an increasingly higher percentage of the portfolio of flows received by NCEs. This would cause NCEs to depend on the United States even further for transnational resources. It would shift even more power into the hands of U.S.-based evangelical actors and allow such actors to leave an even larger cultural footprint on the global evangelical movement.

TRANSNATIONAL FLOWS BEYOND THE EVANGELICAL PROFESSIONAL CLASS

As important as it has become, the evangelical professional class does not capture *all* transnational flows. Some flows bypass this mediating point of entry, including streams contained in transnational migration, church-to-church partnerships, and global mass media.

As has been noted, transnational migration has done much to reorient Salvadoran society and is one of the most formative motors of social change around the world today. Globally, remittances to developing countries exceed the amount of international aid such countries receive. In fact, the World Bank (World Bank 2013) estimates that global remittances to developing countries exceeded $479 billion in 2011.

Evangelicals are also affected by these flows and by the difficulties encountered when trying to carry on relationships across borders. Isa, for instance, moved to Los Angeles with her husband and three children when her husband gained a religious workers visa to pastor a church there. Three years later, Isa's mother fell ill, so she returned to El Salvador to care for her. Several months later, she endeavored to return to Los Angeles, but she was apprehended in LAX and deported because her paperwork was not in order. Her children, now in high school and college, have chosen to stay in Los Angeles, as has her husband, who regularly sends money to Isa in El Salvador. Isa recognizes her family's future is in Los Angeles and with some sadness supports the current arrangement, hoping that at some point the U.S. embassy in El Salvador, which has repeatedly denied requests for a new visa, will eventually relent. Meanwhile, Isa has various causes that she supports in El Salvador. In addition to the money her husband sends her, Isa actively seeks to raise additional funds from other American contacts the family has developed. These kinds of family arrangements and transnational contacts are played out again and again in Salvadoran society and, to a lesser extent, in South Africa and the countries that send migrants to South Africa. Although they spatially distend families in potentially damaging ways, they also enable people in all classes to have access to transnational goods including money, cultural information, and other forms of material goods.

Church-to-church partnerships are a second type of transnational channel that allows flows to go directly to actors that exist outside the evangelical professional classes. These are sometimes originally created by denominational offices. They are also generated by the interchange of short-term mission teams. For example, local Baptist congregations in North Carolina have developed relationships with churches in South Africa. These partnerships are primarily predicated on North Carolina churches sending teams each summer or every other summer to the churches in South Africa. The South African churches are humble but go to some length to receive the teams each year and incorporate them into their ongoing ministries. More importantly, the South African churches that receive teams negotiate directly with the North Carolina churches. There is no in-country intermediary that manages the transnational relationship for them or determines the number of teams they can receive. As the short-term missions movement matures, church-to-church partnerships have become increasingly common. The quantity of transnational flows running through these channels is thus likely to increase over time.

Finally, evangelicalism is quite fond of using tools of mass media to spread its message. Such tools enable messages to be received by anyone anywhere who has a satellite dish or an Internet connection. One Zimbabwean immigrant to South Africa I met lived in a tiny apartment in Hillbrow, one of Johannesburg's most violent communities. He would often go to a local Internet café where he could listen to Christian music produced in the United States or Australia, scan the web pages of his favorite international ministries, and even download or read sermons from internationally known (mostly American) evangelical pastors. Some evangelical media powerhouses such as CBN, the Pentecostal television network, choose to open national offices in NCEs. In these cases, the evangelical professional class mediates the distribution of transnational media products. But as the digital divide is lowered around the world, increasing numbers of evangelicals are able to tap into unmediated flows of evangelical media.

The streams that bypass the evangelical professional class are important because they allow those who are not near cultural, economic, and political centers of NCEs to access resource flows that are critically important in the first part of the twenty-first century. Those who operate outside the networks just described and who are not part of the professional class are structurally disadvantaged in numerous ways, even as they try to use the same religious scripts as their more upwardly mobile co-religionists. But for those who have found alternative transnational streams, at least one component of an uneven playing field is leveled. The implications of these dynamics will be further explored in the chapters that follow.

TRANSNATIONAL RELIGIOUS FLOW CONTENT

It is by now clear that enormous varieties of people and things flow through transnational evangelical networks. Money crosses borders in the form of remittances, offerings, NGO donations, denominational support, and individual gifts, to provide just a few examples. People enter NCEs because they are vacationing, on business, part of a short-term mission team, are missionaries, are providing missionary support, are international evangelists or artists, work for INGOs or other international agencies, are migrating, or are returning to visit friends and family after having migrated. Evangelical goods that land in NCEs include disaster relief, gifts in kind (NGOs often collect material gifts in Western countries to send to NCEs – World Vision El Salvador, for instance, received a large delivery of wheelchairs during the time of this research), new technologies for churches or other kinds of organizations, books, tapes, DVDs, and so on. Services are rendered by dental and medical teams. Information about evangelicals from other parts of the world, global evangelical events, and new trends within the evangelical movement also travels quickly to and through NCEs.

It is difficult to quantify any of these flows, but the volumes are already considerable, and they are growing rapidly. Two examples, those of short-term mission trips and of NGOs, may help to put these streams in perspective. First, the number of adults who go on short-term mission trips is now more than 1.6 million per year (Wuthnow 2009), and most scholars believe the numbers are even higher among youths than adults. Most STM traffic stays primarily between old and new centers of Christianity. Second, many evangelical NGOs have experienced rapid growth in recent years. World Vision now has an annual income of more than $982 million (World Vision 2013), Compassion International's income is more than $648 million per year (Compassion International 2013), and Samaritan's Purse is now a $52 million per year organization (Samaritan's Purse 2012). In addition to the growth of existing NGOs, the number of evangelical NGOs is also growing rapidly. Seventy-five evangelical organizations are now a part of Accord, the most prominent evangelical NGO network in North America. But this does not begin to scratch the surface of the total number of evangelical NGOs that are currently in existence. While short-term missions and NGOs are areas of particular growth, almost all types of evangelical flows are on the rise.

In addition to material items, cultural ideas about how to order society and individual life also flow into NCEs. New organizational forms are important components of this dynamic. According to historian Mark Noll (2009), missionaries and other forces of dispersion helped to distribute around the world an organizational model of religion that was developed in nineteenth-century America. This model is the basic congregational form, and it is characterized by voluntarism and self-directed organization. Other organizational forms have followed – perhaps most recently the standard template of organization that is used by short-term mission teams (Offutt 2011). These organizational forms have wide-ranging implications, but there are also many organizational innovations that are transferred more minutely. For example, some evangelical leaders in Latin America have taken on the title of "bishop." This term is clearly borrowed from Catholicism, but it is rarely transferred directly. One El Salvadoran evangelical leader, to the chagrin of some of his elders and confidants, took on this title after having some personal interaction with a neo-Pentecostal leader in Atlanta named Bishop Earl Paulk. (Paulk has since had legal troubles and has to some extent been discredited.) The point here is that although Salvadorans are immanently familiar with Catholic bishops, the term was not likely to be taken on until it was legitimated as a Protestant moniker in other cultural and national contexts. The congregational organization form, the organizational template of the short-term mission team, and neo-Pentecostal church movements with bishops at their head illustrate that evangelical organizational forms have flowed into NCEs and are now available for use in those contexts. Some such forms are cast off, while others are adopted either consciously or unconsciously.

CONCLUSION

This chapter began with a quote from a South African evangelical leader who is fond of saying that the solution to Africa's problems is not going to land in a jumbo jet at Johannesburg's International Airport. He is right. It is local leadership and homegrown talent that is making Africa a better place today than it was a decade ago. How this works in evangelical communities will be discussed in the following chapter. But the raw materials for such solutions *do* often become available via the airports, train stations, and shipping ports of Africa's pulsing global cities. Those with international connections and adequate education, or those in the professional and transnational classes in Africa and other parts of the emerging world, are receiving these imports and putting them to good use.

It should come as no surprise that evangelicals in the professional classes of NCEs play an important role in global evangelicalism. The fact has, however, gone largely unnoticed. By recognizing the global and national social location of these actors, new ways of understanding global evangelicalism are opened. No longer should the locus of attention be focused exclusively on Western actors. Conversely, when actors in the Global South are considered, they are no longer leaders who seem largely unaffected by other aspects of globalization. Rather, the leaders described in this chapter are urban professionals. Members of transnational evangelical churches in the Global South and East are involved in global commerce. The things they do in their businesses enable Americans to purchase coffee for breakfast and to purchase televisions for their living rooms. Most of these members own smartphones, and many avidly follow global sporting events such as the World Cup. In short, evangelicals in the professional classes of NCEs are global citizens who live in global cities and provide leadership for a global religious movement.

These evangelicals encounter global religious social forces every day. Such forces affect what they can do, how they can do it and, arguably, why they want to do it. In this sense, global religious social forces are overwhelming. But global religious forces also empower those who live at their intersection. Relative to other members of national faith communities, evangelicals in the professional classes are clearly in a position of influence. How they use that influence and what they do with the religious forces at their fingertips is not controlled by people in far-off countries. Rather, these kinds of decisions are made by local actors. And what they decide has both national and global import. Such is the power of contemporary leaders in NCEs.

4

Exercising Local Influence: An Entrepreneurial Approach

Ade, a Nigerian, recently moved to Johannesburg to attend Rhema Bible College. He came to South Africa because of a vision in which God told him to start a church in Cape Town. In Ade's vision, the church grew to be a large, multicultural congregation where people of all different colors could come and worship together. Eventually Ade hopes the church will have international visitors and supporters. Together with his future congregation and his international friends, he wants to build homes where the church can minister to orphans and drug addicts and provide a variety of other social services. Ade said, "for now, my assignment is to stay focused on my studies. Then the vision of God will definitely come to pass and [my wife and I] know that our place of assignment is Cape Town."

Ade's vision has many elements that characterize contemporary evangelicalism. He is inspired and made confident by an encounter with the transcendent to go out and create a new organization. He wants all to be welcome in his new church, and he hopes to build transnational networks of support. He believes that his organization should be relevant to the poor and downtrodden of society. The vision that God has laid on his heart is an entrepreneurial one that shuns barriers of race and distance and that hopes to help the poor.

As new centers of evangelicalism (NCEs) pop up across the Global South and East, they are being built by creative local actors. They are also being affected by local resources, symbols, and methods of social organization. These local religious social forces take many forms, from the rhythmic songs of African worship to the way in which extended families in Latin America work together to build organizations and provide leadership. Local faith communities are grassroots organizations that are embedded in local culture. They thus reflect and draw upon local culture as they create their own community and identity.

Local religious social forces commingle with global religious social forces, the latter of which, as explained in the last chapter, also help to shape NCEs. Indeed, global religious forces exert a powerful and formative influence on NCEs. But global forces are not the primary agents of social construction in local communities, they are not rooted in local cultures and histories, and they are not *ipso facto* meaningful or able to make meaning in local contexts. These are all the domain of local religious social forces, which consequently rival and perhaps exceed the ability of external global forces to shape these emerging faith communities.

Most NCEs share a set of common characteristics that link them together as a single global religious movement. These include a competitive and market-oriented organizational environment, voluntary associations, collections of relationships in which trust can be very high, systems of beliefs that promote confidence, hope and optimism, and a particular collection of religious or cultural symbols. These markers find a place within many different regions and cultures around the world. It is sometimes the case that local actors simply mimic these and other global components of their local faith communities.

But local actors also synthesize their global faith with their local cultures, making each NCE unique. Hence, the evangelical community in Johannesburg is recognizably an African construct, and it occupies a place within contemporary South Africa. It is related to the evangelical community in San Salvador, but it is also different from it. The Salvadoran evangelical community is just as clearly a Latin American construct that holds its own, though somewhat different position, within Salvadoran society.

All NCEs are constantly changing. Different trajectories exist for communities, and the actions taken by local actors, which are always influenced by the global forces around them, dictate these trajectories. Creating intentional change is not easy. People gravitate toward those things and actions that are familiar and trusted. So those who wish to push communities beyond what they already know must find a way to draw people into new patterns and institutions.

The evangelicals who are most effective in these endeavors are entrepreneurs. Evangelical entrepreneurs tie other religious social forces and resources together to create new organizations and social institutions. These creative acts often require what Max Weber called value rational action, which inspires other community members to break established norms and cycles of habitual action. Entrepreneurs also must have a type of charisma that particularly resonates within the evangelical community. It is these three elements – the ability to tie religious forces together, the use of value rational action to break free from habitual activity and to create new forms of action, and the possession of a certain type of charisma – that allows evangelical entrepreneurs to introduce change in the social and organizational landscapes of their faith communities.

Evangelical communities both nurture and resist the entrepreneurs in their midst. They provide the incubators necessary for fledgling entrepreneurs to get their feet on the ground and begin building organizations within their faith communities. But by nurturing entrepreneurs, faith communities become subject to the changes that those entrepreneurs might create. Sometimes faith communities can object to the new directions that entrepreneurs want to take them. When such objections emerge, faith communities can act back upon entrepreneurs and reject their creation, whether it is new organizations, new theologies, or new ways of organizing the community. In spite of such resistance to change, entrepreneurs often successfully serve as the engines by which the constant evolution of evangelical faith communities is powered.

In this chapter I examine the relationship among evangelical entrepreneurs, their local communities, and the global resources to which they now have access. This powerful mix of actors and contexts is the key to social change in NCEs. How they intersect with one another, and the synergies they create, deserve careful analysis.

ENTREPRENEURS IN NCEs

Tying Religious Social Forces Together in New Ways

The creative processes involved in entrepreneurship have been perhaps most ably explained by Joseph Schumpeter (1934). Schumpeter defines entrepreneurs as people who "combine materials and forces within their reach" in new ways (Schumpeter 1934, 65). They are thus not only creating new organizations but often creating new *kinds* of organizations and ways of doing things. Schumpeter points out that economies usually run in cycles that, if left alone, tend toward equilibrium. But, he writes, entrepreneurs can alter economic cycles by coming up with new combinations of resources to create new products or open new markets, both of which signal economic development.

The principles derived from this economic analysis apply to creative activity in other spheres of life. Entrepreneurs in NCEs exercise their skills to build churches, nonprofits, businesses, religious networks, and other types of organizations.

In NCEs, entrepreneurs call upon both global and local resources for almost every creative initiative they undertake. Three categories of resources are most useful to evangelical entrepreneurs: material, symbolic, and ideational. Each resource type is also a social force that on its own can change social realities. This power becomes more directed and more powerful when it is drawn upon by the entrepreneur. To understand how they are used in NCEs, each needs to be described in greater detail.

Material Resources

Material resources are obviously critical to entrepreneurial efforts in NCEs. These include money, people, raw materials, tools, vehicles, knowledge, and technology, to name just a few. Surprising numbers of material resources can be drawn from religious sources or can themselves possess religious meaning. Such material items then qualify as a type of religious social force.

Money is a good example of a resource that may be generated by religious organizations or come from contacts within evangelicalism. Churches are primarily built through the tithes and offerings that they collect locally. At Elim, offerings are carefully orchestrated during the service with something of a business feel, and a large kiosk at the back of the assembly hall allows people to submit envelopes with offerings in them whenever they wish. At Oasis of Life Family Church in South Africa, the morning offering is a celebration moment. People go to the front with their offerings and conspicuously place them in a brightly colored basket, sometimes while dancing or swaying to the music. At Iglesia Josué, the offering time is rather understated. The plates come as people meditate or listen to a musical worship piece being performed on the platform. Across continents, denominations, and cultures, offerings can look very different. But in most cases, they help to infuse money with religious meaning.

Nonprofits and churches can create revenue streams other than offerings. Fundraisers are held locally, such as the one that Feed the Children El Salvador holds in San Salvador each year. Many churches have bookstores on their premises, and some of the larger churches, like Rhema and the Baptist Tabernacle, have radio and/or television stations that generate revenue. These local financial resources often converge with international money flows that can make starting organizations easier. Hilda Bojorquez, A-Brazo's founder, has tapped into funding from religious groups in the Netherlands, the United Kingdom, and the United States. Michael Cassidy, the founder of African Enterprise, has cultivated support offices in ten different countries. Finally, Silvana Valladaras, the School for the Deaf's founder, also works with religious funding from multiple countries. Perhaps none was more critical in the school's early days than the Christopher Blinding Mission, a German foundation, which unexpectedly provided assistance. Stated Valladaras:

They came one day at noon to look for me at the school with all the documentation filled out, [saying] we're going to give you this much. You just have to sign this, do that, and they told me how to do it, and I was there with my plate of food and my tortilla soup ... because I wasn't expecting visitors, and then they said we want to help you. It fell from the sky, honestly, so I think that in our ignorance, God made Himself manifest.

Private sector entrepreneurs can also get money from religious and nonreligious as well as global and local sources. This is partly due to a belief by evangelical businessmen and investors around the world that they can reform or transform the marketplace and ameliorate poverty through private sector initiatives. One Salvadoran entrepreneur, for example, sought to grow and market passion fruit in domestic and international markets. He is deeply embedded in Assemblies of God networks and was able to draw investments from AG businesspeople to pursue this project. In South Africa, Andrew Fasedemi is building a powerful marketing consultancy called Wisdom Keys group. He is part of the Full Gospel Businessman's Association, a global network that provides him with colleagues of a like-minded faith, and it also provides valuable possibilities to look for potential investors. But even in the private sector, religious funding can be found locally. Gustavo Mungia created a partnership of several evangelical Salvadoran businessmen to start a plasti-wrap business at the national airport. The capital for this enterprise was found within the partnership itself.

People are a second material resource that entrepreneurs need to be successful. Entrepreneurs frequently rely on partners and trusted colleagues. Some evangelical entrepreneurs find this trust among co-religionists. They are able to worship, pray, and study the Bible together. For example, Antonio Jarquin and Miguel Ramirez are cofounders of the business Jahve Rafa (which means Jehova, the Healer). Both had tumultuous personal and professional lives, and both have recently sought refuge in the evangelical faith and in this business partnership. Jarquin said, "there is no legal document that says we are partners, only the Lord is in the middle, [Miguel] confides in me, and I confide in him, and we are walking [together]." When asked if they could be partners without involving their faith in Christ, Jarquin said simply, "No, we could not."

Other evangelical entrepreneurs use their faith to engender trust in non-evangelical partners and peers. Tendai Musikavanhu, a cofounder (with other evangelicals) of Umbono Trust, was presented with an award during a meeting attended by the finance minister, the minister of Trade and Industry, and other leading financiers. As he went up to receive it, Musikavanhu said, "I just sensed God telling me ... that I had to give Him glory and so that's what I did. It was very nerve wracking but I even had a Muslim come and congratulate me afterwards." In El Salvador, an evangelical entrepreneur in the coffee sector brought together fifteen to twenty other medium to large coffee farm owners to present a collective marketing plan to them. He opened the meeting with a word of prayer and proceeded to give his testimony before launching into the business portion of his presentation. Most of the people in the room were not evangelicals and most likely did not have religious motivations for attending the meeting. But the entrepreneur's transparency and religious authenticity apparently resonated with them, or at least did not detract from the business side of things, because many stayed afterward to chat with him and his team in a warm and collegial manner.

Entrepreneurs also need people to work for them or to invest labor in their projects. Evangelical churches and ministries often seek out members of the faith to provide administrative or logistical support. For example, while visiting an AG church in the upscale Zona Rosa of San Salvador, I bumped into a man who I met in a poor, rural AG church several months previously. He explained that through AG connections, he had been hired to guard the property of the more affluent church.

In the private sector, not all evangelical entrepreneurs agree with the body of literature that suggests evangelicals are better workers than their non-evangelical counterparts. In fact, one entrepreneur complained that because of the mid-week all-night prayer vigils that a number of his evangelical employees attended, they showed up late for work the next day and were generally unproductive. Still, the prevailing attitude was that, if given a choice between otherwise equal candidates for open positions, evangelical entrepreneurs would tend to hire evangelicals.

Entrepreneurs seeking to build churches in NCEs often benefit from an unexpected labor source: short-term mission teams. As mentioned in the previous chapter, short-term mission teams are ubiquitous in NCEs. Once they arrive at their destinations, they must do something, and the most popular activity of short-term teams is construction work (Priest, Wilson, & Johnson 2010). How do they decide what to build? In many instances, the leader of the hosting church has a project in mind and suggests it to the incoming team. Carlos Ayala, pastor of a Nazarene church in El Salvador, for instance, used a series of teams over several years to put an addition on his church. A church leader in South Africa encouraged a team to build a community center, out of which the church now runs a number of youth programs. The high volume of construction-oriented short-term mission teams makes them a significant material and religious resource that evangelical entrepreneurs in NCEs can uniquely harness.

Symbolic Forces

The importance of symbols to entrepreneurial work may be less obvious than the need for material resources. A brief description of symbols may help. Symbols are basic building blocks of society. They are human products, in that they are created by humans when they socially construct their society. Once created, symbols are fundamental to the ongoing process of social construction. They "are the only means of communication . . . the main instruments of thought, the only regulators of experience" (Douglas 1973, 38). Symbols constitute languages, schemas of action, and social relationships. They represent ideas and help people to make sense of reality. Taken together, symbolic universes are formed that constitute cultural and religious systems (Berger 1967).

As religious symbol systems help humans make sense of reality, they also help them order community. Robert Bellah's (1970) conception of symbolic realism is helpful in understanding how this works. Bellah asserts that symbols "express the feelings, values, and hopes of subjects . . . [and] organize and regulate the flow of interaction between subjects and objects" (1970, 252). Put differently, religious symbols (and the religious forces/deities/realities they stand for) should be understood as real "actors" in the social drama. When symbols are understood to be real, it is no more sociologically appropriate to talk about the actions of "social class" than to talk about the actions of a "god" (Ammerman 2008). Religious symbols are thus both part of the cognitive mapping of individuals and the social mapping of communities.

Evangelical entrepreneurs draw symbols out of their environment just as they draw material resources out of their environment, and use them just as skillfully. Evangelical symbols in NCEs have different origins: some are local, while others are global. Some of the most important symbols currently reverberating in NCEs include the Word of God or the Bible; the idea of a personal relationship with Jesus Christ; the "priesthood of all believers," or the idea that all members of the faith community can carry on sacred functions; and the missionary impulse or call to missions, prayer, and unity. Entrepreneurs are employing these and other symbols in different combinations to create organizations and movements and to draw people into them.

Entrepreneurs in El Salvador have been particularly effective in using the symbol of the missionary call to create a multidenominational movement. Roberto Bustamente, who formulated a Salvadoran missionary agency, and Moises Mejia, head of the Committee for Salvadoran Missions (Comisal) during the time of this research, have been particularly influential in this regard. They draw on many different symbolic images from the Bible. Two examples include the Great Commission, in which Jesus tells his followers to "go and make disciples of all nations" (Matthew 28:19) and Jesus's proclamation that "the Harvest is plentiful but the workers are few" (Matthew 9:37). Bustamente, Mejia, and their colleagues package these symbols in sermons, use them on posters to stage student rallies at universities, and distribute them on church flyers.

Missionary symbols are not in themselves sufficient to generate a nationwide missionary movement in El Salvador. Bustamente, Mejia, and others envision a concerted, multidenominational movement, so they also use symbols of unity. These include common evangelical refrains such as "unity in Christ" or "the unity of the believers." These are necessary because denominational disputes and the competitive nature of El Salvador's religious marketplace could easily have resulted in numerous distinct and rather small denominational forays into missions. Symbols dealing with unity are intended to hold the movement together. Mejia said, "What we want is to [create] bridges of communication, to get to know each other . . . identify with every Salvadoran missionary, to help them, to facilitate [communication with] them . . . to promote them." Mejia takes care not to appear to be placing himself in a position of power but rather as that of a facilitator of a network of likeminded coworkers. By doing so, he becomes more effective at blending together symbols of overseas missions work and symbols of unity.

Evangelical entrepreneurs also harness symbols that have power only within a specific context. For example, pastors in the townships of South Africa often speak to young, upcoming professionals about the ghosts, or the spirits, of apartheid. This phrase was echoed in township churches of Soweto, Alexandra, and Benoni. In each case, it was a call to black South Africans to fight against the spiritual oppression of apartheid that still pervades South Africa and does not allow black South Africans to fulfill their potential. At Grace Bible Church in Soweto, the phrase was complemented by another biblical symbol that is prominent in contemporary South African evangelical circles: the biblical character of Queen Esther, who helped her people avoid persecution. In this context, the Esther reference is used to encourage rising young township dwellers to have the courage to advocate for themselves and for their communities among people of influence and to become people of influence themselves. These references have a kinship to the prosperity gospel message, and entrepreneurs have used them in their efforts to build megachurches in a number of black townships and other peri-urban communities.

Such symbols, especially those referencing apartheid, are of course not useful in El Salvador where local actors draw on their own symbolic contexts. When Carlos Ayala, for example, decided to start a church in an agriculturally based community on the fringes of El Salvador, he used all the symbolism available to him as a Pentecostal pastor. This included displaying the cross and showing the power of the Holy Spirit in various ways. But he also drew upon the local importance of land, especially its ownership (the recent civil war was in part fueled by land issues) and its stewardship. Ayala did so by, among other strategies, naming his church "Mother Earth: Church of the Nazarene."

Organizational Strategies

Entrepreneurs of all types – evangelical and non-evangelical, Western and non-Western – puzzle over what organizational strategies might work the best for them. Business schools provide classes on the topic, the World Bank and USAID provide capacity building seminars for NGOs, and organizational and church growth gurus write books for congregational leaders to help them unlock the potential of their respective institutions.

In NCEs, evangelical entrepreneurs can draw upon numerous organizational models and strategies as they attempt to build their organizations. Just as with material and symbolic resources, the ideational resources surrounding evangelical entrepreneurs have both local and global origins. The institutions that entrepreneurs in NCEs create incorporate strategies and ideas emerging from both locations.

Megachurch founders and leaders in NCEs are cases in point. Elim's current leader, Mario Vega, and its founding pastor, Sergio Solarzano, have looked both locally and globally for organizational models that fit the Salvadoran context. In 1986, Solarzano traveled to South Korea to visit the largest church in the world: David Yonggi Cho's Yoido Full Gospel Church. When he returned, Solarzano asked the twenty-five daughter churches that Elim had planted in or near San Salvador to fold themselves into one large cell group church under his direction. The smaller churches acquiesced, and a cell structure was established that closely copied the South Korean model (Comiskey 2003). Adaptations to the Salvadoran context were quickly implemented, and current leadership continues to tinker with new innovations.

The cell group–based megachurch model worked well in El Salvador because of Salvadoran history and culture. Elim instituted the model when El Salvador was embroiled in civil war. Cell groups thus served as house churches that allowed residents to stay in the safer confines of their houses, avoid the need to break state curfew just to attend prayer meetings, and integrate congregational life with family ties. Today, Salvadoran culture continues to express an affinity for cell group organizational models. Gangs in El Salvador have a strikingly similar organizational template to the evangelical movement; their shared characteristics have helped both to flourish in contemporary Salvadoran society. In short, although a cell group–based megachurch was intentionally imported by

Elim's leadership, it works in El Salvador's context because cells can easily be mapped into existing Salvadoran modes of social organization.

At a more general level, the organizational template of evangelical congregations around the world is strikingly similar. Almost all hold worship services (usually on Sundays), prioritize educational programs for their youth, engage in community formation, and stage activities designed to benefit people outside the congregation (Ammerman 2005). Those building congregations in different NCEs, however, have different visions of what these broad categories should look like. At the Zimbabwean migrant church near Benoni, South Africa, the time of worship is characterized by tribal dancing and singing. Piercing cries punctuate songs in their native tongue, and most congregants sweat profusely as they dance through the morning. This is completely different from the Elim worship experience or 'that of' any other church in El Salvador. At Elim, there is a time in the service when the congregation speaks in tongues. This time is quite emotional, but it is also controlled so that it does not impinge on other components of the service. Such differences are expressed in parts of congregational life across NCEs, as the entrepreneurs who shape churches harness local spiritual and organizational forces.

Evangelical entrepreneurs operating in the private sector also adapt local and global organizational strategies to further their goals. Luis Valiente, for example, has built the sales department of his company on a modified version of Amway's sales techniques. He now employs more than 125 people. This kind of organizational strategy is familiar to church members who use similar strategies in their evangelism efforts. Of course, not all organizational strategies are religious – Andrew Fasedemi's organizational strategies stem more from his university education and his work in global corporations than from his faith community. But the organizational ethos (and the name) of Wisdom Keys Trust is influenced by his faith, and the organizational culture does influence organizational strategies to some extent.

Employing Value Rational Action

A second characteristic that enables evangelical entrepreneurs to create social change is their tendency toward, in Weberian terms, value rational action. Weber (1978) stated that habitual or traditional acts are the most common type of action. In other words, people usually do things they know how to do and that they see other people doing. Acts of this nature maintain the status quo. But people can also execute, among other categories of action, value rational acts. In these scenarios, the actor either embraces a set of values and breaks cycles of habitual action that do not conform to these values, or the actor is motivated by his or her values to accomplish a specific task and chooses to act outside of established norms to accomplish that task. In both cases, people break free from habit to forge new ways of doing things.

Ascetic and Orderly Behavior

In NCEs, values are shaping entrepreneurial action in two ways. First, ascetic evangelical values clear out distractions that keep people from making more direct linkages between their actions and their goals. The social impact of a more upright life is perhaps the most well-documented component of the global evangelical movement. It empowers women, avoids siphoning of meager incomes to unproductive activities, allows families to invest more resources in their children, and creates more social capital in communities, to name just a few advantages (Brusco 1986; Gooren 1999; Martin 1990, 2002; Smilde 1998).

Scholars are not the only ones to notice such dynamics: many evangelicals have enough group awareness to also realize that conversion experiences have social implications. For example, Alejandro Amaya (former president of El Salvador's Evangelical Alliance) states that "when we convert to the Lord our habits change, our interests change, our way of doing things change and believe it or not or whether you want it or not things are going to change in our life in the way we do business, in the way we treat our children."

Amaya's comment points to the broader implications of value driven behavior, but evangelicals also see a very direct link to entrepreneurialism. For example, Mauricio Loucel was the president of both an insurance company and a TV station at the time of his conversion. He described his religious experience in the following way: "I saw myself trapped by a series of circumstances. I was wrapped up in alcoholism, in drug addiction, in adultery, in all of these things. For me they were normal until they reached a crisis, then the Lord came into my life . . ." Loucel subsequently gave up the sins he listed and believes that the impact on his business life and on that of others experiencing this same kind of conversion is significant:

A businessman that arrives at the feet of the Lord now does not lose time doing things of the world that were there previously, in the first place. In the second place he lives an emotional and a spiritual life that is more tranquil, in his house where before there were problems, fights, now there is tranquility . . . . These two things give him a capacity to occupy his brain in more productive things than before because previously he was very busy with thinking about how to trick his wife, for example, or in what bar will I get drunk now, so he has his mind more free, more nimble, more complete, I believe that a Christian must progress more.

Essentially, Loucel is arguing that what social scientists such as Elizabeth Brusco (1986) and Timothy Steigenga and Edward Cleary (2007) have found among poor Pentecostals is also true of upper class Pentecostals and has a similar, positive impact on their economic and entrepreneurial performance.[1]

---

[1] What runs counter to this argument is the fact that an overwhelming majority of evangelical businesspeople do not see any difference in the performance of evangelical versus non-evangelical employees. This is true in spite of the fact that they view their own conversion as significantly improving their own performance. One possible explanation for this incongruence is that, as employers, evangelicals evaluate employees' actions that are directly oriented toward a given task (a strong Catholic, for instance, can lift more bricks than a weak evangelical), and that in their self-reflections they are considering the supporting activities that comprise the evangelical culture.

It should be noted that ascetic principles can also cause evangelicals to miss profit-making opportunities. Geoff, for example, is an entrepreneur in the sexy and often cutthroat telecommunications industry in South Africa. In one of Geoff's initiatives, success hinged on including racy, borderline pornographic material as part of his product. After meeting with his pastor, Geoff chose not to allow this content and faced the market ramifications for this decision. Musikavanhu has also allowed values to negatively affect his company's fortunes. He recounted that "we have lost at least one deal . . . where somebody approached us and they knew the president [of a country] and the short and long of it is we refused to pay a bribe. And we haven't seen them since." Moreover, some evangelicals refuse to inhabit places where other business-people socialize. This practice can exclude them from settings where business gets done. One Salvadoran entrepreneur experienced this when potential colleagues chose to stay in a hotel well known for prostitution, and he chose to stay elsewhere.

The impact on value modified behavior among evangelical entrepreneurs can thus have cross-cutting consequences. A rough and tumble market environment may put a price on some evangelical habits. Still, the process of linking actions more closely to goals, or eliminating bad habits that siphon off resources in unproductive directions, unleashes potential for creative processes to be realized.

Value Driven Organizational Missions and Visions

The second way value rational action affects entrepreneurialism is that evangelicals often create value driven organizations. Whether building churches, nonprofit organizations, or private sector companies, many evangelicals are motivated by the idea that their organizations can serve a greater purpose. Money, power, and influence are part of what motivates evangelicals, but intermingled with these motives are values that shape the way evangelicals engage the world. As Japie LaPoorta, the deputy secretary of the Apostolic Faith Mission, states, "when people are accepting the Lord as their Savior, that's not the only thing they want to do, they want to change society." In NCEs, entrepreneurs now try to forge organizations that can have a transformative impact on areas as diverse as evangelism, leadership, poverty alleviation, environmental stewardship, and reducing crime and violence.

Returning to the example of Musikavanhu and Umbono Capital, the company's principal vision is to transform Africa. The projects they take on and the way that they comport themselves in the marketplace is one part of how they pursue this goal. They also pursue this goal by cultivating leaders for Africa's future. They have created a trust that is used to identify the "brightest black brains in the country," according to Musikavanhu, and to provide them with scholarships to the country's best schools. This usually means bringing black students into white environments. One of their students was recently named the head girl at a private, white school. True to Umbono's evangelical ethos,

Musikavanhu says they also "infuse a Christian ethic [into the students in our program], because our trust is a Christian trust."

Portia Nkutha, a South African lawyer, also builds organizations to pursue evangelical values. Her current "day job" places her in a position of influence: she serves as an advocate at the Sandown Chamber of Commerce, which is part of Johannesburg's financial district. But it usually does not allow her to fulfill a vocational call to heal relationships between people. In her first job out of law school, Nkutha worked for a state body charged with the mediation and arbitration of labor disputes. Nkutha reflected that "God brought that work [to me] . . . I love mediating." From there she opened an independent consultancy on labor law, the success of which opened the door to her present position. But she believes that litigation does not meet people's needs and that mediation is the better option in almost every case. So she recently cofounded a dispute resolution agency. One of the issues they address is divorce, a cause she has taken up after a recent experience in divorce court. "I was sitting in there in shock," Nkutha recounted, "because it was the first time I was in a divorce court . . . It takes five minutes to divorce! They call them in, they ask a few questions, then they say 'yes, divorce granted.' And then people go outside . . . they're crying, they're divorced, but you know, their needs are not met and it's so painful. God begins to say, 'you see [it], now what are you doing about it?'"

To respond to God's challenge, Nkutha draws people and resources together from evangelical professional groups. She is part of a group called Peacemakers, a U.S.-based organization that implements mediation strategies based on biblical principles. She also joined the Christian Lawyers Association, a chapter of the African International Network of Christian Lawyers. That network's agenda in Africa, according to Denise Woods, the South African director, includes peacemaking as well as issues of good governance, corruption, and transparency. Both Peacemakers and the Christian Lawyers Association provide Nkutha with ideas, encouragement, and partners in her efforts to meet the challenge she feels God has placed upon her.

Similar value driven entrepreneurial initiatives can be found in El Salvador. Silvana Valladaras, for example, believed the Lord was calling her to minister to the social, educational, and spiritual needs of deaf children. So she decided to start the School for the Deaf, whose mission is to be "a school that provides dignity to the deaf and brings the deaf community the gospel." Valladaras said, "although we know that the education is an extremely valuable tool, our ultimate goal is to bring the Good News to those that have never heard it." This prioritization is immanently logical within the evangelical ethos. Valladaras, who repeatedly brought up ways in which the deaf are marginalized in society and often made to feel less than human, said, "our mission is to integrate them into society as disciples of Christ . . . so that they can be persons. It is to dignify the deaf person, and the only thing that can provide dignity is the Lord, right?"

When Valladaras started the school in 1987, it was a national novelty. The only other program for the deaf in El Salvador was run through a government ministry as part of a larger institution for the handicapped. That program took a different approach to the issue: Valladaras noted that the government's approach "was purely medical, and their level of training and education [for the deaf] only went up to the second or third grade." Whereas Salvadoran institutions previously assumed deafness was a defect in need of correction, Valladaras believes "there is a sociological element there, also emotional, and of course spiritual." The beginnings of this perspective came from an internship experience she had with a Christian School for the Deaf in the Dominican Republic. But there is also a deductive process at work. Valladaras started with the evangelical value of dignity and perceived that a limited education would limit the deaf's ability to function in society. She thus brings students up to the eighth grade level in her school and has developed relationships with Christian high schools in San Salvador that will then integrate deaf students into their classrooms and encourage them to get a high school degree. This she hopes will enable her students to feel empowered, dignified, and able to fully function in society.

It almost goes without saying that values are going to influence the way people in religious communities think and act. But different values, or the same values in different contexts, can create very different kinds of behavior. Evangelical values have led to a global movement of social change across the Global South and East. Indeed, some have called it a cultural revolution (Martin 2002). Now, values are being modified *within* the movement – to this point, the most notable change has been a broadening of the evangelical social agenda, the implications of which are examined in Chapter 6. Changes in values, then, are critical components of changes that are being worked out in contemporary NCEs.

Charismatic Entrepreneurs

Robert Bellah (1970) wrote about a third concept that is important to evangelical entrepreneurship: charisma. Bellah defined charismatic leadership as being endowed with the authority to utter new commandments. Not everyone in society can persuade others to modify their behavior or open new channels of cognitive activity. This is left to those who display charisma in some way. According to Bellah (1970, 8), charisma "links deeper levels of psychic organization within the charismatic individual and in the members of the group who recognize him with the social process and particularly with radical discontinuities of development." In other words, communities are drawn to people who are endowed with charisma, especially in times of uncertainty. Bellah's charismatic leaders thus become central actors in the processes of change.

In evangelical communities, a synthesis occurs between entrepreneurs and carriers of charisma. Charismatic leaders are particularly good at drawing resources to themselves. Consequently, they are often the ones who get to build organizations and lead movements. In El Salvador, it is widely agreed that three men have the *poder de convocatoria*, or the ability to gather the Salvadoran evangelical masses. These are the heads of the three largest denominations in the country: Jeremias Bolaños of the Assemblies of God, Mario Vega of Elim, and Brother Toby of the Baptist Tabernacle. Alejandro Amaya illustrated the power these men have by stating they are the three Salvadoran evangelicals "that have the ability to fill stadiums." Amaya's words are to be taken literally. Vega, for example, flies in a helicopter to speak at different stadiums around the country when Elim holds a national rally. Bolaños may be the least likely of the three to use the stadium approach; his emphasis is in preaching to the annual conference of AG pastors each year, but he can also mobilize large numbers of lay people. In sum, evangelicals enjoy crusades and mass rallies, but they cannot be called together by just anyone – it takes a particular persona to stage such an event. Most evangelical leaders in El Salvador, even capable leaders at the national level, cannot generate such crowds. This includes even the head of the Evangelical Alliance. Being vested with the *poder de convocatoria* is a necessary element to this evangelical practice.

The *poder de convocatoria* has more significant implications than just the ability to fill stadiums. Vega, Bolaños, and Brother Toby are strategically located to direct the largest and best known evangelical institutions. They can modify the identities of these organizations, and they can channel resources toward new initiatives. Bolaños's position is slightly different, in that while the other two are the heads of independent Salvadoran church networks, he is the highest ranking national official of a global denomination. This has the effect of somewhat limiting his autonomy, but it also provides greater access to international resources. The nuances of his position do not, however, seem to affect the way in which his followers perceive him.

The *poder de convocatoria* is also something that draws attention from political powers in the country. Bolaños, Toby, and Vega have all handled this attention in different ways. For many years, Bolaños and the Assemblies of God discouraged their congregants from participating in politics in any way. Before the 2004 presidential elections, however, Bolaños publicly encouraged AG members to go to the polls. Many observers felt that AG leaders leaned immediately to the right. This is likely true, but the really important change Bolaños made was that he encouraged participation in the political process. It was not the political inclinations that AG voters demonstrated. Brother Toby has long been more vocal about supporting ARENA, the country's conservative party. He prayed at the inauguration of Tony Saca in 2004 and has remained cozy with ARENA political leaders. Vega, on the other hand, has walked a tightrope between maintaining a neutral stance and quietly supporting the FMLN, El Salvador's more progressive party. Before one of Elim's mass crusades, Vega received a request from the president's office to let Saca play a role in the opening remarks. Vega politely declined and during his interview proudly told me of the front page newspaper article on the rally, the title of which was "A Crusade Without Political Flags." Although not confirmed by Vega, there were rumors among other more progressive evangelical leaders that Vega withstood significant pressure from the Saca administration to enter into a dialogue with

Saca. Vega refused. However, when the FMLN candidate, Mauricio Funes, won the 2009 election, Vega welcomed Funes's invitation to offer the inaugural prayer.

Charisma and political influence have a more reciprocal relationship in the South African evangelical community. Unlike El Salvador, there is not a distinct set of two or three people who have significantly greater ability than other leaders to gain a following. Among the wider group of leaders who have star power are Ray McCauley, head of Rhema, David Molapo, founder of the I Can Consortium, and Michael Cassidy, founder of African Enterprise. These individuals are religious leaders, but they are also able to navigate South Africa's political terrain. Unlike in El Salvador, where political influence is a result of demonstrated religious charisma, the relationship between religious charismatic authority and political influence in South Africa is multidirectional. These and other South African leaders gain entrée in the public sphere because they represent evangelicals or some subset of the evangelical community. But the reverse is also true – evangelicals perceive these actors to have charisma at least in part because of their political involvement and accomplishments. Thus, in many cases, their influence within their faith community grows because of their political participation.

Away from politics, one of the more significant religious implications of charisma in South Africa is that those who display it get to help shape the national evangelical community. South African evangelical history is marked by key conferences, including two convenings of the South African Christian Leadership Assembly (SACLA), as well as global conferences hosted by South Africa, including the Global Conference on World Evangelization (GCOWE) and the 2010 Lausanne Conference in Cape Town. Along with several pan-denominational networks and organizations, these conferences have been staging grounds for major evangelical initiatives. In fact, SACLA II was specifically designed to set the South African churches' corporate agenda in the coming years. Michael Cassidy, of African Enterprise, was the architect behind these conferences. Those who were given strategic roles in the conference were those who had developed significant followings within their faith community.

NURTURING ENTREPRENEURS: HOW COMMUNITIES CREATE THE ENTREPRENEURS WHO CREATE THEIR COMMUNITIES

The evangelical entrepreneurs who shape NCEs are themselves produced by the NCEs in which they live. The institutions they create and the evangelical culture they generate will in turn shape the next generation of innovators. Practically speaking, at least two things are necessary for communities to produce entrepreneurs: First, there must be a community ethos that is conducive to creating entrepreneurs within society. Second, there must be incubators in society that serve to foster evangelical entrepreneurial activities.

A Culture That Produces Entrepreneurs

In *The Protestant Ethic and the Spirit of Capitalism*, Weber emphasized several traits that allowed Puritans to help usher in the modern capitalist system. Among the most important was the Calvinist doctrine, which considered all vocations, not just those of priests, to be instilled with religious meaning through a sense of calling. Weber also argued that sixteenth-century Puritans experienced great angst over their salvation status. They thus tried to use achievements in the material world to demonstrate that they were part of God's chosen people and to resolve their psychological angst. The resulting patterns of action led to "an ethos of 'world mastery' and [oriented] their entire lives toward work and material success" (Kalberg 2002, xxxi).

However, Weber's friend and colleague, Ernst Troeltsch, interprets the impact of Calvinism on an individual's psychological state differently. Troeltsch argues that rather than angst, Calvinism produces great confidence in the believer, for once believers achieve the state of grace they cannot lose their salvation. This, according to Troeltsch, allows the Calvinist "to give all his attention to the effort to mold the world and society according to the Will of God" (Troeltsch [1931] 1992, 589). From Troeltsch's point of view, confidence, rather than angst, serves as the psychological and emotional energy behind the spirit of capitalism.[2]

Although they were divided over its origins, Weber and Troeltsch agreed that one of the results of Puritanism's religious energy was that it generated higher levels of material attainment. The strategies Weber highlights (Troeltsch provides a similar list) that made this possible include the duty of the individual to increase his or her wealth, the consideration of labor as an absolute end in itself, the desirability of the acquisition of money and the avoidance of enjoying it, the belief that money's acquisition is the result of competence in a vocational calling, and a frame of mind that strives systematically and rationally to fulfill a calling for legitimate profit (Kalberg 2002).

The culture of contemporary NCEs reflects its Puritan heritage. Many NCEs are characterized by familistic sentiment, frugality, individual accountability, and reliability (Berger 1991), just as the Puritans were before them. All of these facilitate entrepreneurial activity. But there are also differences between sixteenth-century Calvinism and contemporary global evangelicalism. Salvific angst tends not to be a characteristic found in NCEs, the avoidance of enjoying money is found irregularly among evangelicals, and generally speaking, the

---

[2] Both Weber and Troeltsch recognize that Calvinism is not the sole provider of asceticism or behavior conducive to capitalism. Troeltsch in fact highlights a contributing factor that is particularly important to the Latin American evangelical experience, which is that energy conducive to capitalism springs from the persecution, or at least the minority experience, of religious sects. He also notes that the migration experience can spur productive behavior, citing the example of the French Huguenots in the Netherlands – the Huguenots were some of the earliest colonizers of South Africa.

evangelical relationship to money and to its acquisition has a more spiritual feel rather than the practical orientation that appears in Weber's portrayal of sixteenth-century Puritans.

Finally, and perhaps most importantly, the confidence to which Troeltsch refers has been amplified and translated into an optimistic outlook about one's abilities and possibilities for success. This is explained more fully in Chapter 6, but its impact on organization-building initiatives is quite similar to Chesnut's (1997) explanation of how healing actually works in the Brazilian context. States Chesnut (1997, 87):

... the fact that millions of Pentecostals believe that Jesus and the Holy Spirit heal on the basis of faith alone makes *cura divina* a subjective reality. Like the patient whose health improves because of her faith in the curative properties of the little white capsule she takes three times a day, though it is merely a placebo, the *crente* creates the possibility of divine healing through belief.

Similarly, evangelical optimism enables entrepreneurs to overcome personal doubts. Musikavanhu, an evangelical entrepreneur in the South African financial sector, believes that this kind of optimism is desperately needed in Africa: "if you're told over and over again that you're a failure ... then sadly, it's a self-fulfilling prophecy. So, we somehow need a new way of positive-ness in Africa, you know, where the people really have a sense that they can do it." Musikavanhu and other evangelical entrepreneurs have gained this sense through their faith.

In addition to nurturing a healthy self-esteem and an optimistic outlook, the evangelical ethos fosters a moral fortitude in entrepreneurs. Evangelicals believe this is critical to the proper exercise of entrepreneurship. For example, Gumede states:

developing entrepreneurs is about getting a human being to think right and needing something for fixing the soul, addressing the real internals of a human being so they are actually able to get the group principles, to think in the appropriate way, to handle their businesses in a particular way. That is a very difficult thing. It is not as simple as going on a financial course or ... getting a few technical skills. It is complicated and time consuming.

There are multiple ways that evangelicals try to bolster what they see as the intangibles to proper entrepreneurial initiatives. Leadership seminars are the most popular, and they are ubiquitous in NCEs. International speakers often put on these seminars – by far the most well known is Atlanta-based author John Maxwell. His books are prominently displayed in Christian bookstores throughout El Salvador and South Africa, and he has visited both countries in recent years. In both countries, evangelicals frequently discuss his Million Leader Mandate program, which according to the website is a "global initiative to train millions of Christians ... to effectively pursue the Great Commission in their communities, workplaces, and churches." Most of Maxwell's books also espouse basic points of how to become effective leaders. Sample tips Maxwell provides in *The 21 Irrefutable Laws of Leadership* (1998) include: "Trust is the foundation of leadership," "Leaders touch a heart before they ask for a hand," and "Leadership develops daily, not in a day." Both church and business leaders utilize Maxwell's publications: an assistant pastor at the Baptist Tabernacle mentioned Maxwell first when asked which American authors he trusted; in South Africa, Ian Fuller, a business owner in the timber industry, professed to being "very stimulated" by Maxwell's books and was delighted about an opportunity that had arisen to play golf with Maxwell at Pebble Beach a few months after the interview.

Evangelicals in NCEs are also perfectly capable of putting on their own leadership seminars. In a 2011 visit to Iglesia Josué, I noticed flyers for three different leadership-related events in coming months, all of which were locally driven. At the Oasis of Life Family Church on the eastern outskirts of Johannesburg, regular programs were running that were intended to identify and cultivate leadership and entrepreneurial skills.

Entrepreneurial Incubators

The cultural conditions and public rhetoric, then, are right for entrepreneurs to flourish in NCEs. But intentional nurturing of people with entrepreneurial skill is necessary for this potential to be realized. Organizational and relational structures must serve as incubators for entrepreneurs and the organizations and institutions they hope to create. Two types of incubators have proven to be particularly effective within evangelical communities: First, local congregations are often fertile ground for creating new institutions. Second, evangelicals emphasize mentoring relationships among the faithful, and the entrepreneurial spirit is often fostered within these types of relationships. Both types of incubators deserve further elaboration.

Churches

Churches are particularly good at serving in this incubator role. Stephen Warner argues that churches are spaces of empowerment that bring multiple resources together: "churches can combine the symbolic and the material, the cultural and the structural, group morale and social networks" (Warner 1993, 1069). Those interested in creating institutions and organizations can thus thrive in church settings.

Valladaras, for example, decided to start the School for the Deaf when she had just $57 in capital, no physical infrastructure, no teachers, and no support staff. But Valladaras's church wanted to help her realize her vision. So in the early years, the church provided the legal coverage for the school to operate and allowed the school to use several of the Sunday school classrooms during the week. Valladaras's friends in the congregation volunteered their time to be teachers and provided administrative support. Valladaras ran the school within the church for the first ten years of its existence. When the school finally developed the necessary organizational and financial strength, Valladaras moved it into its own building and registered it as its own legal entity. Now in its third decade, the school remains embedded in the social networks of the congregation that helped to birth it, as members sit on its board, provide staff, and attend school fundraisers and other functions.

As Warner (1993) notes, churches also make symbolic and educational resources available to congregational members. Entrepreneurs are able to use these in their creative initiatives. For example, Musikavanhu's early entrepreneurial initiatives may never have come into being were it not for the symbolic work being done at the church he attended during his university days. The church's leaders were calling on its members to carry God's kingdom into the world and to reject any inclination to hide from the world. Musikavanhu and some of his friends in the church wanted to thoughtfully respond to this message. They felt that starting a multiracial consulting firm in South Africa in the late 1990s was a legitimate way to do so. The experiences of Valladaras and Musikavanhu are far from unique; for many who have successfully built organizations, the genesis of their projects can be traced back to people dreaming dreams and receiving the necessary support to realize them in congregational settings.

Churches also serve as incubators for other churches. When a new church is founded, it is often a "daughter church" of another congregation from which it can somehow draw its heritage. Some "mother churches" build church planting activities into their annual budgets and long-term planning activities. The Baptist Tabernacle in San Salvador displays a high level of intentionality about growing in influence through planting churches throughout the country. "Daughter churches" in other contexts emerge almost as if by accident, such as when a church member moves to a new town and starts a Bible study that eventually becomes a church. Roberto Bustamente's Family of God church in San Salvador now has a daughter church in Texas for just this reason. More contentiously, church splits also allow for entrepreneurs to emerge and lead a second church out of what was previously just a single congregation. For instance, in the town of Tinteral, El Salvador, the local Assembly of God church experienced controversy. Eventually, a small group decided to begin meeting just down the road from the larger group. They soon had a pastor, and they were able to normalize relations with the church that they had left. The frequency of church splits in NCEs, whether due to deep bitterness or seemingly haphazard reasoning, is almost dizzying.

Mentoring Relationships

Mentoring relationships, also referred to as discipling relationships, also serve as entrepreneurial incubators in NCEs. These can take many forms but generally include a younger person or someone who is new to the faith and an older, more mature member of the community. Parents can serve as mentors, and they play a recognized role in cultivating entrepreneurship. Elvis Mvulane, South Africa's national director of Walk Thru the Bible, recounted the way in which his father instilled an entrepreneurial spirit in him by teaching him how to sell fruit at soccer games and in other township venues. This served him well as he started a security agency and a church in Soweto before he moved into salaried ministry positions. Alberto, in El Salvador, owns a construction business that builds and sells houses at the higher end of the Salvadoran housing market; they usually sell for about $800,000. Alberto's father was a simple construction foreman. He took Alberto to work when he was very small and, says Alberto, "when the boss came he told him, 'my son is going to be an engineer just like you.' This filled [Alberto's father] with happiness and hope, and for me this was perhaps the biggest motivating factor to follow his dream, and I did it." Life experiences such as these are reinforced by the many sermons that also proclaim the importance of the parent–child relationship.

There are other kinds of mentoring relationships that shape entrepreneurs. The Business Network Forum in South Africa is a good example. The network's founders, Thami and Paul, are self-proclaimed "township boys" and pastors with New Covenant Ministries International. Both have founded their own churches, and Thami has founded several businesses. They started the Business Network Forum to bring struggling black South Africans under the tutelage of more experienced businessmen. The forum targets people who want to start businesses but who don't have a high level of education. "Some of us who know, who have been there, need to impart that knowledge to those who do not know," says Thami. Another example is David Molapo, founder of the I Can Group, who tries to mentor people closest to him within his businesses. He thinks of this model as being something along the lines of how Christ mentored his disciples.

A third kind of mentoring relationship is forged within professional ministry circles. Michael Cassidy, who founded African Enterprise almost four decades ago, now wants to provide guidance to younger leaders. "I find the Lord is bringing younger people, both men and women into purview with me and into relationship where I can encourage them, father them, help them, mentor them, disciple them," stated Cassidy. Similar dynamics are occurring in El Salvador, where Adonai Leiva, former head of the Evangelical Alliance and of Campus Crusade for Christ, disciples a number of younger leaders. One of those is Juan Manuel Martinez, a recent head of the Evangelical Alliance. In sum, evangelicals are intentional about forming parental and other forms of mentoring relationships, and these kinds of social structures act as incubators for creative acts and actors.

CONCLUSION

Local religious social forces are powerful sources of change in NCEs. Local actors are busily engaged in creative processes that introduce new organizations and institutions across the evangelical landscape. To do so, they draw upon other religious forces, many of which also have local origins. But local actors also vigorously draw upon the global forces at work in NCEs. They are often able to redirect these forces, channeling them into their own projects and placing them in the service of their own agendas. This ability shows the potency of local actors in forging their own communities and has implications for theories that posit local actors as dependent upon or in the service of evangelicals in the West.

5

The Social Contours and Global Reach of the New Centers of Global Evangelicalism: Enlarging Organizations, Exporting Religion, and Creating Social Stratification

I met Alejandro and Rogelio near one of the red line metro stops in Washington, DC. Dressed in business attire and speaking in English, Alejandro, whom I knew, introduced me to Rogelio. Both men attended Iglesia Josué, a large, affluent Assemblies of God (AG) church back in San Salvador. Now they were living in the United States. Alejandro moved to Virginia to create an integrated mission program to the Muslim world between Salvadoran and North American churches. Rogelio's government job brought him to Washington; he worked in the Salvadoran embassy. Both expected to return home within the next five years, and each looked forward to worshiping again in their home church.

The two friends chatted with one another as much as they talked to me. They slipped comfortably between languages as they caught each other up on people and events in DC and in El Salvador. As they talked they glanced happily at their smartphones and occasionally took a call, which somehow did not at all disrupt the flow of conversation. At different points in the conversation, their tones became more earnest: Alejandro spoke of the dreams and challenges of developing an integrated mission program, and Rogelio reflected on the opportunities and difficulties of being a follower of Jesus in an embassy setting.

The conversation eventually wound down and the daily hustle and bustle of life crowded back in. I was struck by the fact that I had just witnessed a transnational conversation among members of El Salvador's professional class. The participants perceived themselves, either directly or indirectly, to be emissaries of their San Salvador–based church. Nothing about their presence in DC, their fluidly bilingual conversations, or their level of comfort with the accoutrements of a DC lifestyle seemed odd or out of place to them. In fact, quite the opposite was true: all of these were taken-for-granted aspects of their everyday lives.

Evangelical communities across the Global South and East look different than they did three decades ago, when conversations such as the one just recounted would have been rare indeed. But the global and local religious social forces outlined in the previous two chapters have created dramatic changes. Three of the most important changes include the increasing size of local organizations, the growing ability of NCEs to export religion, and the increasingly stratified nature of national evangelical communities. All of these developments point toward greater influence for evangelicals in their host societies and beyond.

In this discussion of religious change, a caveat is in order. There is still much about evangelicalism in NCEs that remains recognizable. There are also large swaths of evangelical communities in which continuity rather than change is the dominant story. But the changes recounted here are affecting the most visible and prominent parts of evangelical communities. They are thus all the more important.

THE INCREASING SIZE OF LOCAL ORGANIZATIONS

Strong, sophisticated organizations help to propel global religious movements. Evangelicalism is no exception, and churches, NGOs, and evangelically owned businesses in NCEs are all growing – a direct and immediate result of increasingly effective evangelical entrepreneurship. This upward trend is important because bigger organizations allow for higher concentrations of power. This in turn forces evangelicals to learn how to act politically, as other power brokers in society are either attracted to or threatened by the new political actors. Bigger organizations also allow evangelicals to pursue widening agendas more effectively.

Sometimes organizational growth in NCEs is spectacular, outpacing even Western evangelical organizations. The world's largest ten to fifteen churches, for example, exist outside the West.[1] Elim is near the top of this list. Located in San Salvador's eastern urban sprawl, its facilities fit the gritty, working class settings around it. In fact, as one bumps along the rutty dirt road on the way to Elim, it would be easy to mistake its expansive grounds for just another of the neighborhood's industrial warehouse complexes.

Elim was started as a church plant by the original Elim Church of Guatemala, which in turn was founded by a man named Othoniel Rios Paredes. In 1977 Paredes sent one of his assistants, Sergio Solarzano, to start an Elim church in San Salvador. Solarzano started humbly enough: Elim's first meeting counted just nine people in attendance. A year later Elim had grown to 150 people, and by 1983 the church had filled its 1,500-seat hall, causing its leaders to acquire the large piece of land they have now, in what is technically the neighborhood of Soyapongo.

---

[1] This statistic is complicated by the many ways that one can measure the size of churches. But Elim is larger by a very comfortable margin than the largest church in the United States, which is listed by Hartford Seminary's megachurch database as the Lakewood Church in Houston, Texas, pastored by Joel Osteen. Hartford's database estimates Lakewood to have 43,500 congregants (http://hirr.hartsem.edu/, accessed January 2012).

Even in its first years, Elim El Salvador began planting other churches, and by 1985 it had seventy daughter congregations (Comiskey 2003). As mentioned in the previous chapter, this number was reduced when in 1986 the church switched to the cell group model and asked its church plants in the metropolitan area to consolidate into a single entity, but that move was effective in generating rapid growth in the mother church. According to church records, by 1988 the cell groups had grown to include 20,000 people. That number rose to more than 111,000 by 2001 and to more than 129,000 by 2006.[2] It is important to note that only about a third of those who attend cell groups regularly attend the Sunday services, which Elim calls celebration services. But every other year Elim stages an event in which all of its members are called together. To do so, they rent out multiple stadiums within the capital city and in other locales across the country. In 2002 an estimated 200,000 people attended the event; aerial shots of the five stadiums filled to capacity now grace Vega's office.[3]

Congregations like Elim, whose numbers have reached six digits, remain something of a novelty. More common are churches in NCEs that have numbers extending well into the tens of thousands. South Africa's Rhema Church is in this group. Founded in 1979 by Ray McCauley, its first meetings were held in McCauley's parents' house. The family affair quickly attracted enough neighbors to rent space in a nearby cinema. Rhema then moved to an old warehouse (smaller than Elim's current edifice), and from there to its current property in Randburg, a northwest Johannesburg suburb, where McCauley and his leadership team built an entire complex. Rhema now has roughly 40,000 members, and about 14,000 people flow through the doors every Sunday morning, when there are three services. But Rhema's growth has been felt even beyond these spacious premises, as it has partnered with another charismatic megachurch, the Hatfield Christian Church, to start the International Federation of Christian Churches (IFCC) (Anderson & Pillay 1997). The federation (roughly equivalent to a denomination) now has more than 400,000 members.

There are even more churches in NCEs that have between 2,000 and 15,000 congregants. In fact, churches in this range are so plentiful in NCEs as to be commonplace. In El Salvador, the Baptist Tabernacle's church network has several congregations that are between 5,000 and 15,000 people. The Assemblies of God

---

[2] These numbers are taken from statistics in the senior pastor's office. Comiskey (2003) studied Elim in 2003 and showed that when Elim's six Sunday services are combined, the total weekly attendance at Elim tallied 30,000 adults and 3,000 children. There were seventy-six full-time pastoral staff, and total attendance for the weeknight services was 11,000, attendance for the six teaching services during the week was 24,000, and the weekly all-night prayer vigils regularly attracted about 3,000 participants.

[3] Comiskey (2003) distinguishes between Elim's rally, which was held annually until 2002 and is now held semiannually because of the extent of the logistics involved, and a Billy Graham Crusade. Comiskey argues that this meeting is part of the church organizational strategy, and the only people who are in attendance are cell group members. However, in Vega's interview with me, he called the event a crusade and implied that there was an evangelistic component to it.

in El Salvador also has a number of churches that exceed 5,000 members. Other AG churches are not far behind, such as Alejandro and Rogelio's 4,000-member congregation, Iglesia Josué. Even smaller denominations often have cornerstone churches that qualify as megachurches. Independent churches, like the Verbo Church in San Salvador, regularly pull in 5,000 or so members. The situation in South Africa is similar: church networks like His People, church planting movements like New Covenant Ministries, independent churches like Rosebank Union and Grace Bible Church, and traditional denominations like the Dutch Reformed Church all have very large churches in their ranks. In contemporary NCEs, big churches that have significant institutional strength are simply standard fare.

Churches are not alone in their institutional growth. Local faith-based NGOs owned by evangelicals are also growing. Of course, international evangelical NGOs have had big offices in NCEs for decades: World Relief built more than 5,000 homes in El Salvador after the 1986 earthquake, and World Vision's budgets in southern Africa and Central America regularly run into the tens of millions of dollars. But locally grown NGOs have also experienced remarkable growth. Ron and David Bueno started ENLACE, an NGO affiliated with the Assemblies of God, in the early 1990s. Operating on a shoestring budget, ENLACE grew slowly during the first decade of its existence. During that time the Buenos deepened their ties with churches[4] in the impoverished, mostly rural areas of El Salvador and with various donors and churches in the United States. As a result, its second decade of existence was marked by growth: ENLACE went from five formal church training partnerships in 2003 to about forty such partnerships in 2011. They are also transitioning from operating on a $1.5 million budget per year to operating on a $5 million budget per year. ENLACE's growth trajectory is being repeated among local NGOs, schools, and different types of faith-based ministries throughout NCEs.

Local businesses owned by evangelicals in NCEs are also getting larger. Umbono Trust, for example, is hiring more people and expanding its assets. Founded in the late 1990s, cofounder Tendai Musikavanhu stated that the financial services corporation "started off with about four people and no assets under management. Today we manage just under eight billion rand[5] on behalf of our clients, and we have throughout the group, not just in the fund management business, but we have about 336 people and growing quite rapidly." David Molapo, founder of the I Can Group, has encountered similar success: his company has contracts with some of South Africa's largest corporations, like Sasol, an international energy and chemicals company. When multiple contracts run concurrently, Molapo hires more than 100 people at time. Likewise in El

---

[4] About half the churches ENLACE works with are AG churches, but ENLACE works with churches from six other denominations as well. The organization also works with a number of independent churches.

[5] The rand tends to fluctuate between 7:1 and 8:1 against the U.S. dollar.

Salvador, Mauricio Loucel, head of El Salvador's Full Gospel Businessmen's Association, was a founding partner of what has become the largest private university in El Salvador. It now has more than 1,000 employees. In short, for many evangelicals, business in NCEs is booming.

Not all aspiring evangelical entrepreneurs in NCEs create booming churches, businesses, or ministries. Like entrepreneurial projects the world over, most evangelical initiatives in these regions fail. Others that survive hobble along, with just enough revenue streams to keep the doors open. The majority of evangelicals in NCEs, it must be remembered, are still poor. Consequently, the majority of evangelical creative enterprises are located in the crowded downtown marketplaces, where salons, fruit stands, and even buses have biblical names blazoned across the front of their buildings and vehicles. Entrepreneurs in these social settings have grabbed on to evangelical symbols with both hands, but physical resources continue to elude them.

As a result, many who are associated with these efforts remain trapped in poverty. Alicia, an employee of a struggling Salvadoran evangelical NGO, has a university education and earns about $250 per month. Because cuts may need to be made in her employer's budget, even this modest income is not secure. Experiences like Alicia's are far more common than the success stories of ENLACE and Umbono Trust. By focusing on the successful organizations, the point of this book is emphatically not to suggest that any organization started by an evangelical encounters great success. Rather, the point is to show that the number, size, and strength of organizations in NCEs is increasing. Such developments within the population of evangelical organizations increases the ability of evangelicals to get things done, just as it would any other community experiencing similar dynamics within their organizations. The fact that large numbers of initiatives continue to fail does not change this new organizational reality. It does, however, contribute to social stratification, a theme I address later in this chapter.

Diversity in Culture and Growth Strategies

Of the organizations in NCEs that are growing, there is great diversity with respect to *how* they create growth. The pathways of growth taken by Elim and Rhema illustrate these divergences. Elim's dramatic growth began with its exposure to David Yonggi Cho's church growth strategy, which in turn prompted church leaders to adapt a pyramid organizational structure. In Elim's schema, the senior pastor is at the top of the pyramid, followed by district coordinators, zonal pastors, cell group supervisors, and then individual cell leaders, respectively. Rodolfo Chicas is, for instance, a zonal pastor in District Four. The cell group supervisors he oversees have about seventy cell groups in their care. Outside the pyramid structure are two different boards. A group of five elders addresses issues such as budgets and other administrative decisions. The spiritual advisory board keeps a check on church doctrine and has other similar responsibilities. One Elim elder stated that "the elders are those that give administrative support to the general pastor as well as support in making some of the transcendental decisions … this is the Biblical configuration [of what elders should do] and so this is what we put in practice here." Both groups are also charged with keeping the senior pastor accountable.

The level of discipline imposed at Elim reinforces the idea that a need for order is one of the drivers of evangelical growth in the chaotic lower class of Latin America (Willems 1967). Like many Latin American Pentecostal congregations, men and women sit on different sides of the auditorium during Elim's services.[6] Ushers stand in the aisles, attentively watching the congregation. During one evening service, I was busily writing field notes when I was startled by a hand placed gently on my shoulder. "Is everything OK," I was asked. I quickly regained my composure and smiled up at the usher. "Yes brother," I whispered back, and demonstrated that I was paying attention to the service rather than doodling on my paper. He smiled and went back to his post. In other services, I saw ushers gently nudge people who had fallen asleep, ask people to pay attention, and shepherd children to and from the bathrooms. My wife also reported having her head lightly pushed down during prayer, as she apparently hadn't bowed deeply enough.[7]

Discipline of congregants during the service is accompanied by efficiency in other aspects of worship. One weekday afternoon, I walked through the auditorium and saw about twenty-five ladies moving through the empty rows of chairs in semi-choreographed motions. They stopped briefly at each seat before moving on. Puzzled, I asked a lady overseeing this activity what they were doing, and she cheerfully told me that they were practicing for the following Sunday's communion. At Elim that made perfect sense, but it is safe to assume that in most churches, such a full-out rehearsal of communion is seldom exercised. In sum, there are some aspects of the church's culture that are strikingly like that of an army or of a highly efficient corporation. This is one of the keys to Elim's growth in the chaotic environment of lower class San Salvador.

The cell group structure and a focus on discipline and order, combined with an aggressive orientation toward evangelism and Elim's radio and television ministry, has effectively harnessed Elim's Pentecostal energy and generates explosive church growth. Certain contextual factors are also important: in the early years, the anomie created by the civil war was filling all churches, not just Elim, and a fractured Catholic Church made new religious options more tenable.

---

[6] In 2007 Elim created a "family section" in the middle of the seating area where men and women could sit next to each other.

[7] This level of enforcement is not necessarily promoted or appreciated by the church's senior leadership. Vega recounted a story from the pulpit about ushers who refused to let a new couple who was visiting the church for the first time sit together in the back. Vega disapproved of the usher's behavior and said the consequence was that the couple never came back. In a private conversation, Vega explained that the custom of having men and women sit on opposite sides is not a biblical mandate and that in the long term he could imagine Elim lifting this practice.

It is thus the confluence of organizational strategies and contextual factors that have fueled Elim's remarkable growth.

Rhema, like Elim, has a corporate feel, but the two churches have very different corporate identities. Rhema does not use a cell group–based pyramid structure. The personal leadership styles of Vega and McCauley also contrast sharply, as Vega's kind and gentle but ascetic and fairly efficient demeanor is countered by McCauley's folksy, slightly indulgent public persona. But McCauley's charisma is one of the most important factors in Rhema's growth. On stage, McCauley connects so well with his audience that he regularly brings first-time visitors into the church. Ron Steele, Rhema's former media spokesman and assistant to McCauley, stated that Rhema receives about 600 commitments a month. (As in any large church or crusade, only a fraction of those commitments are retained.) An example is Gordon Greaves, who first came to Rhema only because his girlfriend brought him. He describes his own journey to Rhema's altar in this way: "I was . . . critical of Rhema, and I went to that service just [because of my girlfriend] . . . but it felt as if the preacher was talking to nobody else in that auditorium but me, and I just felt so convicted that I didn't walk to the front, I ran [chuckles]." The commonality of this experience has made the altar call, rather than Rhema's leadership or organizational structure, the most frequently discussed engine to Rhema's growth.

The personality differences between Vega and McCauley correspond to the differences in the organizational ethos of Elim and Rhema. Elim continues to meet in a barren warehouse (although plans to move are afoot), whereas Rhema's suburban facilities border on the luxurious. Inside the auditorium, jumbo screens run through the announcements before the service begins, and skilled musicians lead the congregation in praise songs that would be familiar to U.S. evangelicals. As people arrive, they settle into attractive cushioned seats and glance at the polished brochures they have been handed promoting upcoming events. A Bible College is housed on the church grounds, which allows Rhema's property essentially to double as a college or seminary campus. The preparation of future church leaders is an important plank in Rhema's strategy to further extend its organizational influence. There is also a large book shop, a wholesale division, a chapel, a media department, and recreational facilities at Rhema. Each of these enables Rhema to reach beyond the confines of its congregation in some way and attempt to draw new people to its ministry.

Rhema's growth has also been aided by its ability to project a sense that the church and its members are a central piece of society in the new South Africa. Two of Rhema's four aspirations, listed on its website, are to be socially significant and prophetically relevant (the other two goals are to be spiritually vibrant and evangelistically potent). They have been able to project this identity in part through their ability to attract nationally prominent politicians and businesspeople. Nelson Mandela and Jacob Zuma have been spotted at the church at different times, and other national political leaders, including the former ANC chaplain, are members of the church. Lazurus Zim, the former

CEO of Anglo American Corporation, and major actors in South Africa's new business class are also Rhema members.[8] Rhema's many social and political activities and relationships further add to this image. More will be said about these in the following chapter. These two elements – nationally prominent members or visitors and extensive public engagement – draw attention to Rhema and increase its attendance, even as it brews controversy and keeps some evangelicals away.

The Political Implications of Large Organizations

There are political implications to creating large religious organizations. On the one hand, creators and leaders of these organizations attract attention simply by virtue of the fact that they now command large followings or manage significant resources. Such leaders thus must learn to interact with actors and entities that would otherwise ignore them. The unwanted attention that Vega received from the Saca administration, mentioned in the previous chapter, serves as one example of this. Elim has also received attention of a more agreeable nature from UNICEF, which generally does not reach out to evangelical churches in El Salvador. In this case, Vega and Elim were happy to take advantage of the attention their size attracted, and they have cosponsored at least one event with UNICEF.

On the other hand, some evangelical leaders use their organizational platforms to influence public life. The Evangelical Alliance of South Africa (TEASA) is in part designed to pursue this end; TEASA's leaders seek to enter the public debates shaping the country's new democracy. In another example, African Enterprise, a South African NGO, stages mass crusades in many countries throughout Africa. When it does, it calls on leaders of countries to participate. During a crusade in Ghana, for example, African Enterprise included a special dinner for members of Parliament and other distinguished guests. Back in South Africa, African Enterprise has parlayed its ability to reach large masses of people into sustained engagement on a number of political issues. In the days leading up to the end of apartheid, Cassidy was a critical player behind the scenes in bringing Mangosuthu Buthelezi to the negotiating table and thus avoiding terrible postelection bloodshed in the province of KwaZulu Natal. More recently, Cassidy sought to influence members of each branch of government by distributing his *Leadership Letter* to them on a quarterly basis. The letters were intended to encourage those in politics to let moral principles ground their actions and decisions. Cassidy also publicly opposed abortion

---

[8] These kinds of personalities are at Rhema in part because of the strong stand McCauley took against apartheid in the late 1980s. Scholarship on South Africa is divided about the *motives* McCauley had in taking a stand against apartheid, but ANC leaders clearly consider McCauley and Rhema to have been a key ally in the lead up to the end of the apartheid era.

and gay marriage as they were being debated in South Africa and marshaled movements within the faith community to support his positions. Throughout his career, Cassidy has been able to gain an audience with people in political power in part because he can also gather together large groups of people for crusades and other religious events.

In the private sector, the size of an organization more frequently signifies financial muscle than large followings of people, which is the currency of religious leaders. But money can also give people political influence, and conversely, political influence can provide access to capital. David Molapo, for example, has strong relationships with many leading members of the ANC. This has been advantageous to his business interests, as he has positioned his company to take advantage of the government's Black Economic Empowerment (BEE) policies. Molapo has also garnered personal recognition from the government, receiving the National Bridge Builder award for his work with South Africa's youth. This raised the profile of both his company and his foundation. Molapo has refined his political skills to the point that he has not ruled out the possibility of transitioning into the political arena himself at some point. Other South African evangelical businesspeople also move easily within the upper levels of the ANC, such as Oya-Hazel Gumede, the co-owner of Ashira and Shelton law firm and consultant to various government departments; Noli Mboweni, the director of Vela International, which is the Black Economic Empowerment (BEE) partner of Sun International Group, one of South Africa's most powerful conglomerates; and Nomonde Mabuya, a physician and senior member of Vodacom, one of South Africa's telecommunications giants. Mboweni, for example, had a photo in her office of her father and Nelson Mandela standing together. When asked about the photo, Mboweni acknowledged that Mandela and her father were neighbors and that the photo had been taken at her father's birthday party. "Black diamonds," or the emerging black South African elite, have been referenced in a wide variety of media and publications, including *Forbes* magazine (Goyal 2010). It is clear that leading evangelicals can comfortably move in these circles.

The Salvadoran religio-political context makes the kind of relational ease and fluidity on display in South Africa less likely. Even successful evangelicals feel marginalized by their religious identity and sometimes by their ascetic behavior. Francisco Guerrero, an alternate judge to the Supreme Court, for example, reported discussing a difficult case over lunch. One of the other judges suggested that he bring any biblical insights he might have to elucidate the case. So Guerrero began to talk about the book of Ruth, but the chief justice cut him off, noting sarcastically that he didn't realize there was a priest in the court. Another evangelical practiced law for a few years before dropping out of the profession because he believed he could not maintain his integrity within his work environment. A third respondent, a businessman, estimated that more than half of Salvadoran businessmen have affairs (usually with their secretaries) at the office, and he considered that practice to be anathema to his faith. These kinds of moral dynamics can also exist in South Africa. Likewise, in both countries, there are many evangelicals who are also deeply embroiled in morally questionable behavior. More will be said about this in the following chapter. In spite of their own moral failings, evangelicals tend to view moral values within their religiously constructed communities to be at odds with the moral values found in many business settings, especially in the Salvadoran context, and this can be an obstacle to their efforts to exercise influence.

Still, some evangelicals do feel comfortable participating in Salvadoran public and professional life. Those who do have often become evangelicals after their professional networks and activities have been established. Mauricio Loucel, for example, was part of El Salvador's political class before his conversion. With his vibrant personality, he has easily maintained those relationships even as he has re-crafted his religious identity. He has not, however, re-crafted his political activity around an identifiable evangelical political agenda. Rather, he continues to be engaged at a more technical level in public discourse and in overseeing public institutions. On the evening of our interview, he was going to appear in a television program. He stated that "at 8:00 pm tonight, in a program of political opinion, I will be coming out criticizing the government." But Loucel also supports the government in various ways: at the time of the interview, he served on a Presidential Commission concerning national education and on the Board of the National Civil Police. In these various roles, Loucel perceives himself to be a public servant and not an agent of evangelical political interests.

Nonetheless, Loucel willingly puts his faith identity on public display. In addition to presiding over a university, as mentioned above, Loucel is also the president of a television station. Of his own appearances on this station, he stated, "I have said on television that I have accepted Jesus as my personal Savior and as my Lord." He also allows his church to have an hour of airtime on his station free of charge every week. By way of explaining these public displays of faith, Loucel references "the part of the Bible where the Lord says those that are ashamed of me I will be ashamed of them." In short, Loucel is active in El Salvador's political class, both as a technocrat and a public figure. He prominently displays his evangelical identity. He does not, however, use his political influence to pursue a political evangelical agenda.

There are evangelical owners of organizations who do attempt to pursue a specific evangelical agenda. Terri Benner Dominguez owns El Salvador's largest Christian bookstore chain. She grew up in El Salvador as the daughter of an American missionary. After taking over the bookstore chain from her father, who founded it, Benner Dominguez became active among the national evangelical leadership in El Salvador; she was elected vice president of the Evangelical Alliance in 2004. In the twin roles of a prominent businesswoman and an officer for the Evangelical Alliance, Benner Dominguez pursued political solutions to social issues that often concern U.S. evangelicals. For example, it was reported that a Salvadoran UN delegate quietly intended to sign a treaty that would have forced El Salvador to legalize abortion. Dominguez became aware of this and mounted a successful public relations campaign against it. Dominguez also helped to bring gay marriage and religious freedoms into El Salvador's public discourse, mentioning them in a debate between presidential candidates that she helped to organize on behalf of the Evangelical Alliance.

In sum, leaders of evangelical organizations experience political life in different ways. Some feel like non-evangelical actors shun them because of their faith, while others find mainstream culture in public spaces morally offensive and seek to remove themselves from it. But still other evangelicals find a comfort level within the public sphere. Those who do fall into two categories: skilled professionals who happen to be evangelicals, and representatives of evangelicalism in the public sphere. The different encounters that evangelicals have with politics further demonstrate the diversity of social locations that evangelicals now inhabit.

EXPORTING RELIGION

If large organizations expand the national influence of evangelicals in NCEs, they also extend their reach internationally. The two phenomena are connected–to export religious people and products, sufficient organizational abilities are necessary. Today, evangelicals across the Global South and East are able to send people to distant lands, create religious movements, and develop mass media platforms that take their messages around the world. The capacity of evangelicals to develop an increasing array, as well as increasing volumes, of exports is among the most important of the new realities that are redefining contemporary global evangelicalism.

There are three primary audiences or groups of consumers that evangelicals in NCEs hope to reach when they export religious people and products: their own emigrant populations, other Christian centers that usually include neighboring countries or the West, and parts of the globe that are predominantly non-Christian. The audience that is targeted can help to determine the kind of product that NCEs produce and the impact it can have. For example, products sent to emigrant communities can be important in sustaining relationships between family and friends that are stretched across borders. Products sent to Western recipients help to create a modicum of reciprocity in North–South or West–East dynamics that have, to this point, been decidedly uneven. Finally, NCE exports that reach non-Christian regions of the world often arrive without the perceived imperialistic baggage that American evangelical exports might carry, but often with no more, and perhaps less, training in cultural sensitivity than their Western counterparts. Exports in all of these directions extend the influence and visibility of NCEs around the globe.

NCEs differ in the numbers and types of religious products they export. These variations are determined in part by the national contexts in which they are located. Salvadoran evangelicals, for example, focus on exporting different types of people flows, which mirrors the export practices of their national economy. In

South Africa, one of the things evangelicals have exported is a spiritual movement that emphasizes reconciliation: the imprint of South Africa's passage from apartheid to democracy, which was paved by the Truth and Reconciliation Commission, is clear. Other variables that influence what NCEs choose to produce include the relative size of their faith community, the tools of production that are available to them, and the different spiritual, social, and even political emphases within the specific NCE. Some empirical examples of the main types of evangelical exports make these dynamics more clear.

People

People have long been a favorite export of religious groups everywhere. Missionaries, monks, and priests have traveled on pilgrimages, crossed oceans, and journeyed to the world's most remote areas on religious quests. NCEs have picked up this practice, but the types of voyages and actors have changed, reflecting their contemporary cultures and contexts. Today, evangelicals in NCEs often export full-time missionaries, short-term mission teams, faith-based NGO workers, evangelistic crusaders, and emigrants. The different groups of people have different types of knowledge and different goals for their travel. They also require different levels of coordination, support, and organizational strength.

Full-Time Missionaries

Full-time Western missionaries helped to lay the foundations of many of the world's NCEs (Woodberry 2012). In fact, full-time missionaries continue to pour into NCEs, providing various kinds of services to local churches and populations. There is now, however, an outward flow of missionaries from countries like South Africa and El Salvador. Careful planning is necessary to create such flows, and missionary sending agencies across the Global South and East seek ways to meet these challenges. The Southern African Missiological Society (SAMS) has been at this longer than most, and the total number of missionaries sent out by South Africa is high compared to most NCEs. They have anywhere between 2,000 (Peter Hammond, personal correspondence, 2013; Mandryk 2010) and 8,000 (Johnson 2014) missionaries. The low side of this range seems more likely, but even this number would place them above most other NCEs. SAMS has long been a primarily white South African endeavor, and in this respect it could be considered a southern outpost of Western missionary activity.[9] The missionary movement in El Salvador has a

---

[9] Nico Botha, the current general secretary of SAMS, is not white. He may be well positioned to help create a different dynamic within South African missionary networks. Different denominations in South Africa, like the Apostolic Faith Mission, which claims to have a presence in more than twenty African countries, are also increasingly active in missionary work.

different ethos. In Chapter 4, I outlined the way in which Salvadorans use symbols to create and sustain a national missionary movement. It is worth explaining the size and effectiveness of that movement here.

The umbrella network that facilitates Salvadoran missionary activity is called Comisal. Comisal has developed three networks that interlock major evangelical institutions and channel resource flows toward missionary endeavors. The first of the three networks runs among pastors who are interested in missions. The second network coordinates El Salvador's mission agencies, which include locally initiated organizations as well as international organizations that send Salvadoran missionaries overseas, such as Operation Mobilization and Youth With a Mission. Finally, Comisal reaches out to the missionary training institutes in El Salvador. An example is the Miramonte Baptist Church's seminary, which has sent graduates to plant churches in places like Albania and Romania. Each of these organizations has its own networks; through this three-pronged strategy, Comisal brings them into dialogue and collaboration with one another. In doing so, it demonstrates the ability to use symbolic resources that are compatible with the national context to define the contours of the national evangelical community.

Collectively, these networks involve a significant portion of El Salvador's evangelical community. Evidence of this could be seen at one of Comisal's monthly breakfasts which more than forty leaders attended, representing the most important churches, denominations, and ministry organizations in the country (with one prominent exception). The representation at this meeting was more comprehensive than the meetings of El Salvador's Evangelical Alliance during the same time period, making Comisal the only space in which several fiercely independent evangelical actors willingly collaborated with one another. In all, more than 135 missionaries from El Salvador have been sent overseas through nine different Salvadoran organizational vehicles (denominations, mission agencies, or churches). This places tiny El Salvador as the seventh highest sending country in Latin America, something they consider to be an achievement.[10]

Money is needed to support missionary personnel. In El Salvador (and elsewhere), sending missionaries is primarily a middle and upper middle class endeavor. Many churches in these social strata include missionary support in their annual budgets. In 2006, Iglesia Josué had a foreign outreach budget of $165,000. As churches in these sectors multiply and grow, more funding for missionaries becomes available. Funding also comes from businesspeople: a company owned by a consortium of evangelical businesspeople sees 10 percent

---

[10] There are certainly more than 135 Salvadoran missionaries currently in the field, as congregations simply decide to send out missionaries without reporting their activities. This undoubtedly occurs in every country. World Christian Database (Johnson 2014) estimates that there are 220 Salvadoran missionaries, but they do not look only at evangelical missionaries.

of its profits go immediately to support overseas missions. Some Salvadorans had hoped they could enter into a financial partnership with U.S. churches to send Salvadoran missionaries overseas, but they have been disappointed by the U.S. response to this idea. Hence, except where Western organizations are directly involved in sending Salvadoran missionaries, the money for the Salvadoran missionary movement comes from domestic sources.

Short-Term Mission Teams

Any growth in full-time missionaries is being far outstripped by the exponential growth of short-term missionaries. Previous chapters noted that South Africa and El Salvador are inundated with short-term mission teams each year. It is also true that NCEs increasingly send short-term teams of their own to other destinations.

There is no reliable data about how many short-term teams NCEs send each year. A clue, however, is provided by Robert Priest (2007), who conducted a survey of urban churches in Lima, Peru. Priest's study found that 52 percent of pastors surveyed reported that their members go on mission trips. Some of these trips were done domestically. Even so, the number hints at the magnitude that this growing movement has already achieved.

Like full-time missionaries, many short-term teams are sent by affluent congregations. Iglesia Josué, for example, has sent teams to Kosovo, Equatorial Guinea, Honduras, the Niger, Nicaragua, and Vietnam. In South Africa, Alan Frow, pastor of a white Johannesburg-based congregation, reported that his church sends short-term missions to "... Zimbabwe, Mozambique, Malawi. We're working into Poland, we're working into France ... there are teams going out all the time." One of his congregants had recently come back from India and was hoping to return there on a more permanent basis.

On a more limited scale, lower or lower middle class congregations also send short-term missions across borders. For example, a pastor's wife in Alexandria, a Johannesburg township, has taken teams to Uganda. Likewise in El Salvador, less affluent churches generate enough energy and resources to send an occasional short-term mission to Nicaragua, the United States, Spain, or even Africa. Such churches are more likely to send teams to in-country destinations, but transnational relationships can motivate and facilitate efforts to send teams farther afield.

NGOs and ministry organizations located in South Africa and El Salvador also send teams across borders. Greg Smerdon, the head of African Enterprise's South African office, stated, "It's time for Africa to send missionaries to First World countries, and I believe youth teams are the way to go. [In fact] we have a youth team in Germany at this moment." In El Salvador, a ministry called Castillo del Rey, run by U.S. missionaries, sent more than 900 Salvadoran young people to other countries in 2009 to evangelize or to do service projects. The overwhelming majority of youths, most of whom were from poor communities, went to neighboring countries in Central America. But some were sent to places like the United States, India, and Cambodia. Western-based organizations, like Operation Mobilization, Campus Crusade for Christ, and Intervarsity also regularly send Salvadorans and South Africans across borders on short-term mission trips. The organizational strength of local churches and ministries, as well as international organizations, is thus critical to the fast-growing short-term missionary movement in NCEs.[11]

Micro Religious Movements

NCEs generate what might be referred to as micro religious movements within global evangelicalism. Particular ways of church planting, spiritual emphases, ways of singing, reading the Bible, or praying can emerge anywhere on the planet and then spread throughout the global faith community. Sometimes this can happen unintentionally; other times leaders promote the phenomenon more systematically. In both scenarios, NCEs are now trend setters as well as trend receivers.

An example of this is the Global Day of Prayer (GDOP), which began in Cape Town in 2001. Businessman Graham Power, after receiving a vision from God,[12] rented Cape Town's largest national rugby stadium and invited Christians from all denominations to engage in a day of repentance and prayer. About 45,000 people responded to the invitation. The next year, rallies took place in eight stadiums around South Africa, and 330,000 people participated. GDOP then spread first into the rest of Africa and quickly across the globe. In 2006, between 400 and 500 million Christians in 204 countries participated, according to GOD TV,[13] which televises the event.[14] In 2010, 220[15] countries participated in a formal, coordinated event, and since then the movement's strategy has changed to emphasize smaller locales and lifestyles of prayer. Regardless of the strategy, the movement literally spans the globe.

GDOP's leadership is distinctly South African, but it has sought assistance from international partners. In late 2002, World Vision and Global Action, a U.S.-based evangelical ministry, hosted a retreat near the GDOP headquarters in

---

[11] Data in the previous three paragraphs appeared in an earlier article I wrote about short-term mission teams (Offutt 2011).

[12] Power was also animated by a video he saw of prayer transforming Cali, Colombia, in the wake of the drug cartels located there.

[13] These numbers would appear to be fairly speculative. The number of countries is difficult to dispute, as GDOP organizers have names of organizers in every participating country and visit or in other ways communicate with them. But the number of participants could be hard to defend, and what it means to participate is not well defined. Even if God TV is only half right, though, the movement is involving a remarkable number of people.

[14] In South Africa it is also televised by SABC 2, SABC Africa, and TBN, as well as some smaller stations.

[15] Most official sources state that there are between 194 and 196 countries in the world. GDOP includes a series of territories and colonies in its list of participating countries, including Puerto Rico.

Cape Town. Almost 300 prayer network leaders from around the world (China, India, Latin America, etc.) came together to see how they could be better connected. In Latin America, for example, follow up to the Cape Town meeting occurred in 2004, when the GDOP leadership teamed with John Robb of World Vision to stage a retreat in Bolivia. Thirty-five leaders from around the region attended. A regional prayer network later named CLAMOR was organized, with individuals from the various regions being charged to generate GDOP participation in their locales.

Salvadoran Mercedes Dalton was among the conference's attendees and was named CLAMOR's regional representative for Central America. To generate interest in El Salvador, Dalton aired television and radio commercials on the country's primary evangelical stations and contacted many evangelical leaders. In May 2006, the Evangelical Alliance held a special session to consider a larger and more coordinated GDOP participation. Promotional videos about GDOP were shown. Dalton and her colleague, Juan Carlos Hasbun, proposed a unified rally, such as a mass march downtown or a stadium event. They were ultimately unsuccessful in this kind of event, but other activities were held. Juan Manuel Martinez, the founder of a Salvadoran network of churches called Campamento de Dios, martialed churches together in his own neighborhood, and the pastor of Elim asked 8,000 children in his church to participate as he folded the project into a previously planned focus on Children's Month. The Baptist Tabernacle also honored the occasion, as did Bautista Miramonte and some of the country's wealthiest congregations, including Iglesia Josué and two neo-Pentecostal churches, La CIA and CCI. This South African initiative clearly drew a response in the Salvadoran evangelical community, as it has around the world.

Organizations

Organizations in NCEs are thus demonstrating the capacity to send people across borders and to generate religious movements that reverberate globally. But such organizations are more than just launchpads; their own infrastructure and organizational activities also straddle borders. Organizations built in NCEs are now transnational actors in their own rights.

In some cases, the transnational extension of organizations in NCEs is made possible by a third people flow emanating from NCEs: emigrants. Evangelical emigrants usually leave NCEs for reasons other than faith. Yet they powerfully extend the influence of religious organizations in NCEs. Other scholars have also witnessed this trend: Cristina Mora (2008) studied Brazilians in New York who watch media produced by a Brazilian megachurch, and Helen Rose Ebaugh and Janet Saltzman Chafetz (2002) noted the transnational reach of Mexico's Luz del Mundo church. Peggy Levitt (2007) has further shown that this trend occurs in numerous religions, including Eastern religious organizations that are following emigrants from Asia and the Middle East to other parts of the world. Returning, though, to evangelical organizations from El Salvador and South Africa, one aspect of organizational expansion to emigrant communities is dominant: the transnational extension of local denominations or church networks.

When migrants begin their lives in a new place, they often choose to re-create the faith communities they left behind. Transnational migrants who do this can then create formal linkages back to their original congregations. This allows denominations and church planting movements that were begun in NCEs to become transnational. Elim, for example, oversees more than forty churches outside of El Salvador. Most such churches are planted by Salvadoran migrants who initiate contact with the "mother church" in San Salvador. Once Elim El Salvador accepts their overture, the migrant churches fall under Mario Vega's spiritual authority. This is worked out in very tangible ways: when I visited the Elim church in Los Angeles, for example, several booklets authored by Vega were on display in its bookstore, and the Elim organizational culture was evident in the Los Angeles congregation.

Similar dynamics are evident in other independent Salvadoran and South African churches. The Bautista Miramonte near San Salvador's city center has numerous daughter churches around the world. Even younger congregations, like the neo-Pentecostal church CIA, have planted churches beyond national borders. In South Africa, church networks also follow emigrants across borders. New Covenant Ministries, the International Federation of Christian Churches, and other South African–based Pentecostal movements have taken up residence in countries like Australia, New Zealand, Canada, and the United Kingdom as (usually white) South Africans migrate to these locations. Such denominational extensions are important, as they establish outgoing channels through which evangelical culture can consistently flow, and they help keep people who are living abroad connected to their home country.

Organizations built in NCEs also operate outside of migrant communities as they expand internationally. Local faith-based NGOs, for example, have long been considered exactly what their name implies: local counterparts to Western international faith-based NGOs. But many such evangelical NGOs have developed international programs of their own. ENLACE now works in Guatemala and will soon begin work with English- and Spanish-speaking churches in the United States and with churches in Nepal. ENLACE is further exploring opportunities to operate in several African countries as well. Its mission in these new countries will remain the same: to help congregations in poor neighborhoods reach out to their communities. Another local Salvadoran evangelical NGO, A-Brazo, became active in Haiti after the 2010 earthquake. A-Brazo's previous work with El Salvador's 2001 earthquake gave it personnel experience and technical expertise, as well as relationships in the international relief and development community. A-Brazo's director was thus stationed in Haiti for more than three years to direct reconstruction programs of various evangelical NGOs, the primary one being Compassion International. A third Salvadoran evangelical NGO, Association Amiga, has been working with the Garifunas on

Honduras's north coast since the late 1990s, after Hurricane Mitch destroyed Garifuna houses and villages. Once the disaster relief period was over, Associacion Amiga decided to launch long-term development programs in the area. Similar dynamics are evident within South African evangelical NGOs: just one example is African Enterprise, which has offices in ten different African countries.

If local NGOs have become active internationally, it comes as no surprise that businesses built by evangelicals in NCEs also have an international reach. Abi Molele's commodities business has mining concessions in Angola, investors in the United Kingdom, and customers in China. Oya-Hazel Gumede's organization, Ashira Legal Advisors, now does business in several East African countries. In El Salvador, an evangelical businessman who is in the shipping industry has a warehouse that serves Nicaragua and Honduras. Another Salvadoran has industrial projects in Honduras and sources scrap metal from California. Most businesses that have a presence in other countries do not create religious products (although some do, like the Christian bookstore that Benner Dominguez has opened in Nicaragua). They nonetheless reflect the evangelical ethos of their founders.

Mass Media

A favorite evangelical tool for exporting religion the world over is mass media. Like their Western counterparts, evangelicals in NCEs have become adept at using television, radio, Internet, and all other forms of telecommunications to share their message. This is a well-known and much chronicled component of evangelical identity, but the fact that NCEs, in addition to evangelicals in the West, have developed the ability to reach people around the world using these tools has been less noticed.

Radio stations are ubiquitous in NCEs. El Salvador's airwaves are crowded with independent and competitive Christian radio stations, some of which claim international listeners. Radio Truth, which is owned by the Assemblies of God in El Salvador (not by the AG U.S. headquarters), is one such station. Radio Truth can be played wherever there is Internet. The AG Superintendent, Jeremias Bolaños, reported that people write into the radio station from places as far afield as Australia, Brazil, and Sweden. Radio Truth is even translated into Hindi for listeners in northern India. Likewise, evangelicals also keep South Africa's airwaves busy. The Association of Christian Broadcasters of Southern Africa now has more than seventy-five members, many of them from South Africa. These stations serve both national and international audiences.

Evangelical television stations and production studios in NCEs also send their messages across borders. In El Salvador, there are fewer barriers to creating television stations. This has allowed several of the more affluent churches to own stations. The Baptist Tabernacle's station is perhaps the strongest, and it can be viewed in most of Central America. In South Africa, where costs prohibit even large churches from owning stations, Rhema buys airtime from secular or state-owned television stations. Rhema's programming, usually featuring McCauley, is viewed throughout Africa, Australia, parts of Asia, and the Middle East. Ade, a Nigerian studying at the college, assured me, "No, no, no, no, no, Rhema *is known* in Nigeria!" These kinds of reactions are not uncommon among African Pentecostals. Churches in El Salvador and South Africa may soon have even wider access to global viewers, as they have begun to develop digital television programming and they are making it available on their websites.

HIERARCHICAL SOCIAL NETWORKS

Success in building large organizations furthers the stratification that is beginning to characterize NCEs. When most evangelicals were poor and marginalized, an egalitarian ethos existed within their faith communities. It could legitimately be argued that small house churches were social cells that could facilitate democratic values (Freston 2008; Martin 1990; Martin 2011). Likewise, pastors of churches might compete against one another for potential members, but they also could collaborate as peers on equal footing (Berryman 1999; Martin 1990). These egalitarian-oriented evangelicals long referred to one another as "brother" or "sister," which was an outward expression of a new kind of relationship. Surveying the scene in 1990, Martin argued that evangelical communities are constituted by those who have recently left or been freed from "constraining vertical and horizontal ties." For Martin, the re-formation of ties within the evangelical schema had wide-ranging implications, as he argued that these voluntaristic, participatory, mutually respecting relationships were "part of the rapid expansion of the range of cultural communication and the differentiation of society" (Martin 1990, 108).

In contemporary NCEs, multiple trends toward the stratification of evangelical communities are eroding these social arrangements. Most broadly, globalization creates winners and losers in almost every sector of society. This widens the gap between the "haves" and the "have-nots," making inequality the social norm. As evangelical communities grow, they map their national faith communities over these existing social features. Thus, social class now competes with religious identity among evangelicals rather than reinforcing it, as it did when evangelical communities were smaller and more socioeconomically homogenous. An upper class evangelical Salvadoran may be part of the same general faith community as a *campesino*, but the two are likely to have little else in common. The same can be said for an affluent, white South African who might share a set of evangelical beliefs with a poor, black South African. Important aspects of evangelicalism's egalitarian attributes have thus been victimized by the movement's growth into other social sectors and exacerbated by the more general socioeconomic trends wrought by globalization.

Evangelicals do not just passively map themselves onto socioeconomically divided societies. Rather, they propel such trends into the religious sphere by concentrating power and resources at the top of their own social order. As mentioned in the previous chapter, just three Salvadoran evangelical leaders have the power to call evangelicals together for crusades or other mass events. This places them in the highest strata of evangelical leadership, and other layers of stratification are being forged beneath them. Heads of other denominations and lead pastors at other megachurches also often act with complete autonomy and can dictate terms to other pastors underneath them. Mutual accountability structures among some pastors certainly still exist, but they do so within a broader hierarchical framework.

In South Africa, stratification between churches can be seen in the way evangelicals perceive Rhema. This is true within the congregation and in the relationships Rhema and Rhema members have with other kinds of evangelicals. It is widely asserted that an inner circle exists within Rhema, and that it receives preferential treatment. One affluent, black South African who does not attend Rhema stated that Rhema "is one church that's got celebrities and non-celebrities ... if you are an unknown, the pastor will not come to you, he will send other people. But if you are a celebrity, he will [pay attention] to you." Some members of the Rhema community have felt spurned by its most active members and have left the church. This was the case for two graduates of Rhema's Bible College who are now pastors in another denomination. While reflecting on their relationship with Rhema, one of them said, "... we enjoyed the time we were (at Rhema) ... they are our fellow brothers, but not necessarily like we would say 'hey guys, remember us?' It is like we have moved on, you know?" Some South Africans who do not attend Rhema feel intimidated by it. I was, for example, discussing Rhema with a poor but fairly well educated Zimbabwean who now lives in Johannesburg. After he affirmed that Rhema holds a prominent place in South Africa, I suggested that we attend the church together the following Sunday. He immediately indicated that he would not feel comfortable in that environment.

Rhema clearly holds a place of privilege within evangelical and Pentecostal circles in South Africa. Class plays a role in creating this dynamic. To the extent that it does, other affluent churches, such as Rosebank Union, join Rhema in the upper tiers of evangelical society. But class is not the whole story. After all, plenty of poor South Africans attend Rhema, and even rich South Africans can feel excluded by Rhema. Cultural attributes also help churches accumulate power within evangelical communities. These differ among NCEs, but they can include particular doctrines, levels of spiritual activity or commitment, and the quality of church programs. Still, in most NCEs, wealthy megachurches with political influence find their way to the top.

Inequality continues to persist within South African churches, not just as churches relate to one another. In earlier literature, especially in the literature on Latin American Pentecostalism, those who argued against the evangelical egalitarianism school did so by pointing to the strong authoritarian leadership evangelical pastors exert in their churches (Bastian 1983, 1986). My research uncovered further evidence of this view. Before I interviewed the head pastor of a black megachurch in one of Johannesburg's townships, a lay leader in the church was casually enjoying conversation with us. I could tell that something he said displeased the pastor, who in response gave a barely perceptible signal to the lay leader. He quickly and politely excused himself from the room and was still sitting outside the pastor's office, looking duly chastened, after the interview was over. Larger churches and organizations only tend to exacerbate these tendencies; leaders are in charge of more people and more resources, and authoritarian styles of leadership can be more efficient. This is especially so when churches use organizational strategies based on leadership pyramids.

Not all of evangelicalism's tendencies toward egalitarianism are dead. There continue to be structural constraints limiting the extent to which stratification translates into social power. Rich, large churches may be both influential and resented, but they cannot force other churches to actually *do* anything. Systematic social hierarchies that could afford this kind of power will likely never be seen in NCEs. The participatory and voluntaristic nature of evangelical churches also persists. This means that a poor church could very well continue to be an incubator of democracy, as Martin (1990) asserts, by giving people opportunities to speak publicly, to practice social organizational skills, and to act collaboratively. The existence of extremely rich churches in the adjacent neighborhood does not alter these religious practices. The evidence in this study shows that stratification in NCEs is an empirical reality. It also suggests that vertical, oppressive relationships have to this point been avoided.

Such mitigating dynamics do not entirely take the bite out of stratification. Affectionately referring to other evangelicals as "brother" and "sister" was once a hallmark of evangelical interaction in NCEs. Today, the monikers are used with less frequency. In one interview, a subject left the intended topic of conversation to explain why such terms were too parochial and why he actively encouraged other evangelicals to stop using them. Perhaps such ways of relating simply don't fit among the globally active, professionally astute, less egalitarian evangelical communities of today.

CONCLUSION

Organizations are how people (not just evangelicals) get things done. This means that when organizations grow, so too does the power to solve problems. In fact, organizations can help people acknowledge and try to address problems in distant lands. Because of their assiduous attention to building organizations, NCEs now possess these abilities.

Two primary problems accompany the organizational strength of NCEs. Ruth Padilla DeBorst, Latin American evangelical leader and critic, points to the first problem by referring to NCEs as "the New North." She implies that some of the unhealthy relational dynamics that have long characterized relationships between the Global North and the Global South are being replicated. This time leaders of NCEs are in positions of power, and they unduly influence evangelicals in rural areas, who are less educated or in other ways remain disempowered. Rather than celebrating a new equality between North and South, Padilla DeBorst points to a familiar problem that has simply shifted its social location.

Second, and related, newly powerful evangelical organizations draw attention away from the fact that most organizations fail. Failure has its own set of consequences, which can include poverty. Even as some evangelicals ride their growing organizations into positions of influence, other evangelicals struggle with the fact of failure, the inability to make ends meet, and in some cases, resentment against those who have had success.

Problems such as these have the potential to pull the global movement apart. As yet, however, the glue of a shared religious identity has outweighed these polarizing forces. It has helped that some benefits of flourishing organizations can be shared by the broader faith community, such as increased social legitimacy and broader social influence for the movement. So for now, the cross-cutting trends are creating socioeconomic diversity within the movement, rather than multiple movements moving in different social directions. It will be interesting to see if, and for how long, this remains the case.

6

New Strategies of Public Engagement: Integrated Political Engagement, Increasing Social Engagement, and Shifting Beliefs

It has become commonplace in the new centers of global evangelicalism for evangelical leaders to pray at presidential inaugurations, participate in community leadership activities, and provide basic social services through their church ministries.

This has not always been so. Today's emerging new centers of evangelicalism (NCEs) followed a pattern of social withdrawal through much of the twentieth century. This made sense to people for whom conversion to Christianity meant a radical break from their culture. In Africa, Latin America, and elsewhere, evangelicals stopped engaging in existing cultural practices, frequenting newly objectionable public spaces, and participating in newly perceived corrupt political and social power structures. Separatist tendencies were often encouraged by U.S. missionaries who were coming out of their own separatist experience. But even further magnifying these trends were the oppressive or war-torn social contexts in which many NCEs grew quickly. Evangelicals were mostly poor and sometimes a persecuted minority religion. They felt powerless in the midst of social strife. The basic human desire to survive thus encouraged them to keep a low profile (Smilde 1998; Stoll 1990).

Evangelical eschatological beliefs, particularly within Pentecostal denominations, fit with a separatist ethos. They believed that Christ's return, and thus the end of the world, was near (Fields 1985; Williams 1997). Starting from this premise, evangelicals exercised simple logic when they concluded that addressing the problems of this world was a waste of time. Saving souls thus became the only really worthwhile endeavor for a faith community that was so attuned to the temporal nature of this world. Although Pentecostals have always responded to the poverty that surrounds them, they relied heavily on evangelistic activity as their primary strategy for engaging with society.

For many evangelicals, an intended but secondary effect of evangelism was the reduction of social ills. Christian Smith (1994) notes that evangelicals in Latin America were often interested in social and political change even as they sought isolation. Indeed, a strong belief among evangelicals was that if they were able to save enough souls, society and social structures would become more just and less corrupt as the individuals shaping those structures embarked on a journey of becoming more Christ-like. This belief still lingers in NCEs: one leader I interviewed in El Salvador expressed open confusion as to how social ills could grow apace even as the evangelical community expanded.

For the most part, however, NCEs no longer fit this description. Today, Salvadoran and South African evangelicals run programs designed to alleviate poverty, protect the environment, recover from disasters, provide medical care, promote leadership development, facilitate racial reconciliation, and improve business ethics. They reach out to victims of crime and violence, alcoholics, drug addicts, gang members, and prisoners. Silvana Valladaras, founder of El Salvador's School for the Deaf, explained that evangelicals now want to "be an answer to the needs of gangs, street children, orphans, AIDS . . . to enter into all the [country's] social problems and to present an integral evangel." In South Africa, David Molapo (I Can Foundation) also demonstrates this broadening agenda, stating that future evangelical leaders should not just develop spiritually but also "politically, academically, psychologically, and economically." As he preaches sermons, gives motivational talks, and puts on leadership seminars for teens, Molapo tries to instill in them the skills and attitudes necessary for integrating into society. There is no shortage of empirical evidence within this study or in others that evangelicals are expanding their interests and engaging with society's most pressing social issues.[1]

Sometimes, though, evangelicals lose their way. Very seldom do evangelicals have a collective and systematic strategy when they enter the public sphere, and sometimes they do not have clearly defined goals. Rather, independent evangelical actors enter the public arena from various social locations, political perspectives, and particular interests. Occasionally, evangelicals coalesce around a single issue or within umbrella institutions, but autonomy is the norm. This keeps the evangelical political voice muted, and it causes evangelical social action to favor a program orientation. Global and local religious social forces may be helping evangelical entrepreneurs build larger institutions, and these institutions are often used to serve the needy, but the competitive orientation of their religious community keeps them from addressing macro political, economic, or social issues. Building organizations that do good

---

[1] There have been hints of this for some time (Freston 2001; Martin 2002; Smilde 1998), but it was not until Donald Miller and Tetsunao Yamamori (2007) published *Global Pentecostalism: The New Face of Christian Social Engagement* that the trend became more commonly acknowledged by North American audiences. The empirical snapshots provided by the authors showed Pentecostals engaged in humanitarian aid, community transformation, leadership development, and other social activities around the world. Miller and Yamamori concluded that Pentecostals are a critical component of the future of global social engagement. Future publications connected to Miller's research center at the University of Southern California are likely to deepen our understanding of these dynamics (Street 2013).

things is an evangelical strength; gathering that organizational strength to advocate for policy changes is not.

Changes in the evangelical approach to social and political action are accompanied by changes in evangelical beliefs. The rise of the prosperity gospel is the most ubiquitous signal that evangelical beliefs are no longer strictly otherworldly. It is also a reminder that a single story does not capture the complexity of trends within evangelicalism. Positive normative tones accompany the most dominant accounts of evangelicalism's social engagement (Miller & Yamamori 2007), while most writings on the prosperity gospel carry at least a hint (and sometimes more) of derision. However, not all evangelical social engagement is positive. Likewise, some of the more influential versions of the prosperity gospel do not fit popular scholarly accounts. Careful empirical work is needed to understand these cross-cutting trends in actions and beliefs.

In this chapter, I show *how* these changes are occurring and the directions they are taking. Evangelical entrepreneurs, in classical Schumpeterian form, tie global and local resources together in new ways to create goods in the public sphere. At times they channel religious resources toward an intractable social or political problem. At other times they enter the public sphere in search of resources for their own projects. Likewise, evangelical theological innovators sometimes promote beliefs that appear entirely self-serving; at other times they promote beliefs that encourage their adherents to more faithfully serve their community. It is thus that evangelicals in NCEs both contribute to, and take from, the broader societies that host them.

Converging trends facilitate evangelical public engagement. The religious organizations built by local entrepreneurs are now strong enough to take on social and political activities. The social location of some evangelicals is such that they are no longer intimidated by those who hold power. The international connections of evangelicals provide further legitimacy, leverage, and resources for those who wish to be socially and politically active. New theologies make it logical for believers to care about the things of this world, including increasing one's health and income and helping the less fortunate in society. Collectively, these are the principal dynamics propelling evangelicals into the public sphere. As will be shown below, evangelical participation in such arenas produces diverse results.

THE POLITICAL SPHERE

In both El Salvador and South Africa, the political preferences of evangelicals span the entire political spectrum. In El Salvador, where the political party system looks somewhat similar to that of the United States, ARENA is the primary party on the right, and the FMLN is the primary party on the left. The Salvadoran evangelical vote is segmented by denomination, with the Baptist Tabernacle being strongly politically conservative and much of the Assemblies of God also leaning in that direction. Elim, however, is moderately progressive, as are other evangelical churches and denominations, including a strategically located independent church called Tabernaculo Avivimiento Internacional (Ayala 2008). A 2008 poll done by the Instituto Universatario de Opinion Publica (IUDOP) showed the FMLN getting 41.8 percent of support from evangelicals, compared with 30.9 percent who supported ARENA. This effectively reversed what IUDOP found in a 2004 poll, when ARENA garnered support from 44.1 percent of evangelicals, compared with 28.6 percent of evangelicals who supported FMLN (Ayala 2008). Such a swing suggests that, while it is possible to identify the political leanings of denominations and their leaders within the evangelical community, religion is not necessarily a driver of political preference for El Salvador's general public, including evangelicals.

In South Africa, the dominance of the African National Congress (ANC) creates a different topography of political preferences. Most evangelicals support the ANC, which was the party that led the struggle against apartheid. Within that large tent, evangelical activists have taken a stand for conservative sexual ethics, including opposition to abortion and gay marriage. Evangelicals have also advocated for more action against poverty, crime, the HIV/AIDS epidemic, and other challenges facing the country. Like El Salvador, in South Africa one must ask "which evangelicals?" when considering their political leanings.

While the question of how evangelicals vote is interesting, this study is more interested in how evangelicals look for resources and produce public goods in the political arena. The answers to these questions show actions that are consistent with the entrepreneurial mode of social action and organization, even as they reveal very different types of political engagements, relationships, and contributions.

Dubious Resource Seekers

Evangelicals who are gaining new access to the public sphere often do so looking for more resources to help build their organizations. They sometimes are also looking simply to enrich themselves. They often borrow time-honored and culturally appropriate strategies, such as clientelism, bribery, and being a free rider.

One of the dominant characteristics of Latin American political systems has long been clientelistic relationships. In clientelism, a political leader or *patron* enters into a relationship with a group of people. The relationship is predicated upon the exchange of goods: usually the leader is interested in votes, and the group is interested in financial or material goods, or possibly employment opportunities.

Political clientelism can be found in many societies, including the United States. However, in societies where a political class exists alongside large numbers of poor, uneducated citizens who are precluded from most forms of political engagement, clientelism takes a different hue. Party identification matters a lot to the political class and to ex-combatants in the country. But for a great many poor communities, they do not. During voting season in El Salvador, political parties will visit poor communities and hand out shirts with the colors that symbolize their parties. Community members are happy to have a new shirt and gladly put it on. The next week another political party comes with shirts of a different color. Community members are equally happy to have another shirt and gladly wear that one as well. It is in this environment that clientelism can be particularly effective and often manipulative.

The Latin American version of political clientelism is also often accompanied by a political "strong man" – in Latin America, this figure is known as a *caudillo* – who governs the political party. Strong men and clientelism are found in parties from the far right to the far left and everywhere in between. The Nicaraguan political scene, for example, has been dominated by two personalities. On the right, Arnoldo Aleman has presided over a coalition of parties, sometimes from prison. On the left, Daniel Ortega consolidated power into his own hands. As the country's president, he determines who gets to participate in politics and commerce in the country. Aleman and Ortega serve as central figures in a highly clientelistic political system.

The idea that Latin American evangelicals might be involved in clientelistic relationships is not new. Some of the oldest literature on the movement makes this claim. However, where evangelicals were particularly marginalized or where their retreat from society was most complete, they eliminated the possibility of participating in clientelist systems. Any relationship with politics or political actors was considered untoward. El Salvador's experience can be so characterized. One Salvadoran evangelical leader says that "it used to be the mentality that being involved in politics was sin. Even going to vote was sinful." Political actors thus did not stand to gain from relationships with evangelicals and so left them alone.

When Salvadoran evangelicals began the journey "back into" civil and political society, some became enmeshed in clientelistic relationships. The 2004 presidential elections marked the greatest spike in this strategy. ARENA, the country's conservative party, made aggressive moves to capitalize on the new evangelical voting bloc. ARENA found a willing partner in Brother Toby, the founding pastor of the Baptist Tabernacle. It is rumored that he bussed congregants to polling stations on the day of the elections. In return, Saca invited Brother Toby to pray at his inauguration.

It was also in 2004 that the massive Assemblies of God denomination encouraged their members to vote. ARENA thus courted AG churches, and some AG pastors responded by inviting Saca campaigners into their churches to speak. The denomination did not formally support ARENA, but a number of pastors within the denomination did. These pastors assumed their support would be rewarded. One AG leader said, "Yes, oh yes. There was talk. [It went something like] 'Okay ... AG will give [Saca] their votes, but [Saca] will have one of our people in as a Minister of Education.' It was very interesting."

After Saca won the election, he set up an informal department designed to liaise with evangelicals. Those who staffed the office were charged with fostering a network of evangelical leaders and with developing loyalty to the ARENA party. An evangelical leader described the approach the staffers took in this way: "[They came and said] okay, we're going to give you milk, and you can give that away to the people in your communities and we're going to do this for you and that and that and that." It was clear to this leader that the implication of accepting the goods that were brought was that the congregation was to vote for ARENA in return. Some evangelical pastors found nothing wrong with such an arrangement. They subsequently joined the network. However, the AG's denominational leadership found it problematic. One of its leaders explained, "it became so controversial that in the last General Conference we finally made a decision that they were not going to permit any pastors to be involved ... nor were they going to allow political proselytizing in the churches. [As a result] there was a huge conflict between the pastors." The denomination held firm, however, and the decision represented a blow to the ARENA initiative.

In South Africa, clientelism may also exist, but a more obviously unseemly evangelical political involvement is that of bribery. South Africa is a country beset by corruption (*Economist* 2013b; Country Corruption Assessment Report: South Africa 2003). Many evangelicals, especially those who hold positions in the government bureaucracy, fully participate in this aspect of the culture. Abiel, a South African pastor and a businessman, laments this problem: "The reality, Steve, is this: guys are corrupt. I mean you can go to any office of the state today, and you can find that 80 percent are professing Christians. But also you will find that out that 80 percent, 100 percent of them, they accept bribes. You see so, that's the thing that we are doing as the church." It is rare for a North American researcher to find this kind of candor among evangelical leaders. Other respondents acknowledged that this is a problem but tended to suggest that members of their churches are not involved.

A third issue in evangelical political involvement is that they are susceptible to the free rider problem. Evangelicals in El Salvador and South Africa, even those who are not involved in clientelism or bribery, do not greatly support institutional initiatives that are intended to engage national or macro-level issues (Grace Goodell, personal correspondence, 2012). Evangelical advocacy groups generally do not exist in NCEs. The evangelical alliances are sometimes called upon to function as the evangelical voice in the public square. But they have difficulty attracting strong commitment and participation by evangelical leaders. One young Salvadoran leader, for example, is intent on building a megachurch and an international ministry. When asked if he attended the Evangelical Alliance meetings, he responded that he didn't think that would be helpful in furthering the project that God had put on his heart. Likewise in South Africa, an evangelical was asked to assume a leadership position for TEASA. He did so but then stepped down after just a few months. He explained that he had assessed whether he could "give the time, energy, and leadership to really take it to where it should be going and ... my conclusion was to say, am I called to do this at this time of my life? And the answer was no." For those who do commit to the Evangelical Alliances, the conclusions arrived at by the two leaders just mentioned can be exasperating. One officer of the Salvadoran Alliance said, "that's part of my frustration with the Evangelical Alliance. The pastors are still saying, 'we'll be a part but what are we going to get out of this?'" Even those who refuse to participate are generally supportive of Alliance activities, but the prevailing attitude of nonparticipation places limits on how effective Evangelical Alliances can be.

Evangelical Alliances are not alone in this struggle. The competitive structure of evangelical communities ensures that most voluntary, collaborative initiatives struggle. The Network for Integral Mission's history provides another example. El Salvador suffered significant earthquakes in 2001. The Association of Evangelical Relief and Development Organizations (AERDO) in the United States, since renamed the Accord Network, wanted to coordinate the responses of their member organizations and the evangelical churches in El Salvador. They sponsored a conference that drew more than 100 leaders of various churches and ministries. At the conference, it became evident that no money would be transferred by AERDO to participating local entities. The conference was then followed by monthly meetings, at which attendance dropped precipitously. Within twelve months, the initiative had almost completely stalled until four leaders decided to revive it under a new name, which was the Network for Integral Mission. Ruth Padilla DeBorst, who is influential in the Latin American Theological Fraternity, and Ron Bueno, director of ENLACE, were largely responsible for reshaping the organizational strategy and content of the movement. Attendance at the meetings climbed again to between twenty-five and thirty leaders. But at one of these meetings a leader publicly asked, "How am I helping my organization by attending this meeting?" The answer centered on cultivating a vision for holistic mission, which did not seem to satisfy the gentleman. He did not attend the following meeting.

Producing Public Goods in the Political Sphere

While some evangelicals in NCEs enter the public sphere simply looking for resources to further their own entrepreneurial endeavors, other evangelicals seek to produce public goods in the political sphere. This is done in culturally appropriate and context-specific ways, based on the NCE in which the evangelical resides.

Political influence in contemporary South Africa remains tied to the position that groups or individual actors took during the struggle against apartheid. A few evangelical leaders took courageous stands against apartheid in the 1970s and 1980s, including Ray McCauley and Michael Cassidy. McCauley came into the struggle in the late 1980s, which was a little later than most. He brought with him (what was at that time) an all-white church. Several scholars, including Paul Freston (2001), have openly wondered at McCauley's motives in getting involved. Perhaps McCauley could already see the end of the apartheid regime and was making a tactical and opportunistic play. He might also have been trying to salvage white privilege in the coming political dispensation. Freston is not convinced that either were part of McCauley's calculus; Freston points out that McCauley's subsequent actions and policies seem to bear out a true interest in facilitating a transition to democracy. Rhema has since become an over-whelmingly black congregation, and McCauley has willingly borne the cost of seeing many of his white members leave the church.

During the struggle against apartheid, McCauley and Ron Steele, who long served as McCauley's spokesman and right-hand man, hosted private dinners for political leaders from all sides of the conflict. Steele previously pastored a church in Lusaka that was attended by exiled ANC members as well as Angola freedom fighters, and so he lent further credibility to the Rhema team. The dinners were an important element in a chain of events that brought the principal protagonists of the apartheid conflict together: Nelson Mandela of the ANC, Mangosuthu Buthelezi of the Inkatha Freedom Party (IFP), and Prime Minister F. W. DeKlerk, of the ruling National Party (NP). Once the foundations of these talks were established, leadership was handed off to members of the civic and business community. They ultimately led to the 1991 National Peace Accord, which was a step toward South Africa's peaceful transition to democracy in 1994 (see Gastrow 1995).

Rhema's political involvement in the years leading up to democracy brought its leadership into a wider gambit of relationships than is normally maintained by Pentecostals. Rhema continued these trends in the new dispensation, when in 1997 McCauley was one of the founding members of the executive committee of the National Religious Leaders Forum (NRLF). The NRLF brought together Muslims, Jews, Baha'is, Buddhists, Hindus, African Traditional Religions, and Christians and has addressed such issues as corruption, the HIV/AIDS pandemic, and problems in the national education system. After Jacob Zuma won the 2009 presidential election, McCauley helped to form and then chaired the National Interfaith Leadership Council (NILF), which is composed of Christian, African Traditional, and Muslim churches.[2] Providing ecumenical leadership is highly unusual for an evangelical Pentecostal pastor, but Rhema has found these relationships politically useful. Steele stated: "We've learned to work with [people of other faiths], I mean, when the abortion issue was debated ... we had an alliance with the Muslims and the Jews and the Hindus in opposing abortion .... So we've learned to form alliances without compromising our faith. It's not about your faith; it's about common values."

Michael Cassidy, founder of African Enterprise, a local evangelical NGO, and the honorary chairman of the Lausanne Congress for World Evangelization, which is global evangelicalism's most extensive formal global network, also fought against apartheid. Cassidy teamed with Nobel Prize winner Desmond Tutu to run the National Initiative for Reconciliation (NIR) in the 1980s, which

---

[2] Some view the NILF to be in competition with the NRLF, which McCauley continued to participate in after starting the NILF. Both bodies are ecumenical.

founded a network of about 400 church leaders from all races and denominations. Cassidy was also a major player behind the scenes in ensuring that KwaZulu Natal did not ignite in violence in the run-up to the first democratic elections. He regularly put himself in opposition to apartheid government policy and in danger from its security forces as he created alliances, moved in and out of townships, and lost colleagues to the struggle.

Cassidy and McCauley were among a few evangelical "heroes" who teamed with "heroes" in other faith traditions to fight apartheid. They did not represent a strong tide of popular evangelical dissent against the apartheid government. Cassidy himself did not feel that the evangelical community was supporting him in the most difficult times. Says Cassidy of his pre-1994 experience, "I was moving with many fellow travelers who would not have attached to themselves the label 'evangelical.' And in fact evangelicals, one could say, by and large were not with us. Their stance was very weak . . . other than some black evangelicals. And even at that, not a great number of those." Thus, in those days Cassidy tried to avoid the 'evangelical' label. It was not until he helped to create the Evangelical Association of South Africa (TEASA) that he moved decisively into the evangelical camp.

In recent years, TEASA has increased its role as a public voice for evangelicals. TEASA may not receive much active support from its membership, but its leaders, such as General Secretary Moss Nthla and cofounder Michael Cassidy, provide it with legitimacy in the leadership circles of the new South Africa. TEASA also teams with other religious groups; some TEASA leaders have strong personal ties to the South African Council of Churches (SACC) leadership. The two umbrella groups have worked together to push the government to do more about poverty. Independently, TEASA has also recently tried to highlight the Millennium Development Goals (MDGs) in its conversations with government leaders, particularly those MDGs that are related to health indices. Advocacy against poverty and for traditional sexual values are issues that black and white evangelicals in South Africa support. These are the issues that most commonly animate TEASA's activities.

Evangelicals serving in national leadership positions have even greater access to South Africa's decision makers than formal evangelical organizations. In addition to the private sector actors who have political clout and who were mentioned in the previous chapter, examples of evangelicals in the public sector include Frank Chikane, the son of an Apostolic Faith Mission pastor. He has been part of the ANC's National Executive Committee since 1997 and is considered part of the ANC's inner circle. Noko Kekana is a seminary professor. He also serves as a political consultant at high levels of government. Such strategically positioned evangelicals do not formally represent the evangelical community or consistently advocate for an evangelical agenda. But their presence means that the pluralistic cultural ethos of South African political and economic elites necessarily includes an evangelical element.

In El Salvador, political contributions by evangelicals are scarce. The executive branch makes political overtures to evangelicals and has made decisive plays to create clientelistic relationships with evangelical pastors. But no senior-level members of the executive branch claim to be evangelicals. Token evangelicals do populate El Salvador's legislative branch. They are not, however, key power brokers, nor are they particularly well known within the evangelical community. No members of the Supreme Court publicly claim to be evangelicals; one alternate to the Supreme Court is an evangelical. Any response by the state to evangelicals is thus that of a bureaucratic institution responding to a social movement, with the exception of a very few evangelicals in the business classes, such as Mauricio Loucel, who have been able to foster networks among political actors. Evangelicals do not wield state power in El Salvador.

Moises Mejia, head of the Salvadoran missionary network, said, "there is still a chapter lacking [in Salvadoran evangelicalism] I believe, one that shows a political impact. I believe that there have not been men like Daniel, like Joseph, in the Old Testament, Esther, that God placed them to be of national impact." This is, in part, because many evangelicals still consider politics to be dirty. One evangelical who has done well in business stated that two different political parties had approached him about running for a seat in El Salvador's legislative assembly. He declined both overtures because:

I cannot work in the way that they work ... politics has been turned to the art of deceit. You say one thing and you do another. Politicians do not respond to general interest, but rather they respond to economic interests and to groups of power, so you enter into this environment, and if you don't take an umbrella, all of the rain will fall on you, so it is a lie that someone will go there and be able to guard his integrity.

The number of evangelicals who do not view politics in this way, however, is beginning to rise. In fact, in 2012, the Evangelical Alliance held a prayer meeting for evangelical congressional candidates. The candidates who attended were running for five different political parties, including ARENA and the FMLN. None of those running were aspiring to leadership positions within their respective parties. But the change in evangelical attitudes toward the political arena since the end of the civil war in 1992 makes it increasingly likely that evangelicals may soon produce more significant public goods in El Salvador's political sphere.

SOCIAL ENGAGEMENT

Evangelical social engagement in NCEs is easy for a researcher to spot. In El Salvador and South Africa, homegrown ministry organizations are plentiful. Just a few of these include El Salvador's Asociacion A-Brazo, Orphan Helpers, Amilat Orphanage, and Asociacion Amiga. A sampling of South Africa's ministry organizations include Inserve, Rays of Hope, HOPE, and Cierra Romeli. These ministries exist alongside the many international NGOs, such as World Vision, Samaritan's Purse, and Compassion International. Local churches are also often venues of social engagement, regardless of denomination or church size. Finally, individual evangelicals often look for ways to assist the poor without getting involved in formal organizations. This could mean stopping by after work to help at a soup kitchen, developing a relationship with a street urchin, or using professional skills to help in volunteer centers. Evangelicals in NCEs are caring about the poor.

An evangelical theological rationale, often referred to as integral mission, accompanies this intense activity in the social arena. Ruth Padilla DeBorst and her father, author Rene Padilla, have been key players in developing this theological outlook. Padilla DeBorst states that evangelicals are now "able to say in the same breath, 'We need Jesus Christ's saving action *and* he calls us to his kingdom of justice.' [Some evangelicals continue to say], 'Oh no, those things have to be separate.' Well, no, they don't. In the gospel both things come together, they are not to be pulled apart." The Padilla family has developed church networks, publishing houses, and training institutes throughout Latin America to elaborate and spread their message among evangelicals. They have been joined by other leaders in NCEs around the world in this endeavor, and they are gaining an ever wider audience.

Leaders of some of the most important churches in NCEs are adopting the integral mission message. The Dutch Reformed Church in South Africa is a major case in point. This was the church from which the theology justifying apartheid flowed, helping to uphold the apartheid system during the second half of the twentieth century. However, in recent years the denomination has entered into a "major identity transformation phase becoming a missional church" (Jurgens Hendriks, personal correspondence, 2014). Japie LaPoorta, deputy secretary of the Apostolic Faith Mission (AFM) and chairman of the board of TEASA, references a similar trend in his denomination, stating, "we have had this problem in evangelicalism of being so heavenly minded that we are no earthly use ... but we have discovered that this world is the world for which Jesus came, that God sent his son to die. In this world, people are in dire need. If you take the parable of the Good Samaritan and a lot of other biblical texts, you cannot simply preach the gospel to people in need without helping them." In El Salvador, Elim's head pastor, Mario Vega, is a member of Padilla DeBorst's Network for Integral Mission in El Salvador. Vega says his church is undergoing an evolution in which it is no longer "a church that is only dedicated to the salvation of souls ... [it is now] a church that sees its mission in a more complete form and searches for the salvation of people, not only souls, but of human beings that are immersed in social problems." LaPoorta and Vega are both prominent leaders in their contexts, but they are just two among many leaders who are adopting this particular strain of evangelical theology.

Producing Public Goods in the Social Sphere

The evangelical impulse to social engagement is consistent with an integral mission approach. The programmatic strategies evangelicals use include (but are not limited to) skills-building workshops, drug and alcohol rehabilitation programs, HIV/AIDS ministries, orphanages, and work with gangs and prisons. A few evangelical entrepreneurs target national audiences or attempt to influence national government policy through social media or effective case studies.

Skills-building efforts in NCEs are consistent with evangelicalism's entrepreneurial orientation. In El Salvador, A-Brazo provides training in brick masonry when it begins a housing project in the community. It also provides basic training in computer literacy to urban youths, with the hope that they will become more employable. In South Africa, Rhema, using its own funds as well as government funds, has built care centers in several large townships around South Africa. These are intended to help with social service provision – a particular weakness of post-apartheid governments. Rhema runs numerous programs through its care centers, including basic skills-building programs such as literacy, bookkeeping, sewing, and computer skills. Meanwhile, an Apostolic Faith Mission (AFM) church south of Durban trains local residents to grow their own gardens. This is a commonly accepted community development strategy that is intended to fight malnutrition in the area.

Evangelicals are particularly interested in creating drug and alcohol rehabilitation centers and programs. There are indications that those in crisis situations are more likely to become evangelicals than the working poor (Mariz 1994). There are also indications that faith-based programs for addictions are more effective than similar programs that do not have a faith component (Cnaan 2002). Accordingly, in El Salvador, Elim, Iglesia Josué, and the Baptist Tabernacle, to name just a few, have drug and alcohol rehabilitation centers and programs. In South Africa, an AFM church in KwaZulu Natal runs a rehabilitation center, and numerous churches in Johannesburg and Cape Town have ministries of this sort as well.

Evangelicals are also highly involved in ministry to gang members and prisoners, especially in El Salvador. Robert Brenneman (2012) has powerfully outlined the affinities and interactions between evangelicals and gangs in Central America. My data supports Brenneman's thesis that gang leaders allow their members to leave the gang if they have an authentic conversion experience and find God in an evangelical or Pentecostal church. Many who make such a conversion become leaders in their local church contexts. Elim, for example, has longstanding and successful ministries to gang members – numerous former gang members are now Elim pastors. This is also true in various other Salvadoran denominations. Jorge Mira, the head of an evangelical television station in El Salvador, has developed a ministry to gang members and ex-gang members. Brother Toby's Baptist Tabernacle is well known for its extensive prison ministries, and Alejandro Amaya, the chaplain of Iglesia Josué's Christian school and former head of the Evangelical Alliance, visits a detention center in San Salvador each week to minister to former gang members.

HIV/AIDS remains one of the most important health and social issues in South Africa, and evangelicals have responded accordingly. The South African Leadership Assembly II named AIDS as one of the seven giants South Africa is currently facing and set up a task force to see what the South African church could do about it. At the local level, Isaac Asithole's independent megachurch in the township of Alexandria provides an education and feeding program to about 120 children orphaned because their parents died of AIDS. They also have a hospice ministry for AIDS patients who are near death, with the hope that they can provide them with dignity in their last days. In Durban, an evangelical Methodist church started an AIDS center and has a lay program designed to assist with various components of AIDS ministries. Baptist churches in Cape Town, KwaZulu Natal, and Johannesburg all run AIDS ministries. Although modestly good news about AIDS has begun to surface in the nation's health reports, the problem remains vast, and many local churches feel called to respond.

Caring for orphans is also high on the agenda in NCEs. South Africa's Rosebank Union church has a ministry for child-headed homes. They partner with a local NGO to feed up to 400 children a day. Local churches in Cape Town have a ministry for abandoned children, and an innovative ministry partnership between young American and South African evangelical professionals invested heavily in building and running AIDS orphanages. In El Salvador, Amilat Orphanage is owned and operated by Terri Benner Dominguez and Oswaldo Dominguez, who also own the Josué bookstore chain. An AG pastor, Roberto Sorto and his wife, Sandra, support a children's home near San Salvador. Evangelicals in NCEs frequently recite the mandate to care for the widow and the orphan, and in these instances they take the command quite literally.

Attention can also be given to evangelical efforts in health care and care for the environment in NCEs. LaPoorta's wife, for example, is a nurse. She trains community members in basic nursing principles. Other churches in South Africa and in El Salvador provide medical clinics, some of which are mobile, as well as dental clinics. At Elim, a young pastor has started such a clinic for his neighborhood and has tried to develop a scheme through which community members subsidize their own health care. Elim also demonstrates care for the environment by running a recycling program at the church, which is still something of a novelty in Salvadoran society. World Vision El Salvador has teamed with the Evangelical Alliance to run a leadership seminar on the country's ecological concerns and how church leaders can be engaged in these issues.

Consistent with evangelicalism's entrepreneurial model, all of these examples are program driven. The programs they create are often not the most technically sound or the most efficient, but they remain at the grassroots level. In several of these examples, international religious resources are used – for example, one Salvadoran reports using curriculum created by Saddleback Church, a California based megachurch, in its prison ministries. But they remain consistent with the framework of a local entrepreneur who creates an organization or a program and uses religious resources to solve a local problem.

A few evangelical initiatives are larger and move beyond a grassroots or community-level orientation. Heartlines is one of them. Heartlines was founded in 2002 with the goal of promoting better values in South African society. The primary platforms Heartlines uses to achieve its goal are mass media, social networking media, and partnerships with churches and faith-based organizations. Heartlines' breakthrough initiative was a 2006 television series called, appropriately enough, *Heartlines*. The eight-week series aired on South Africa's state channel, SABC (the most watched channel in the country), in a prime time evening slot. Each week featured a different value such as compassion, forgiveness, or honesty. Heartlines also distributed workbooks to churches around the country, so they could discuss the value featured on that week's program in their church services. The project resonated with many South Africans, not just evangelicals, such that SABC decided to rebroadcast the series in 2007. Heartlines followed this with a campaign called *Six Weeks of Values in Action* in 2009, which in its movie form garnered an international Emmy nomination, and a 2013 production called *Nothing for Mahala: A Campaign on Values and Money*, which was viewed by a wide audience.

Heartlines is the brainchild of Dr. Garth Japhet, a member of Rosebank Union Church, one of the leading (mostly white) evangelical churches in Johannesburg. A number of influential evangelicals serve on the board, including Oya-Hazel Gumede and Esme Bowers, the latter of whom has also served as the Southern Africa regional leader for the Pan African Christian Women's Alliance and as the international chairperson for the board of African Enterprise. Heartlines is not an exclusively evangelical endeavor – it has multiple resource streams for its productions, including South Africa's First National Bank and the John Templeton Foundation. But it was founded by evangelicals and is largely controlled by the evangelical community.[3]

There are also times when evangelicalism's program-driven projects are successful enough to affect national policy. The educational strategy Silvana Valladaras implemented at the School for the Deaf, for example, represented a major innovation in Salvadoran educational opportunities for the deaf. The school's innovations have led the way for change at a national level. Valladaras said, "In 2001, the Ministry of Education called us so that we would give them the recipe of how we have achieved what we have achieved with so few resources and in such little time." One of the school's board members, Ricardo Hernandez,

---

[3] Not all evangelicals rushed to support Heartlines' vision of producing a public good that was not overtly evangelistic in nature. During the *Heartlines* production process, Heartlines created a number of focus groups to gain input from evangelical leaders. At one of these focus groups, some of the discussion focused on whether the series would lead viewers to Christ. Most leaders had no doubt it was good for society, but they were unsure if that was enough to warrant evangelical support for the endeavor. Heartlines' representative at the group, who was a senior member of Youth for Christ in South Africa, said afterward that he expected this concern. However, he and other Heartlines leaders strongly believed that their evangelical faith could motivate a values-driven media product that didn't explicitly invite an audience into a relationship with Christ.

stated, "We have been an example for the Ministry of Education for many years and for other private schools for the deaf." In 2011, Valladaras was named the Avon Lady of the Year in El Salvador, an award that seeks to honor women who spend their careers assisting vulnerable populations in the country.

SOCIETY ACTS BACK

Successful efforts at producing public goods in the social sphere exist alongside times when evangelicals in NCEs do not find consonance with existing culture. Evangelicals may be naïve to how things work in the marketplace, or they may not understand how their religious initiatives will interact with social cleavages based on race, class, or gender. Sometimes this is the result of their relative innocence, and other times it is the fault of their inattention to issues of power and oppression in their own faith communities.

Evangelicals may be particularly vulnerable in the marketplace. Hilda Bojorquez, for example, partnered with an American entrepreneur to create Telemax, a start-up company in the telecommunications sector. They developed a new product that could help to lower the digital divide in El Salvador by providing easier access to cell phone usage. For their idea to work, they needed to partner with one of the three major multinational telecoms operating in the country. But once the contract was signed, the multinational corporation simply stole their idea, contracted other vendors to distribute the product, and aggressively forced Telemax out of the market. In another case, an evangelical owner of a hardware store and delivery services company contracted with the Salvadoran government to move raw materials to a construction site. The owner reported that someone in the government then stole the raw materials from the construction site and claimed they were never delivered. The owner of the store called it a double theft, as he was not paid for the services rendered, and the government charged him for the missing raw materials. This blow severely damaged his small company.

Evangelicals can also struggle with the dynamics of the social arena. The Global Day of Prayer (GDOP) provides an example. Its rapid international expansion was discussed in the previous chapter, but GDOP has been a lightning rod for racial tension in South Africa, where it originated. GDOP's first rally was held in 2001 on Human Rights Day, a day set aside to reflect on the abuses that occurred under the apartheid system. GDOP organizers chose the date because of stadium availability and because people were more likely to come on a holiday. However, some public figures believed the high level of participation in GDOP (some 45,000 people came) drew attention away from human rights themes, and the following day a firestorm of protest was unleashed in the press. The sensibilities of GDOP's founders, who are white, to the country's past were openly questioned. Black evangelical leaders have since widened these initial criticisms by claiming that the GDOP movement only pursues action in the spiritual realm and ignores South Africa's bleak social realities.[4] A senior black member of the South African Council of Churches, for example, became visibly annoyed when I asked about GDOP, stating, "There are some theological events in the country that we do not know about. There are also some of the events in the country that we are very disturbed about." Thus, as Michael Cassidy, a patron of GDOP, says, the movement "has revealed, in a way, a fairly ongoing level of not huge but modest cleavage between white and black Christians [in South Africa]."

Although the relationship between class and race in South Africa is becoming more complex, there is still strong overlap, and as GDOP grew it also encountered class-based critiques. One national director of an international evangelical ministry explained that movements that have attracted support from wealthier churches do not have much relevance to the "second South Africa." He notes that "You have the South Africa which is predominantly black and poor ... and you have the South Africa which is predominantly white and wealthier, and this South Africa which is primarily black and poor still grapples with issues of post-colonialism, issues of poverty and all those things." This is contrasted by the social concerns of the upper class which focus especially on crime. Crime also affects the poor but in different ways and is lower on the poor's social agenda.

It is true that GDOP has been initiated by South Africa's business class: GDOP's visionary, Graham Power, was once named South Africa's Businessman of the Year. It is again true that part of GDOP's agenda is to pray about crime in South Africa: Davie Spangenberg, GDOP's coordinator, has claimed that crime in Cape Town has receded because of GDOP.

To point this out is not, however, to imply that GDOP has only mobilized rich, white participants. On the contrary, GDOP participation is much larger than the comparatively small white population in South Africa. And although the personnel in the movement's international headquarters is white, this is not true of the critically important city or regional levels of leadership. In Johannesburg, high-profile black evangelical leaders such as David Molapo and Elvis Mvulane, national director of Walk Thru the Bible, have been extensively involved. In Cape Town, respected black pastor Barry Isaacs serves as the regional chair. Whites who have been on the cutting edge of the race issue, such as Cassidy, are also involved. States Cassidy, "One of the reasons I identified with it was that I really felt I was seeing a thermal of the Holy Spirit here .... It might be led by whites, but there are lots of things God raises up that are led by blacks. It is not a crime. He can use whomever He likes." And while poor black South Africans are often more attuned to social concerns than their richer counterparts, it is emphatically true that neither they nor their leaders reject spiritual exercises such as prayer. It is within this context, then, that Moss Nthla, a black South African who is the general secretary of the Evangelical Alliance of South Africa (TEASA), evaluates GDOP:

[4] A more radical accusation heard in the African community is that the GDOP is a last-gasp effort by whites to maintain a position of influence and to make impoverished blacks easier to govern.

So I think it has been good in the sense that it has helped mobilize Christians globally for prayer and really if you are an evangelical, if you believe prayer does something in terms of allowing God's involvement in the lives of people, it's a good thing. I've always thought though that it has to be managed better because people can pray as a way of running away. And unless the leaders of that movement guide or help the churches and leaders worldwide to use the power of prayer to find meaningful ways of engaging their community, it will become a joke after a while and nobody will take it seriously.

Alexander Venter, a white evangelical leader who gained credibility by living in a community with black Africans under the apartheid regime and who continues to live in a commune with three white families, three black families, and some single adults, underscores the need to balance both the social and the spiritual. He states, "the perception [of GDOP] has been that it's a charismatic white escapist thing. The idea is that prayer can change everything, whereas we've learned through the struggle for justice that its prayer and social engagement and protest and justice work that changes everything, not just prayer. It's never either/or, it's 'and' and 'both.'" Thus, while many black South Africans have helped to fill stadiums each year, some of the black and progressive evangelical leadership have been slow to get on board.

In fairness to GDOP, it must be pointed out that reconciliation as well as crime reduction has been a central part of its programming. GDOP moved away from stadium events in 2006 to create greater involvement in local towns and cities. But churches in South Africa often do not cross social lines (Erasmus, Mans, & Jacobs 2006). To create a unified movement, GDOP conducted reconciliation workshops in many of the 650 towns in which it operated. Spangenberg said in some communities church leaders "started to repent to one another ... and they started to cry and beg one another for forgiveness." These processes, which were also evident in other countries, showed that GDOP has had some success in overcoming the social cleavages that so challenged the movement at its inception.

SHIFTING BELIEFS

Evangelicalism has never had a highly unified, specific set of doctrines. Rather, it represents a movement across traditions and denominations that has held tightly to a few core beliefs but has considered the details of a given denomination or tradition as interesting but optional. This approach has allowed a range of theologies to percolate in NCEs. The integral mission theology is growing in importance, but a theology with a larger popular following is the prosperity gospel. In certain manifestations, these gospels are diametrically opposed to one another. But it is also surprisingly common to find a synthesis of the two positions, as local religious leaders pull symbolic resources from their environments and tie them together in new ways.

The Prosperity Gospel

Globally, the prosperity gospel is part and parcel of the Word of Faith movement. The Word of Faith movement originated in the United States (Coleman 2000) and is a subgroup of the broader evangelical community. Its current leaders include the Kenneth Hagin Ministries, Kenneth and Gloria Copeland, South Korean Paul Yonggi Cho, Joel Osteen, Joyce Meyer, Fred Price, Kreflo Dollar, John Avanzini, Markus Bishop, and Leroy Thompson (Bowler 2013; Harrison 2005). Although these personalities operate within Pentecostal and charismatic evangelicalism, their teachings raise the ire of many evangelicals who find elements of the prosperity gospel to be deeply problematic.

In spite of objections from more traditional evangelicals to the prosperity gospel, the germ of the Word of Faith movement can be found in some of Protestantism's earliest teachings. Ernst Troeltsch argued that a confidence (not the angst that Weber saw) characterized the earliest adherents of Calvin's doctrines. As noted in Chapter Four, the key doctrine in this regard was that once believers achieve "the state of grace" they cannot lose their salvation. For Troeltsch, confidence, rather than angst, served as the emotional catalyst behind Calvinism's creative (capitalist) spirit.

David Martin finds other antecedents to the prosperity gospel in eighteenth- and nineteenth-century Wesleyanism. In 1749, Charles Wesley wrote a hymn titled "All Things Are Possible," and Martin states, "in that claim one recognizes an exuberance which with only a change of key can yield a theology of success and power" (2002, 7). The Wesley brothers believed Jesus's biblical claim that he came so that his followers could "have life, and have it abundantly" (John 10:10, NIV Version). Wesleyan scholars, however, argue that the Wesleys' teaching had nothing to do with themes of prosperity. Rather, the Wesleys believed that abundant life was attained through the restoration of broken relationships and the creation of communities characterized by shalom (Snyder & Scandrett 2011). Even so, argues Martin, the confidence that emanates from Wesleyan teaching unintentionally served as a precursor for the Word of Faith's hermeneutic of success and power.

The contemporary prosperity gospel is tremendously malleable around the globe and across time, constantly reinventing itself as it breaks into new contexts or as familiar contexts begin to change. In a study of the prosperity gospel in Nigeria, George O. Folarin states, "the prosperity gospel is the teaching that the solutions to people's problems of sin, sickness, poverty, and demon oppression are in Jesus Christ. Many Charismatics even believe that these blessings are fully available to all Christians now" (2006, 1). Folarin notes that no single Nigerian denomination develops all the elements of the prosperity gospel – that is, the solutions to all the problems mentioned in his definition. In fact, a specialization has occurred in which churches focus either on healing, financial breakthrough, or exorcism. A common thread is that all the churches and denominations in Folarin's research include provisions for spiritual growth in their teaching – an important point because many prosperity critics suggest that prosperity-oriented churches focus only on promising material gain for their congregations. While there are some important differences between all NCEs, making parts of Nigeria's experience unique, Folarin's definition provides an excellent starting point for understanding the prosperity experience in the South African and Salvadoran cases.

There is, of course, a strong material element to the prosperity gospel. This includes bald assertions by televangelists that they have found large sums of money in their car or in their pockets. It also includes people who claim to find gold fillings in their teeth or who find gold dust sprinkled on their wallets, cell phones, or other personal effects. The things that trigger such unexpected blessings are often putting sacrificial sums of money in the offering plate or going to a revival and receiving prayers from charismatic leaders. Martin calls this a "bargain with Providence," in which people "give in order that [they] may receive" (2002, 10). Claims about the effectiveness of these strategies can be heard while watching TBN in the United States, talking with believers in Johannesburg, or enjoying dinner with a missionary to Mozambique. Not all adherents of the prosperity gospel claim to have such experiences, but they are a prominent characteristic of the movement.

Almost as strong as this material element is the therapeutic or self-help theme that courses through prosperity teachings. States Martin (2002, 17):

The Protestant Ethic has switched from the currency of virtue to a conspicuously financial currency and, as [Simon] Coleman recounts it, the proper service of others has become a form of helping oneself. What was a discipline of self has become a form of self-management collectively promoted as a religious version of the "feel-good" factor.

The switch to which Martin refers is evident in sermons that can be heard in the religious markets of South Africa and, to a lesser extent, El Salvador. The producers of these sermons and other religious products more directly (and more crassly) address material and emotional needs than earlier forms of Protestantism or, for that matter, Pentecostalism.

There is considerable speculation with regard to how many people adhere to the prosperity message. The Pew Forum surveyed delegates to the Third Lausanne Congress of World Evangelization, held in Cape Town in 2010 (this event is discussed in Chapter 3). Only 7 percent of respondents affirmed that "God gives wealth and good health to those with enough faith," which was the question on the survey. This result has more to do with which evangelicals get to come to the Lausanne Congress than with the percentage of evangelicals who adhere to the prosperity gospel. But the results balance a 2006 Pew Survey that found that a stunning 80 percent of all Christians in South Africa believe in the prosperity gospel, with 90 percent of Pentecostals and 85 percent of Charismatics falling into that category. In that survey, Pew's question read: "God will grant material prosperity to those who have enough faith" (Pew 2006, 30). It may be clear to the educated Western mind that the question is trying to uncover a belief that would link poverty's resolution directly to faith. But when impoverished Africans were asked the question, it is highly likely that they understood it to mean, "Does God care about your material and physical well-being?" To which most will, and of course did, answer a resounding yes.[5] The results of that survey nonetheless sent traditional evangelicals into something of a frenzy. *Christianity Today*, North America's flagship evangelical publication, ran a cover story lamenting the problem revealed by the survey, and other evangelical leaders launched campaigns against prosperity teachings. The true percentage is clearly somewhere between those provided by the 2006 and 2011 surveys. But even if that number could be successfully derived, it would not reveal much, as there are so many different prosperity gospels with such wide ranges of beliefs.

Extreme Examples

Although much of the hand-wringing about the prosperity gospel is unwarranted, there are times when faith communities manifest such beliefs in the extreme. In Johannesburg, reports emerged in 2006 of members of one small, impoverished church that decided to act on the premise that if they demonstrated enough faith, God would materially reward them. They thus gave away the little they did have, and then fasted and prayed, believing that God would send them more material blessings than they could imagine. This kind of action is clearly consonant with teachings that can be found in American prosperity circles, and one could draw direct lines of causality between their prosperity beliefs, many of which were exported by the U.S. Word of Faith movement, and the decision to divest themselves of their belongings. But this event also carried echoes of South African history: in 1856 the Xhosas killed all of their cattle and destroyed all of their corn. They did so because two girls reported that spirits came to them and said this would bring forth greater numbers and more beautiful cattle than the tribe currently owned (Theal 1904).[6] Contemporary communities are often caught in the vortex of local and global forces that create prosperity gospels. Recognizing the synthesis of global and local culture within prosperity circles is consistent with the conclusions Meyer (1998) reached after studying the movement in Ghana.

---

[5] Pew's numbers are even more disputable considering that Jurgens Hendriks (2006), using data from the 2001 South African census, stated that 14 million South African Christians are members of main-line denominations. If the Pew numbers are correct, it would mean that a remarkable percentage of Anglicans, Lutherans, Presbyterians, and members of the Dutch Reformed Church are also adherents of the prosperity gospel.

[6] There is a political reading of this story that centers on Xhosa attempts to set fierce, hungry warriors on the British colonists. That may be true. The point here is that many people in the tribe simply acted in obedience to the prophecy they were told.

Integration of Prosperity Teachings and Holistic Mission – A More Dominant Trend

Prosperity teachings can also move communities in decisively more pro-social directions. An interesting synthesis between the prosperity gospel and social outreach is under way in some of the most prominent prosperity-oriented churches. Rhema, for example, is the signature South African church of the prosperity movement. In the late 1970s and 1980s, its founder, Ray McCauley, was heavily under the sway of his mentor, Kenneth Hagin, Sr., and consequently "there was a bit of an over-emphasis" on the message that faith brings financial gain, according to Steele. But as Rhema South Africa quietly distanced itself from the Kenneth Hagin ministries, its leaders repackaged their prosperity message. According to Steele, McCauley's current stance begins with the precept that God wants to bless his followers. McCauley supports the claim with various biblical references, including the passage in which Jesus says: "Therefore I tell you, do not worry about your life, what you will eat or drink; or about your body, what you will wear .... Look at the birds of the air; they do not sow or reap or store away in barns, and yet your heavenly Father feeds them" (Matthew 6:25, 26). McCauley, according to Steele, explicates this to mean that God knows that we need clothes and food and that money is necessary to acquire these goods. God is therefore not against money, an impression gained when Scripture is misquoted. It is rather the love of money that God warns against.[7] Steele notes: "Ray will often say, 'If poverty was such a great blessing, then why aren't the Ethiopians the greatest nation in the world? They probably have the greatest poverty of all.' You know ... that's a silly illustration, but it ... emphasizes the point."

This last aspect of Rhema's presentation shows an important turn in theodicy that the prosperity gospel in general makes. It removes the "plus sign" that much of Christianity assigns to suffering and appears to "provide the theodicy of good fortune to those who are fortunate" that more primitive religions provided by understanding "suffering as a symptom of odiousness in the eyes of the gods and as a sign of secret guilt" (Weber 1946, 271).

Rhema does not teach that poverty is a sin. Rather, it embraces the impoverished and hopes they can participate in God's plan to address the material needs of the poor. Rhema also directs the action of those who have acquired material wealth to both continue in their wealth procuring ways *and* to reach out to those who have yet to be materially blessed.

The prosperity/integral mission synthesis becomes evident in the holistic conceptualization of the prosperity message that many South Africans put forth. Paul

---

[7] It was clear that Steele believed the love of money could in fact be an obstacle to the evangelical's faith. When I asked him if there were evangelicals in prominent positions in the country, he responded: "So there are, a lot of them are, are, have come under the influence of the gospel or even have made decisions for Christ, but have just got sucked into the whole thing about making money. So, that's the temptation. It comes very easy."

Tsai pastors a New Covenant Ministries church. Tsai understands the prosperity gospel as a reflection of God, not a get-rich-quick scheme.

I don't see a God that is sitting there and looking at people who are very poor and He's happy that they are poor and oppressed, they don't have anything. I don't see that kind of a God. And so I think that prosperity gospel, in a sense, it would be the very part of the nature of God ... I would simply say that prosperity gospel is that God is a God that simply wants people to be prosperous in all spheres of life ... physically, spiritually, financially. In all these things, he wants people to prosper.

Tsai further contends that distortions to the gospel arise when preachers focus only on financial issues. Says Tsai: "If you are talking about the factional part of prosperity and you are talking about material things, and money ... then you say, man, this is what they are talking about when they say prosperity gospel. I think that it is error. I think that it is not true."

Thami Klassen, another pastor of a New Covenant Ministries church, agrees with the holistic understanding of prosperity. He establishes a picture of God as one who looks after His children, and ultimately God wants His children to be able to care for others. States Klassen:

In terms of articulating who God is, a God who cares, a God who says I'm the provider.... He says to us, I have given you the ability to create wealth, so that my covenant can be established, and the covenant hasn't been broken ... it's just part of who God is, that as Creator, I should learn to be prosperous, I should learn to thank Him when I don't have [anything].... He has given us gifts and talents to help others and help ourselves and our families.

This, believe Tsai and Klassen, is the proper interpretation of the prosperity message: a holistic belief in the relationship between God and humanity and an understanding that the empowerment of the self is only meaningful when the self can serve and enable the community. Within African circles especially, where Western individualism is found only in syncretic form with indigenous culture and African understandings of Christianity have long included the material world, the duality of focus between self and community is organically synthesized. These reflections are fundamental to understanding what the prosperity gospel is in South Africa and to seeing how the synthesis has drawn South Africa's prosperity gospel away from the North American presentations, which can be viewed almost daily on TBN or in churches around America.

CONCLUSION

Evangelical entrepreneurs in NCEs are looking for opportunities to enter the social and political arenas of their countries. They are motivated by new theologies, and they are made more effective by increasing resource availability and strengthening organizations.

The results of these entrepreneurial incursions have been mixed. Due in part to the competitive structural characteristics of NCEs, clientelism, bribery, and free riders are all part of the evangelical political experience. Broad-based collaborative initiatives among evangelicals generally are not. One discouraged evangelical leader summed up the situation thusly: "Right now, the very image of the evangelical church is saying 'Give me, give me, give me. What can I get from the government? We give them our vote, and they give us this.'"

Fortunately, other evidence shows generally more positive efforts of evangelicals to engage government and the *polis* more generally. Public goods are also produced by evangelicals, including initiatives in reconciliation, multitudes of programs for the poor, and the infusion of pro-social values into the community. Public engagement by evangelicals is thus a mixed bag. For better and for worse, people across the Global South and East can expect that bag to get bigger in coming years.

Conclusion

The religious social forces framework offers a fresh look at the internal dynamism of global religious movements. It identifies the many different kinds of religious resources that are available in a local faith community. It examines the networks through which such resources pass, and the people of faith to whom these resources are made available. All of these elements – material, symbolic, and ideational resources, as well as networks and people – have the capacity to change local faith communities; they are all religious social forces.

Change created by religious social forces can be pervasive. Forms of worship, emphases on different religious values, methods of educating children and newcomers, ways of socializing or of being a community, attitudes toward those outside the faith community, and messages from the pulpit can all change. So too can the size of a religious movement's organizations, the strength and type of its transnational networks, and the total number of people who choose to be part of a faith community. Further changes include the way religious movements conduct themselves in public spaces, the kind of political participation in which they engage, and the scope and type of social services and outreaches they provide. These aspects of religious social movements are constantly in flux, and religious social forces within the movement are usually most responsible for the changes that occur.

Religious social forces do not act alone. Economic, political, and other social forces also create change in religious communities. Global financial crises, spikes in food prices, and innovations that improve wealth creation are just some of the economic activities that affect religious groups. Likewise, the deepening of democracy or, conversely, authoritarian political systems determines the political climate to which religious groups must adjust, or against which they must protest. Such political systems may even persecute religious actors and activities. Finally, nonreligious aspects of civil society affect religious groups. Local school systems, networks created by rotary clubs, culture produced by contemporary artists, and the quality of education provided by school systems can enable or constrain the endeavors of religious communities. Scholars tease apart the different elements of life to analyze them, but humans live in a complex and interconnected world where there is constant give and take between all sectors of society.

In spite of the interconnected nature of human experience, the religious social forces framework argues for the primacy of religion in creating religious change. This is because religious social forces are constitutive elements of the religious communities they act upon. At a practical level, religious social forces include the person in the pew who decides to start a new ministry in the church, thus changing the church's identity. They refer to new thoughts about how God wants his followers to live, which can change the lifestyles of those who hear those thoughts. Religious social forces also include short-term mission teams that forge relationships across borders and cultures, thus expanding the universe of those who participate in those networks. All of these examples are not just intimately connected to faith communities, but they *are* faith communities in action. Their activities create the constant evolution that characterizes global religious movements.

GLOBAL EVANGELICALISM AND THE RELIGIOUS SOCIAL FORCES FRAMEWORK

Several traditional questions have long governed studies of evangelicals in Asia, Africa, and Latin America. Students of the movement have been interested in why people convert to evangelical Christianity, the relationship between the spread of Christianity and the spread of modernity, the potential links between American empire building and global evangelicalism, and how evangelicals vote when they go to the polls. In considering such topics, scholars have provided important insights and furthered our understanding of the global movement.

By using the religious social forces framework, I have moved away from such questions. I have instead inquired about internal sources of change in a global movement. The question led me to study those who receive transnational flows of religious goods, messages, and services when they arrive in NCEs, and to notice that these goods are captured by local entrepreneurs, who are helping to create social change now precisely because global resources are newly available to them. Entrepreneurs' synthesis of global and local forces has generated currents of change across different elements of the movement. The questions pursued by this study clearly distinguish it from other analyses of Global Christianity.

Evangelicalism's religious social forces have created at least six new trends in NCEs. They are explained in Chapters 5 and 6, respectively, but it is worth listing them once more. First, NCEs have become increasingly effective at exporting religion. It is now commonplace to see South African missionaries in India and Salvadoran missionaries in Spain. Second, organizations in NCEs have become large, sophisticated, and effective. Megachurches with television and radio stations, social outreaches in poor communities, primary and secondary schools, and bookstores on their campuses dot the landscape of NCEs. Their reach too is increasingly global. Third, as inequality has increased around the globe, it has changed the nature of evangelical communities. Not all evangelical pastors have megachurches to shepherd. Many still meet in humble storefront churches. The relationship between the megachurch pastor and the storefront pastor is far from equal. Fourth, evangelicals are still interested in sharing Jesus with those who have not heard about Him, but they would increasingly prefer to do that while caring for widows and orphans. As others have noted, evangelical and Pentecostal social engagement in NCEs is increasing and becoming more diversified. Fifth, evangelicals are entering the political domain of their host countries with increasing regularity. Evangelical political perspectives are as diverse as their level of political competency. But whether they are well prepared or ill prepared, evangelicals are increasingly entering, rather than fleeing, political life. Finally, evangelical beliefs are shifting. Evangelicals in NCEs are both more likely to provide theological support for social engagement and more likely to believe some derivation of the prosperity gospel than they were a decade ago. Some evangelicals are doing both simultaneously.

FIVE PRINCIPLES

By identifying the religious social forces at work in NCEs and the directions of social change they are creating, I have sought to create a deeper awareness of how NCEs are being built. It is a sophisticated process that defies one-sided answers. It is not true, for example, that American political and military interests are the primary drivers of evangelical growth in Latin America and elsewhere, as the Imperial Expansion school of thought contends (Brouwer, Gifford, & Rose 1996; Stoll 1990). It is equally erroneous to conclude that Christianity in Africa was only free to grow when Western influence receded, as the New Faces argument has posited (Jenkins 2002, 2006). To accurately portray the current realities of NCEs, scholars need to consider the synthesis that local and global factors undergo when they collide.

In Chapter 1, I alluded to five basic principles upon which the argument outlined in this book is predicated. These principles help us to understand how and why NCEs are developing so quickly. They show that the model of evangelical growth makes sense in a world where global cities have become critical centers of cultural and commercial exchange. These principles are also consistent with what international development theorists have learned about developing countries. As such, they could cause any other religious or nonreligious global movement to grow just as effectively. It is worth looking at each of these principles more closely.

First, *local actors are building NCEs*. Much like other aspects of social, economic, and political development, local citizens in the Global South and

East are primarily responsible for the progress of their own faith communities. Leading evangelicals in NCEs often come from the transnational professional class. Such actors build their communities' largest and most influential organizations. But evangelicals from all social classes and walks of life help to create and sustain their faith communities, and they often use local resources in the process. The simplest and most pervasive parts of community life support this claim. Most sermons in NCEs are, for example, preached by local pastors, and most lay members are residents of NCEs. Evangelicals in these locations are part of a global religious movement, but the responsibilities they have are primarily local. They decide what those responsibilities should be and subsequently fulfill them with almost complete autonomy.

Second, *religious forces emitted from the West greatly influence NCEs.* In El Salvador, South Africa, and most other NCEs, the imprint of North American evangelicalism is clear. This is especially the case for countries that have opened their political economies to globalization. One measure of this is the organizational presence that Western entities have in NCEs. Many North American denominations, like the Assemblies of God, have spread across the Global South. U.S. ministries such as Campus Crusade for Christ or Walk Thru the Bible are also conspicuous. Western NGOs like World Vision and Samaritan's Purse are tremendously influential: they have large budgets, they are well connected locally and internationally, and they provide desperately needed services to the poor. The organizational presence of North America in NCEs is simply unmistakable.

The flows of people, knowledge, and material resources that come through these and other organizations and networks from the West to NCEs are voluminous. Short- and long-term missionaries, tourists, businesspeople, friends, and family flow freely into NCEs. Western hymns are sung in the worship services, Western curriculum is used in Sunday Schools, and Western degrees confer legitimacy on local evangelical leaders who have had the chance to study abroad. The human and cultural presence that North America and other Western powers have in NCEs is clearly quite significant. To imply, as Jenkins (2002) and others have, that NCEs have grown as (and perhaps because) the Western presence has receded in these regions is not empirically defensible.

Third, *as local actors build social institutions and organizations, they organically synthesize local and global resources.* It bears repeating that the central image in this book is that of the local entrepreneur who is pulling the local and global religious resources that populate his or her environment together in new and unique ways. As has just been pointed out, there are indeed many global resources circulating in NCEs. The goal of most local entrepreneurs is to attract as many of these resources as possible. Local actors do not fear global religious forces. Rather, they know how to channel such forces into their projects alongside more familiar local religious forces and resources. As global and local forces are synthesized, Western evangelical culture becomes embedded in the culture of NCEs. It also becomes transformed, sometimes to the point that it is almost unrecognizable, and recast as ingredients of products and organizations that are locally initiated and which are enmeshed in local culture.

Fourth, *the organizations and institutions that local actors create are more sustainable than those built by outside actors*, however sympathetic and supportive outsiders might be. International development initiatives often end in abject failure. Hospitals built by Western donors and then handed over to local authorities can quickly cease to be operational. Western technologies that are introduced in developing countries – anything ranging from farm equipment to computers – can be quickly broken or sit simply unused, rusting away. Initiatives by religious Westerners can be equally ineffective. Take the example of American evangelical leader Bruce Wilkinson, author of the bestselling book *Prayer of Jabez* (2000). In 2002, Wilkinson moved to South Africa hoping to build an orphanage that could house 10,000 AIDS orphans in Swaziland. However, Wilkinson encountered numerous difficulties, and in 2005 he returned to the United States, admitting that his plan had failed. Whether secular or religious, development projects are far more likely to succeed when they are wholly owned by local actors who know the local context and understand the local culture.

NCEs could not be flourishing as they are if they were being controlled and planned by Western actors. Local autonomy is central to their growth. Even international evangelical organizations have learned this lesson. For example, after earthquakes hit El Salvador in 1986, World Relief, a U.S.-based evangelical NGO, opened a large office in San Salvador. It worked closely with local churches to respond to the disaster and built more than 5,000 houses for earthquake victims. However, when the disaster response project was over, World Relief closed its office. It fired its local staff and severed ties with its partnering churches. This was a difficult process. In 2001, earthquakes again hit El Salvador, and World Relief again responded. This time, however, World Relief decided to minimize its own official presence and to cultivate a local partner organization. The local NGO never became as large as the World Relief office of the late 1980s, but it continues to be a viable organization more than a decade after the earthquakes, and its relationships within Salvadoran evangelical circles remain intact. World Relief discontinued its El Salvador funding just a few years after the earthquakes hit, but this time it did so on good terms with its local partners.

Finally, *global religious forces can be imperial, but they can also be sources of empowerment*. Places like Brazil, Russia, India, and China are achieving economic development at a dizzying pace. They are using Western capital, knowledge, human resources, and technology to do so. The United States sometimes bullies these countries, forcing them to change certain policies or accept terms on certain agreements. But these states can and do fight back. Concessions from the United States and other Western countries to states with emerging economies are also common. These relationships are no longer as one sided as they once were, and many forecasters predict that China will someday overtake the United States in its global reach and power.

Just as the West does not control the trajectory of emerging economies in the Global South and East, Western evangelicals do not control evangelical leaders in NCEs. The most effective of these leaders are culturally savvy, technically capable, and religiously inspired. They are embedded in global networks and have close relationships with Western actors. They also have close relationships with evangelicals in neighboring countries and, although less frequently, with evangelicals in regions other than their own outside the West. These are the actors that are most responsible for building the new centers of global evangelicalism, and they are using transnational networks and global resources to do so.

FUTURE DIRECTIONS?

Given the basic principles just outlined and the internal dynamics that govern global religious movements, what can we expect as new centers of evangelicalism become the world's established centers of evangelicalism? Much like the present, the future will be determined by global and local religious social forces and the social, political, and economic context in which NCEs find themselves.

Such contingencies make peering into the future a tricky business. What is certain is that NCEs will continue to evolve. Just as numerical growth and increased social standing helped to precipitate the current trends in NCEs, these newer trends will join existing religious social forces in pushing NCEs in still other directions. The goals of future entrepreneurs will be based on the successes and failures of today's entrepreneurs. Tomorrow's cadre of decision makers will be operating in contexts that we do not yet fully understand, and they will be able to draw from resources that we cannot yet fully imagine. An evangelical culture could even emerge that no longer places such a premium on entrepreneurs.

It is also possible that current trends will continue to move in their current direction. Evangelical communities could continue to grow in number and in organizational sophistication. They could increase their ability to export religion across borders and to have an impact on their national societies. They could increase their already sizable share of the global Christian community and maintain their pace against the world's other major religions. These kinds of projections assume that the religious fervor that now characterizes the Global South and East will continue unabated.

But as Martin (2002) notes, secularization could also be the dominant story of evangelicalism's future. As evangelicalism grows, its religious distinctive could become more obscured. This is already happening in many places. Evangelicals could make compromises so that they are accepted in pluralistic settings. The public face of evangelicalism could become benign. The impulse to evangelism, and thus growth, could begin to fade. The strategies of asceticism and of rational thought that the movement has promoted could be redirected to pursue more material and secular ends. If the movement were to mature in this direction, it would not be the first to do so.

A less distinctive religious community does not necessarily mean increased secularism. Religious life could still be important to evangelicals even if they begin to blend more organically into other aspects of local or global culture. If the sociology of religion has taught us anything in recent decades, it is that religious change is not the same thing as religious decline.

These are just a few of the possible scenarios that could play out. There are others. The tale will not be known until it is told by local actors who are using global resources and are embedded in transnational networks. It should be an interesting tale to hear.

Appendix I

Methodology

Most of the current literature on global evangelicalism extracts information from either a single case study or multicountry surveys that are not fortified with ethnographic or qualitative research. This dissertation's contribution rests in its deep empirical grounding, its cross-continent comparative nature, and its unique emphasis on national-level evangelical leaders in strategic churches, NGOs, and businesses.

I selected the national evangelical communities of El Salvador and South Africa for cross-continent comparison. These two countries emerged because both have vibrant and growing evangelical communities that comprise well over a quarter of the national population (IUDOP 2009; Teichert 2005; Johnson 2014). El Salvador and South Africa are rendered more comparable because they are both transition economies and states that share a surprisingly similar social structure and recent history. It is thus no accident that Elisabeth Wood (2000) chose these same two countries to compare the paths states take to democracy. Concerning religion, David Martin (1990) included a chapter on South Africa in his path-breaking analysis of Latin American Pentecostalism because he felt it was an important parallel case. Also, Paul Freston (2001) stated that South Africa is particularly well suited to comparison with Latin American countries in his book on evangelicalism and politics.

South Africa and El Salvador have both opened their political economies in recent years. The dynamics described in this book are particularly applicable to countries that have made similar policy choices. Global religious social forces are most powerful when they cross unfettered borders. In political economies that remain closed, global religious forces do not play as strong a role. Clearly, they play *some* role, as even in a place like North Korea some cultural radiation seeps through the cracks. But transnational resources and networks are simply scarcer for the house church movements in some of the closed countries in Asia and elsewhere than they are for the many countries with more open political economies. To be applicable for closed contexts, the argument presented here would need to be modified.

To access the evangelical communities in El Salvador and South Africa, I relied heavily on in-depth interviews and employed a two-pronged subject selection process. First, I interviewed key national evangelical leaders. To identify a pool of each country's most strategic evangelical leaders, I relied on knowledge I had gained of the communities in my previous in-country work and on investigations I conducted by phone and e-mail in the months before going to the field. Once I created this leadership pool, I attempted to interview as many of these people as possible. In both cases, I successfully contacted and interviewed a majority of the most important national leaders, which included the directors of the Evangelical Alliance (an umbrella group for independent evangelical entities), senior pastors of megachurches, and leaders of some of the principal evangelical denominations, NGOs, media outlets, and academic institutions. Please see Appendix II for a list of the evangelical institutions represented in the study.[1]

The second prong of my selection process was to interview entrepreneurs in the private sector, focusing on those operating in the transnational business classes. To select these subjects and to set up the ethnographic portion of my research, I chose *Iglesia Josué* in San Salvador and the Rhema Church in Johannesburg. Both are considered to be leading churches in their countries because they exercise significant influence in crafting their national evangelical ethos. Within these churches, I first interviewed members of the pastoral leadership team and asked them to point me to entrepreneurs within their congregations. In *Iglesia Josué*, I joined a cell group and interviewed all of the entrepreneurs in that group, as well as others that were referred to me. In both churches, I asked entrepreneurs I interviewed to point me to other entrepreneurs within the congregation. On occasion I received names of evangelical entrepreneurs who were not part of these congregations; if they attended a church with a kindred ethos, I proceeded with the interview.[2]

In all, I conducted 115 interviews. Eighty-six of those were formal; thirty-two were informal. The formal interviews were split evenly between countries (forty-three in each). I conducted seventeen informal interviews in El Salvador and twelve informal interviews in South Africa. Seven of the forty-three formal interviews in each country were conducted with female evangelical leaders and entrepreneurs; three of the informal interviews in El Salvador and two of the informal interviews in South Africa were conducted with women. In South Africa, where race is also a factor, I conducted formal interviews with twenty

---

[1] Because of the tight interlocking in the evangelical community, one interviewee often represents more than one institution. For example, Adonai Leiva served as the director of Campus Crusade for Christ in El Salvador for twenty-seven years and is now the director of Walk Thru the Bible. Both organizations appear in Appendix II.

[2] I have received permission to use the names of most of my interviewees. Where I do not have permission, I refer to the individual using a first name pseudonym. Whenever last names appear in the text, they are names of real people.

TABLE 1: *Gender in the Interview Sample*

	ES Men	Women	ES Total	SA Men	Women	SA Total
Formal Interviews	36	7	43	36	7	43
Informal Interviews	14	3	17	10	2	12

TABLE 2: *Race in the South African Interview Sample*

	Black	Coloured	White	SA Total
Formal Interviews	20	6	16	43*
Informal Interviews	4	0	7	12**

* I interviewed one Asian American serving as a missionary.
** I interviewed one African American serving in economic development.

black evangelical leaders and entrepreneurs, six interviews with "coloureds," sixteen interviews with whites, and one interview with an Asian American missionary serving in the country. (The four primary race groups in South Africa are black, coulored, Asian, and white. These categories are a holdover from the apartheid system.) Of the informal interviews I conducted, seven were with white respondents, four were with blacks, and one was with an African American who worked in economic development in South Africa. I did not try to control for gender in my sample. In South Africa, I attempted to get a racially balanced sample by pursuing interviews on both sides of the racial divide. However, this was of secondary importance to gaining access to national evangelical leadership, which is represented by all racial categories. Tables 1 and 2 summarize the gender and racial breakdown of my sample, respectively.

To gain access to key evangelical leaders, I used personal contacts and networks that I had developed during my previous experiences in these countries. I clearly identified myself as a fellow evangelical when I introduced myself to my interviewees. My status as a co-religionist had a bearing on the kind of feedback I received during the interview; I received more "insider information" in the context of responses that were not sanitized by filters people often employ when speaking to others outside their faith communities. Some distance between the interviewee and the interviewer did exist, however, because of our different national identities. That is, my identity as an American academic may have been secondary to my identity as a co-religionist, but it certainly was not left outside the interview process.

Concern is sometimes voiced concerning how a researcher might treat and process the data collected from co-religionists. To address such concerns, let me mention that this project has been conducted in the midst of ongoing dialogue with other members of the mainstream academic community. I have taken seriously suggestions from other scholars concerning how to collect and analyze the data. Because sociology is fundamentally an interpretive enterprise (Wuthnow 1987), it is impossible to completely overcome the dynamic created by my religious identity. But all sociologists have individual identities that interact with their interpretive analysis. In this sense, we must all be attentive to such issues.

During the interviews, I employed a semi-structured interview strategy. Open-ended questions allowed me to explore a consistent set of topics with each interviewee. In each interview, we discussed the subject's personal testimony; church; religious beliefs; questions about the national evangelical community and the evangelical agenda; an exploration of the subjects' personal, professional, or religious networks (especially networks that cross borders); and an extended discussion of the organization the subject founded or leads. Formal interviews lasted between sixty and ninety minutes, with a few falling on either side of that range. Some interviews were conducted over a series of visits due to time constraints on given days. In most cases, I met subjects in their places of work, but sometimes the interviews were conducted in their homes or neutral sites, such as cafes.

To buttress information gained by interviews, I also engaged in participant observation. I attended a bevy of meetings at the national level, including those staged by the Evangelical Alliances, NGO networks, and national missionary networks. I also attended meetings for national business fraternities and went to seminars and devotionals hosted by specific evangelical NGOs. In addition to attending meetings, I read evangelical newspapers and periodicals and listened to evangelical radio and television broadcasts. Finally, I spent part of my time in both countries living in the houses of leaders who are recognized at the national level; this proved to be a particularly rich source of ethnographic data.

Congregations, both rich and poor, were a second important setting for participant observation. In addition to doing interviews at Iglesia Josue and Rhema, I also conducted participant observation in these churches. I also conducted participant observation among more economically humble environs. In El Salvador, I found this in the megachurch Elim;[3] in South Africa, I frequented a small group of churches located in marginalized communities around Johannesburg.[4] Within these churches, I attended Sunday and weekday services, gathered printed materials that were distributed by the churches, had tea or lunch with pastors, joined a small group, and attended men's breakfasts and a men's retreat. Also, I casually visited some of the other churches in the business classes of El Salvador and South Africa.

---

[3] Elim is discussed at length in Chapter 5.
[4] The two poor churches that I focused on most closely were part of the Church of God denomination. They were pastored by Zimbabwean immigrants, and Zimbabweans were well represented in their congregations.

I conducted the El Salvador research in 2006. Previous to my research, I lived in El Salvador for nearly three years, working professionally there. I also made return visits to the country in 2007, 2008, 2009, 2011, 2012, and 2013. Four more trips to El Salvador in 2014 helped to confirm the findings of this book. I had further trips to Nicaragua in 2010 and Costa Rica in 2007 and 2012, which were useful in developing a sense of regional comparison. I conducted follow-up e-mail messages and phone calls to a number of subjects while I was in the United States from 2006 to 2008. During the formal field research in 2006, I collected all of the data in the capital city, San Salvador, and except for interviews with missionaries or other English speakers, all of my communication was conducted in Spanish.

I conducted the South Africa research in the latter part of 2006. Previous to my research, I lived in South Africa for roughly eighteen months, also working professionally there and learning a great deal about the social context. In 2010 and 2011 I hosted a key informant from South Africa in the United States. In 2010, I visited East Africa and interfaced with a number of South African evangelicals there. I pursued follow-up e-mail messages and phone calls with South African subjects from 2006 to 2008 and again in 2013 to 2014. A trip to Southern Africa in 2014 also helped to confirm the findings in this book. My research in South Africa concentrated on the Johannesburg/Pretoria region, but interviews of national leaders and organizations took me to Cape Town for three interviews and to KwaZulu Natal for six interviews.[5] I conducted all communication in English.

Finally, I conducted a small amount of follow-up research with U.S.-based evangelicals and evangelical entities. First, I interviewed the vice president of governmental affairs for the National Association of Evangelicals in Washington, DC, to understand the global connectedness of the World Evangelical Alliance. I also conversed with a Salvadoran evangelical consul working in Washington. Second, I followed Elim's transnational ties up to its daughter church in Los Angeles, which I visited in August 2007. These U.S.-based activities were attempts to understand transnational ties as they pertained to the evangelical communities of El Salvador and South Africa.

---

[5] All field research, especially in Africa, has its humorous moments. During a particularly busy stretch, I drove six hours from Johannesburg to Pietermaritzburg for a Wednesday afternoon interview and flew back to Johannesburg for a Thursday morning interview. While I was there, I learned that the house where I was staying had been robbed that night. To address the concerns arising from the robbery, I missed my return flight to KwaZulu Natal in the early afternoon but caught the next flight out an hour and a half later, just in time for an interview in Durban that evening. Meanwhile, a church leader had strongly suggested I meet an entrepreneur back in Johannesburg Friday morning. So I slept for two hours at a pastor's house in Durban before driving six hours back to Johannesburg for an 8:00 am appointment. Unfortunately, there were two people with the same name in this leader's church, and I had been given the contact information of an unwed teenage mother in need of employment rather than the up and coming entrepreneur. After realizing what had happened, I gamely conducted an interview with her but did not include it in my sample.

Once I collected the data, I had it converted into text to analyze it. Eighty-five interviews had to be transcribed; almost half of those had to be translated. I had sufficient funding to contract out about half of this work; the other half I did myself. Once this considerable task was completed, I used Atlas.ti, a qualitative research software package, to do the analysis. I created 4,048 quotes and organized them into 156 codes. These original codes emerged inductively from the data. From there I created various families of codes, coding networks, and memos. Analysis of evangelical discourse was thus the central, but not the only, method of data analysis that I employed.

This study reflects both the strengths and weaknesses of my methodological strategies. Its strength is the ability to compare cases through qualitative sets of data. Its weaknesses include a general lack of quantitative data, the absence of an Asian case in the study, and the impossibility of providing "thick description" (Geertz 1973) of two entire national religious communities, even at the leadership level.

Appendix II

Institutions Represented in the Study

EL SALVADOR
CHURCHES & CHURCH DENOMINATIONS
Denominational Leaders

	Position(s) Interviewed
Assemblies of God	Regional Director
Central American Mission	Missionary

Churches

Assemblies of God – A Miracle Comes	Senior Pastor
Assemblies of God – Josué Church	Senior Pastor, Assistant Pastor
Camp of God Church	Bishop
Christian Community of Faith & Adoration	Senior Pastor
Church of the Nazarene – Madre Tierra	Senior Pastor
Elim Church	Senior Pastor, Zonal Pastor, Board Member
Family of Jesus Church	Senior Pastor
Baptist Tabernacle – Friends of Israel	Associate Pastor
Seventh Day Adventist Church – Merliot	Founder/Senior Pastor

PARA CHURCH ORGANIZATIONS
Networks or Movements

Channel 25 Pastors Network	Facilitator
Church Growth International (ELIM)	Board Member
El Salvador Missionary Network	Director
Evangelical Alliance	President, Vice President, two Ex-Presidents
Full Gospel Businessman's Association	Director
Latin American Theological Fraternity	Director
National Network of Pastors in El Salvador	Participant
Network for Integral Mission	Coordinator, four Participants
Rivers of Life Network (out of Argentina)	Participating Pastor

International NGOs or Mission Organizations

Campus Crusade for Christ	Ex-Director
Christian Reform World Mission	Missionary
Convoy of Hope	National Representative
Future Hope	Founder/Director
Operation Blessing	Ex-Director
Partners for Christian Development	Director
Samaritan's Purse	Evangelism Director
Walk Thru the Bible	Director
World Relief	Latin America Regional Director
World Vision	Coordinator, Board Member

Local NGOs & Ministries

A-Brazo	Founder/Director, Board Member, Employee
Amilat Orphanage	Two Co-Directors
Association Amiga	Ex-Director
ENLACE	Founder/Ex-Co-Director
MIES	President of Board, two Ex-Directors
Orphan Helpers	Assistant Director

Schools & Universities

Baptist Tabernacle Seminary	Dean
Evangelical University	Board Member
Josué Bible Institute	Teacher, Students
School for the Deaf	Founder/Ex-Director, Board Member

CHRISTIAN MEDIA OUTLETS

A Miracle Comes (TV/radio mini-show)	Producer
Josué Book Stores	Owner
La Hora de La Reforma (TV/radio show)	Director
TV Channel 25	Director

BUSINESSES

Alsesa (warehouse)	Founder, Owner
American Enterprise (export primary materials)	Founder, Owner
Compuayuda (computer store)	Founder, Manager
Escamillas & Co (house construction)	Founder, Manager
Evangelical & Other Universities	Law Professor
Exporcasa/SafeWrap (airport baggage wrap)	Co-Owner
Ferreteria (hardware store)	Founder, Manager
Furniture Company	Ex-Founder, Owner
Grupo Rayo (car battery distributer, car repair)	Owner, Manager
Jahevrafa (mechanical engineering)	Co-Founder, Co-Manager
Supreme Court	Alternate Judge
Tea Shop	Founder

Texaco gas stations	Owner
TV Channel 7	President
Universidad Technologica	Co-Founder, Rector
Valdivieso (repair/construction)	Founder, Owner
Vapegroup (health products)	Co-Founder, Co-Owner
Window Tinting Company	Owner in El Salvador

SOUTH AFRICA
CHURCHES & CHURCH DENOMINATIONS

Denominational Leaders	**Position(s) Interviewed**
Apostolic Faith Mission	Director
Assemblies of God	General Secretary
Baptist Union	General Secretary
New Covenant Ministries	Apostle
The Vineyard	Superintendent

Churches	
Church of God	Assistant Pastor
Cosmo City Church	Founder/Senior Pastor
Harvestime Evangelical Ministries	Founder/Senior Pastor
Life Transformation Church	Founder/Senior Pastor
Manning Road Methodist Church	Co-Pastor
Oasis of Life Family Church	Founder/Senior Pastor
Pietermaritzburg Central Baptist Church	Senior Pastor
Rhema Church	Two Assistant Pastors
Roodeport Baptist Church	Senior Pastor
Rosebank Union Church	Assistant Pastor, Organist
Uniting Reformed Church of Southern Africa	Senior Pastor

PARA CHURCH ORGANIZATIONS

Networks or Movements	
Christian Lawyers Association	Director
Lausanne Congress on World Evangelization	Director, Founder, Honorary Chair
The Evangelical Alliance of South Africa (TEASA)	Director, two Co-Founders
South African Council of Churches	Director
Southern African Missiological Society (SAMS)	General Secretary
Thank Goodness Its Friday	Two Speakers
Transformation Africa/Global Day of Prayer	Coordinator, Co-Patron
Willowcreek Association Network	Participant
World Evangelical Alliance	International Chair

International NGOs or Mission Organizations	
Billy Graham Association	Ex-Director
Campus Crusade for Christ	Ex-Employee
Focus on the Family South Africa	Ex-Director
OC International – Africa	Missionary
Promise Keepers	Ex-Director

Scripture Union	Ex-Director, Ex-Employee
Walk Thru the Bible	Regional Director, Country Director
Youth for Christ	Director

Local NGOs & Ministries

African Enterprise	International Team Leader, South Africa Team Leader
HOPE	Founder
I Can Foundation	Founder/Director
Inserve	Director
Rays of Hope	Director

Schools & Universities

His People Bible Institute	Co-Founder/Ex-Director
Rhema Bible Institute	Teacher, Students
UNISA Missiology Department	Chair
Unit for Religion & Development, Stellenbosch University	Director

CHRISTIAN MEDIA OUTLETS

Heartlines	Leadership Team Member
Rhema Television	Ex-Director
TVPC Media	Founder/Director

BUSINESSES

ACDP (political party)	Johannesburg Rep
Ashira & Shelton Law	Co-Owner
Commodities Trader	Co-Founder
Department of Labor	Political Consultant
Dimatha Phatso (car wash)	Founder
Ian Fuller Agencies (lumber)	Founder
I Can Group (incudes I Can Consulting and I Can Telecommunications)	Founder/Director
LGI Foods (health foods)	Founder
MAID (domestic services)	Founder
Mobilezine (telecommunications)	Founder
Opus Dei Advisory Services (law)	Co-Founder
Private Law Practice	Founder
Sandown Chamber of Commerce	Advocate
Soweto Tourism Association	Founder
Umbono Capital	CEO
Umzantsi Creative Marketing	Founder
UN, Beijing +5 Participant	Representative of South Africa
Vela International (investment firm)	Director
Vodacom (telecommunications)	Physician
Wisdom Keys Trust (advertising/media)	CEO
Wits, ICT (universities)	Professor

Bibliography

Acosta, Pablo. 2006. *Labor Supply, School Attendance, and Remittances from International Migration: The Case of El Salvador*. Washington, DC: World Bank, The World Bank Development Research Group Trade Team.

Adam, Heribert. 1996. *Comrades in Business: Post-Liberation Politics in South Africa*. Cape Town: Tafelberg Publishers Limited.

Adam, Heribert & Kogila Moodley. 1986. *South Africa without Apartheid: Dismantling Racial Discrimination*. Berkeley: University of California Press.

Allen, John L. 2006. "Evangelical Strength in Latin America is Homegrown." *National Catholic Reporter*. http://findarticles.com/p/articles/mi_m1141/is_37_42/ai_n16740715. Accessed February 2008.

Ammerman, Nancy T. 1982. "Operationalizing Evangelicalism: An Amendment." *Sociological Analysis* 43, no. 2 (Summer): 170–171.

———. 1994. "Accounting for Christian Fundamentalisms: Social Dynamics and Rhetorical Strategies." In *Accounting for Fundamentalisms*. Eds. Martin E. Marty & R. Scott Appleby. Chicago: University of Chicago Press, 149–172.

———. Ed. 2007. *Everyday Religion: Observing Modern Religious Lives*. New York: Oxford University Press.

———. 2008. "American Evangelicals in the Landscape of American Religion." Unpublished.

Amstutz, Mark. 2005. *The Healing of Nations: The Promise and Limits of Political Forgiveness*. New York: Rowman & Littlefield Publishers, Inc.

Anderson, Allan. 2004. *An Introduction to Pentecostalism*. New York: Cambridge University Press.

Anderson, Allan & Gerald Pillay. 1997. "The Segregated Spirit: Pentecostals." In *Christianity in South Africa: A Political, Cultural, and Social History*. Eds. Richard Elphik & Rodney Davenport. Oxford: J. Curry, 227–241.

Anderson, Thomas P. 1992. *Matanza: The 1932 Slaughter That Traumatized a Nation, Shaping US-Salvadoran Policy to This Day*. Second Edition. Willimantic, CT: Curbstone Press.

Appadurai, Arjun. 1996. *Modernity at Large: Cultural Dimensions of Globalization*. Minneapolis: University of Minnesota Press.

Ayala, Benjamin. 2008. Contra Punto – El Salvador – Edicia "N100: del 16 al 22 de Febrero de 2008." *Contra Punto – El Salvador.* http://archivo.contrapunto.com.sv. Accessed May 4, 2012.

Baker-Cristales, Beth. 2004. *Salvadoran Migration and Southern California.* Gainesville: University Press of Florida.

Balcomb, Anthony. 2001. "Evangelicals and Democracy in South Africa: Another Look, Another Method." *Journal of Theology for Southern Africa* (March): 109–129.

—. 2007. "From Apartheid to the New Dispensation: Evangelicals and the Democratization of South Africa." In *Evangelical Christianity and Democracy in Africa.* Ed. Terence O. Ranger. Series Ed. Timothy Samuel Shah. Oxford: Oxford University Press, 191–224.

Bastian, Jean-Pierre. 1983. *Protestantismo y sociedad en México.* Mexico City: Casa Unida de Publicaciones.

—. 1986. *Breve historia del protestantismo en América latina.* Mexico City: Casa Unida de Publicaciones.

Bebbington, David. W. 1989. *Evangelicalism in Modern Britain: A History from the 1730s to the 1980s.* Boston: Unwin Hyman.

Becker, Howard S. 1973. *Outsiders: Studies in the Sociology of Deviance.* New York: The Free Press.

Bediako, Kwame. 1995. *Christianity in Africa: The Renewal of a Non-Western Religion.* Edinburgh: Edinburgh University Press, and Maryknoll, NY: Orbis.

Bellah, Robert. 1970. *Beyond Belief: Essays on Religion in a Post-Traditional World.* New York: Harper & Row.

Bender, Courtney. 2003. *Heaven's Kitchen: Living Religion at God's Love We Deliver.* Chicago: University of Chicago Press.

Benford, Robert D. & David Snow. 2000. "Framing Processes and Social Movements: An Overview and Assessment." *Annual Review of Sociology* 26: 611–639.

Berger, Brigitte. Ed. 1991. *The Culture of Entrepreneurship.* San Francisco: ICS Press.

Berger, Peter L. 1967. *The Sacred Canopy.* Garden City, New York: Anchor Doubleday.

Berger, Peter L. & Bobby Godsell. Eds. 1988. *A Future South Africa: Visions, Strategies, and Realities.* Boulder, CO: Westview Press.

Berger, Peter & Thomas Luckmann. 1966. *The Social Construction of Reality: A Treatise in the Sociology of Knowledge.* New York: Doubleday.

Berryman, Phillip. 1984. *The Religious Roots of Rebellion: Christians in Central American Revolutions.* Maryknoll, NY: Orbis Books.

—. 1999. "Churches as Winners and Losers in the Network Society." *Journal of InterAmerican Studies and World Affairs* 41, no. 4 (Winter): 21–34.

The Holy Bible, New International Version. 1984. Copyright by International Bible Society. Grand Rapids, MI: Zondervan.

Binford, Leigh. 1996. *The El Mozote Massacre: Anthropology and Human Rights.* Tucson: The University of Arizona Press.

Boli, John & George M. Thomas. 1999. *Constructing World Culture: International Non-Governmental Organizations since 1875.* Stanford: Stanford University Press.

Booth, John. 1991. "Socioeconomic and Political Roots of National Revolts in Central America." *Latin American Research Review* 26: 33–74.

Bouillon, Antoine. 2001. "Francophone African Migrants in South Africa: A Broad Overview." In *African Immigration to South Africa: Francophone Migration of the 1990s.* Eds. Alan Morris & Antoine Boillon. Pretoria: Protea & IFAS, 112–149.

Bowen, Kurt. 1996. *Evangelism and Apostacy: The Evolution and Impact of Evangelicals in Modern Mexico.* Buffalo: McGill-Queen's University Press.

Bowler, Kate. 2013. *Blessed: A History of the American Prosperity Gospel.* New York: Oxford University Press.

Brenneman, Robert E. 2012. *Homies and Hermanos: God and Gangs in Central America.* New York: Oxford University Press.

Brignoli, Hector & Yolando Martinez. 1983. "Growth and Crisis in the Central American Economies, 1950–1980." *Journal of Latin American Studies* 15, no. 2: 365–396.

Brockett, Charles. 1990. *Land, Power, and Poverty.* Boulder, CO: Westview Press.

——. 2005. *Political Movements and Violence in Central America.* Cambridge: Cambridge University Press.

Brouwer, Steve, Paul Gifford, & Susan D. Rose. 1996. *Exporting the American Gospel: Global Christian Fundamentalism.* New York: Routledge.

Browning, David. 1971. *El Salvador: Landscape and Society.* Oxford: Clarendon Press.

Brusco, Elizabeth. 1986. "Colombian Evangelicalism as a Strategic Form of Women's Collective Action." *Feminist Issues* 6, no. 2: 3–13.

Bueno, Ronald. 2007. "White Paper: The Church as Effective Agent of Community Transformation." Presented at the Compassion Forum 2007.

Burdick, John. 1993. *Looking for God in Brazil: The Progressive Catholic Church in Urban Brazil's Religious Arena.* Berkeley: University of California.

Burgerman, Susan. 2006. "Making Peace Perform in War-Transition Countries: El Salvador, Guatemala, and Nicaragua." In *Short of the Goal: U.S. Policy and Poorly Performing States.* Eds. Nancy Birdsall, Milan Vaishnav, & Robert L. Ayres. Washington, DC: Center for Global Development, 245–284.

Bushnell, David & Neill Macauley. 1994. *The Emergence of Latin America in the Nineteenth Century.* New York: Oxford University Press.

Cadge, Wendy & Elaine Howard Ecklund. 2007. "Immigration and Religion." *Annual Review of Sociology* 33: 335–357.

Cardenal, Rodolfo. 1990. "The Martyrdom of the Salvadorean Church." In *The Church and Politics in Latin America.* Ed. Dermot Keogh. New York: St. Martin's Press, 225–246.

Carpenter, Joel. 2005. "Preface." In *The Changing Face of Christianity: Africa, the West, and the World.* Eds. Lamin Sanneh & Joel Carpenter. Oxford: Oxford University Press, vii–ix.

Carrol, Glenn & Michael T. Hannan. 2000. "Density-Dependent Processes I." In *The Demography of Corporations and Industries.* Eds. Glenn Carrol & Michael Hannan. Princeton: Princeton University Press, 213–238.

Cassidy, Michael. 1989. *The Passing Summer: A South African's Response to White Fear, Black Anger, and the Politics of Love.* Ventura: Regal Books/African Enterprise.

Castells, Manuel. 1996. *The Rise of the Network Society.* Cambridge: Blackwell Publishers.

Central Reserve Bank of El Salvador. 2014. "US $3.9691 millones recibio el pais en remesas familiars durante 2013." Published January 15, 2014. www.bcr.gob.sv. Accessed February 17, 2014.

Chesnut, R. Andrew. 1997. *Born Again in Brazil: The Pentecostal Boom and the Pathogens of Poverty.* New Brunswick: Rutgers University Press.

CIA World Factbook. 2011. "Central Intelligence Agency of the United States of America." https://www.cia.gov/library/publications/the-world-factbook/fields/2011.html. Accessed May 3, 2012.

Cnaan, Ram A. 2002. *The Invisible Caring Hand: American Congregations and the Provision of Welfare*. New York: New York University Press.

Coleman, Kenneth, Edwin Eloy Aguilar, José Miguel Sandoval, & Timothy Steigenga. 1993. "Protestantism in El Salvador: Conventional Wisdom versus the Survey Evidence." In *Rethinking Protestantism in Latin America*. Eds. Virginia Garrard-Burnett & David Stoll. Philadelphia: Temple University, 111–142.

Coleman, Simon. 2000. *Globalisation of Charismatic Christianity: Spreading the Gospel of Prosperity*. New York: Cambridge University Press.

Comaroff, Jean. 1985. *Body of Power Spirit of Resistance*. Chicago: University of Chicago Press.

Comisíon Nacional del Centenario. 1996. *Cien Anos de Presencia Evangelica en El Salvador*. San Salvador: Confraternidad Evangélica Salvadorena (CONESAL).

Comiskey, Joel. 2003. *Passion & Persistence*. Houston: Cell Group Resources.

Compassion International. 2013. "Annual Report: Honoring our Legacy: Advancing Our Call." http://www.compassionmedia.com/pdf/compassion-international-2013-annual-report.pdf.

"Country Corruption Assessment Report: South Africa." 2003. Cape Town: Government of South Africa & United Nations Office on Drugs and Crime – Regional Office for Southern Africa. http://www.westerncape.gov.za/text/2004/4/sacorruptionassessmentreport2003.pdf

Coutin, Susan Bibler. 2007. *Nations of Emigrants: Shifting Boundaries of Citizenship in El Salvador and the United States*. Ithaca: Cornell University Press.

Crush, Jonathan & David A. McDonald. 2000. "Introduction." *Canadian Journal of African Studies / Revue Canadienne des Études Africaines* 34, no. 1, Special Issue: Transnationalism, African Immigration, and New Migrant Spaces in South Africa: 1–19.

Crush, Jonathan, Eugene Campbell, Thuso Green, Selma Nangulah, & Hamilton Simelane. 2006. *States of Vulnerability*. Southern African Migration Project. Cape Town: Idasa.

Crush, Jonathan, Vincent Williams, & Sally Peberdy. 2005. *Migration in Southern Africa: A Paper Prepared for the Policy Analysis and Research Programme of the Global Commission of International Migration*. Geneva: Global Commission on International Migration.

Csordas, Thomas J. 1997. *Language, Charisma, and Creativity: The Ritual Life of a Religious Movement*. Berkeley: University of California.

Danielson, Robert. 2013. "Independent Indigenous Protestant MegaChurches in El Salvador." *Missiology: An International Review* 41, no. 3: 329–342.

Deflem, Mathieu. 1999. "Warfare, Political Leadership, and State Formation: The Case of the Zulu Kingdom. 1808–1879." *Ethnology* 38, no. 4 (Autumn): 371–391.

De Gruchy, John. 1990. "The Church and the Struggle for a Democratic South Africa." In *Christianity Amidst Apartheid: Selected Perspectives on the Church in South Africa*. Ed. Martin Prozesky. New York: St. Martin's Press, 219–232.

DGACE. http://www.rree.gob.sv/sitio/sitiowebrree.nsf/pages/ssalvext_dgace. Accessed November 2007.

Diani, Mario. 2003. "Introduction: Social Movements, Contentious Actions, and Social Networks: 'From Metaphor to Substance?'" In *Social Movements and Networks: Relational Approaches to Collective Action*. Eds. Mario Diani & Doug McAdam. New York: Oxford University Press, 1–18.

Dickson-Gomez. 2002. "The Sound of Barking Dogs: Violence and Terror Among Salvadoran Families in the Postwar." *Medical Anthropology Quarterly* 16, no. 4: 415–438.

DiMaggio, Paul. 1988. "Interest and Agency in Institutional Theory." In *Institutional Patterns and Organizations: Culture and Environment*. Ed. L. G. Zucker. Cambridge: Ballinger Publishing Co., 3–21.

——. 1991. "Constructing an Organizational Field as a Professional Project: U.S. Art Museums, 1920–1940." In *The New Institutionalism in Organizational Analysis*. Eds. Walter W. Powell & Paul J. DiMaggio. Chicago: University of Chicago Press, 267–292.

Douglas, Mary. 1973. *Natural Symbols: Explorations in Cosmology*. London: Barrie and Jenkins.

Duarte, Jose Napoleon & Diana Page. 1986. *Duarte: My Story*. New York: G.P. Putnam's Sons.

Ebaugh, Helen Rose & Janet Saltzman Chafetz. 2002. *Religion across Borders: Transnational Immigrant Networks*. Walnut Creek, CA: AltaMira Press.

Economic Intelligence Unit. 2008a. "El Salvador Country Report." http://store.eiu.com/product/50000205SV.html?ref=featuredProductHome. Accessed March 2008.

——. 2008b. "South Africa Country Report." http://store.eiu.com/product/50000205ZA.html?ref=featuredProductHome. Accessed May 2008.

——. 2011a. "El Salvador Country Report." http://store.eiu.com/product/50000205SV.html?ref=featuredProductHome. Accessed March 2012.

——. 2011b. "South Africa Country Report." http://store.eiu.com/product/50000205ZA.html?ref=featuredProductHome. Accessed March 2012.

The Economist. 2012a. "Disappointment." January 14, 2012. http://www.economist.com/node/21542798. Accessed May 4, 2012.

——. 2012b. "Still Dysfunctional." January 21, 2012. http://www.economist.com/node/21543214. Accessed May 2012.

——. 2013a. "El Salvador's Gangs: The Year of Living Less Dangerously." March 9, 2013. iPhone Edition.

——. 2013b. "The African National Congress: A Sad and Sorry Decline." June 29, 2013. iPhone Edition.

——. 2014. "El Salvador's Gangs: Breaking Good." February 8, 2014, 35.

Ellis, Stephen & Gerrie ter Haar. 2004. *Worlds of Power: Religious Thought and Political Practice in Africa*. New York: Oxford University Press.

Elphick, Richard & Rodney Davenport. Eds. 1997. *Christianity in South Africa: A Political, Social, and Cultural History*. Berkeley: University of California Press.

Emirbayer, Mustafa. 1997. "Manifesto for a Relational Sociology." *American Journal of Sociology* 103: 281–317.

Erasmus, Johannes, Gerbrand Mans & Cindy Jacobs. 2006. "Transformation Africa: Pray and Work – The Role of Research." In *South African Christian Handbook*. Ed. Johann Symington. Wellington: Tydskriftemaatskappy van die NG Kerk.

Escobar, Cristina. 2007. "Extraterritorial Political Rights and Dual Citizenship in Latin America." *Latin American Research Review* 42, no. 3: 44–75.

Fields, Karen E. 1985. *Revival and Rebellion in Colonial Central Africa*. Princeton: Princeton University Press.

Finke, Roger & Rodney Stark. 1998. "Religious Choice and Competition." *American Sociological Review* 63, no. 5 (October): 761–766.

Folarin, George O. 2006. "The Prosperity Gospel in Nigeria: A Re-Examination of the Concept, Its Impact, and an Evaluation." Presented at the Conference of Theological Education held from March 8 to 10, 2006, at the Nigeria Baptist Theological Seminary, Ogbomoso, Nigeria. http://www.pctii.org/cyberj/. Accessed June 2007.

Goyal, Malini. 2010. "Black Diamonds." *Forbes.* http://www.forbes.com\2010\06\21\forbes-india-black-diamonds-middle-class-spending.html. Accessed May 4, 2012.

Forum of Young Global Leaders. 2012.World Economic Forum. http://www.weforum.org/community/forum-young-global-leaders. Accessed May 3, 2012.

Fredrickson, George M. 1997. *The Comparative Imagination: On the History of Racism, Nationalism, and Social Movements.* Berkeley: University of California Press.

Freeman, Richard B. 2006. "People Flows in Globalization." *Journal of Economic Perspectives* 20:145–170.

Frere, Bartle. 1889. "Historical Sketch of South Africa." *Transactions of the Royal Historical Society*, New Series 4: 221–284.

Freston, Paul. 2001. *Evangelicals in Politics in Asia, Africa, and Latin America.* Cambridge: Cambridge University Press.

——. Ed. 2008. *Evangelical Christianity and Democracy in Latin America.* The Evangelical Christianity and Democracy in the Global South Series. Series Ed. Timothy Shah. Oxford: Oxford University Press.

Galaskiewicz, Joseph, & Wolfgang Bielefeld. 1998. *Nonprofit Organizations in an Age of Uncertainty: A Study of Organizational Change.* New York: A. de Gruyter.

Garson, David G. http://www2.chass.ncsu.edu/garson/pa765/links.htm. North Carolina State University. Accessed March 2005.

Gastrow, Peter. 1995. *Bargaining for Peace: South Africa and the National Peace Accord.* Washington, DC: U.S. Institute of Peace.

Geertz, Clifford. 1973. "Religion as a Cultural System." In *The Interpretation of Cultures.* New York: Basic Books, 87–125.

Gifford, Paul. 2004. *Ghana's New Christianity: Pentecostalism in a Globalising African Economy.* London: Hurst & Company.

Gill, Anthony. 1998. *Rendering Unto Ceasar: The Catholic Church and the State in Latin America.* Chicago: The University of Chicago Press.

Glick Schiller, Nina, Linda Basch, & Cristina Blanc-Szanton. Eds. 1992. *Towards a Transnational Perspective on Migration: Race, Class, Ethnicity, and Nationalism Reconsidered.* Annals of the New York Academy of Sciences, Vol. 645. New York: New York Academy of Sciences.

Global Policy Network. 2005. "Economic Development and the Labor Market in El Salvador, 2004–2005." San Salvador: Fundacion Nacional para el Desarollo Area Macroeconomia y Desarrollo. www.gpn.org. Accessed May 2008.

Godsell, Gillian. 1991. "Entrepreneurs Embattled: Barriers to Entrepreneurship in South Africa. In *The Culture of Entrepreneurship*. Ed. Brigitte Berger. San Francisco: ICS Press, 85–98.

Gomez, Ileana & Manual Vaszuez. 2001. "Youth Gangs and Relgion in Washington and El Salvador." In *Christianity, Social Change, and Globalization.* New Brunswick: Rutgers University Press, 165–187.

Goodell, Grace. 1999. "Entrepreneurs in the Asian Tigers." Lunch bag series, Department of Social Change & Development. SAIS-Johns Hopkins University.

Goodman, David. 1999. *Fault Lines: Journeys into the New South Africa.* Berkeley: University of California Press.

Gooren, Henri. 1999. *Rich among the Poor: Church, Firm, and Household among Small-Scale Entrepreneurs in Guatemala City.* Amsterdam: Thela.

Granovetter, M. 1985. "Economic-Action and Social-Structure – the Problem of Embeddedness." *American Journal of Sociology* 91: 481–510.

Hagopian, Frances. 2009. "Social Justice, Moral Values, or Institutional Interests?" In *Religious Pluralism, Democracy, and the Catholic Church in Latin America.* Ed. Frances Hagopian. Notre Dame: University of Notre Dame Press, 257–331.

Hallum, Anne Motley. 1996. *Beyond Missionaries: Toward an Understanding of the Protestant Movement in Central America.* Lanham, MD: Rowman & Littlefield Publishers, Inc.

Hamilton, Carolyn Ann. 1992. "The Character and Objects of Chaka: A Reconsideration of Shaka as 'Mfecane' Motor. *The Journal of African History* 33, no. 1: 37–63.

Hannerz, Ulf. 1996. *Transnational Connections: Culture, People, Places.* New York: Routledge.

Harrison, David. 1981. *The White Tribe of Africa: South Africa in Perspective.* Berkeley: University of Berkeley Press.

Harrison, Milmon F. 2005. *Righteous Riches: The Word of Faith Movement in Contemporary African American Religion.* Cambridge: Oxford University Press.

Hendriks, Jurgens. 2006. "Census 2001: Religion in South Africa with Denominational Trends 1911–2001." In *The South African Christian Handbook.* Ed. Johann Symington. Wellington: Tydskriftemaatskappy van die NG Kerk, 27–84.

Hernandez, Ester & Susan Coutin. 2006. "Remitting Subjects: Migrants, Money and States." *Economy & Society* 35, no. 2: 185–208.

Hexham, Irving & Karla Poewe. 1997. "The Spread of Christianity among Whites and Blacks in Transorangia." Eds. Richard Elphik & Rodney Davenport. *Christianity in South Africa: A Political, Social & Cultural History.* Oxford: James Curry.

Hildreth, Ann. 1994. "The Importance of Purposes in 'Purposive' Groups: Incentives and Participation in the Sanctuary Movement." *American Journal of Political Science* 38, no. 2: 447–463.

Holland, Alisha C. 2008. Senior Thesis. Woodrow Wilson School, Princeton University. Unpublished.

——. 2013. "Right on Crime? Conservative Party Politics and Mano Dura Policies in El Salvador." *Latin American Research Review* 48, no. 1: 44–67.

Hsu, Becky, Amy Reynolds, Conrad Hackett, & James Gibbon. 2008. "Estimating the Religious Composition of All Nations: An Empirical Assessment of the World Christian Database." *Journal for the Scientific Study of Religion* 47, no. 4: 678–693.

Hunter, James Davison. 1982. "Operationalizing evangelicalism: A review, critique and proposal." *Sociological Analysis* 42: 363–372.

Hussein, Solomon. 2003. *Of Myths and Migration: Illegal Immigration into South Africa.* Pretoria: University of South Africa.

Index Mundi Country Facts. 2009. Index Mundi. http://www.indexmundi.com/facts/el-salvador/income-distribution. Accessed May 3, 2012.

India National Census. 2011. http://censusindia.gov.in/. Accessed July 2013.

Instituto Universitario de Opinión Pública Encuesta de Evaluación. 2009. IUDOP El Salvador. http://www.uca.edu.sv/publica/iudop/Web/2009/boletinrel_2009.pdf. Accessed May 3, 2012.

Jenkins, Philip. 2002. *The Next Christendom: the Coming of Global Christianity.* Oxford: Oxford University Press.

——. 2006. *The New Faces of Christianity: Believing in the Bible in the Global South.* Oxford: Oxford University Press.

Johnson, Scott. 2009. "Fleeing from South Africa." *The Daily Beast.* February 13. <http://www.thedailybeast.com/newsweek/2009/02/13/fleeing-from-south-africa.html>. Accessed May 4, 2012.

Johnson, Todd. Ed. *World Christian Database.* Leiden/Boston: Brill. Accessed February 2014.

Johnson, Todd & Kenneth Ross. Eds. 2009. *Atlas of Global Christianity.* Edinburgh: Ediinburgh University Press.

Juhn, Tricia. 1998. *Negotiating Peace in El Salvador: Civil-Military Relations and the Conspiracy to End the War.* New York: St. Martin's Press.

Kalberg, Stephen. 2002. "Introduction to *The Protestant Ethic.*" In *The Protestant Ethic & The Spirit of Capitalism.* By Max Weber. Translated by Stephen Kalberg. Los Angeles: Roxbury Publishing Company, xi–lxxvi.

Kellner, Douglas. 2002. "Theorizing Globalization." *Sociological Theory* 20: 285–305.

Kincaid, A. Douglas. 1993. "Peasants into Rebels: Community and Class in Rural El Salvador." In *Constructing Culture and Power in Latin America.* Ed. Daniel H. Levine. Ann Arbor: University of Michigan Press, 119–154.

Kuyper, Abraham. Center for Public Theology. http://libweb.ptsem.edu/collections/kuyper/Default.aspx?menu=298&subText=470. Accessed December 2007.

Lancaster, Roger. 1988. *Thanks to God and the Revolution: Popular Religion and Class Consciousness in the New Nicaragua.* New York: Columbia University Press.

Landolt, Patricia, Lilian Autler, & Sonia Baires. 1999. "From Hermano Lejano to Hermano Mayor: The Dialectics of Salvadoran Transnationalism." *Ethnic and Racial Studies* 22, no. 2: 290–315.

Landolt, Patricia & Wei Wei Da. 2005. "The Spatially Ruptured Practices of Migrant Families: A Comparison of Immigrants from El Salvador and the People's Republic of China." *Current Sociology* 53, no. 4: 625–653.

Levine, Daniel H. & David Stoll. 1997. "Bridging the Gap Between Empowerment and Power in Latin America." In *Transnational Religion and Fading States.* Ed. Susanne Hoeber Rudolph & James Piscatori. Boulder: Westview Press, 63–104.

Levitt, Peggy. 1998. "Local-Level Global Religion: The Case of U.S.-Dominican Migration." *Journal of the Scientific Study of Religion* 37, no. 3 (September): 74–89.

——. 2001. *The Transnational Villagers.* Berkeley and Los Angeles: University of California Press.

——. 2004. "Redefining the Boundaries of Belonging: The Institutional Character of Transnational Religious Life." *Sociology of Religion* 65, no. 1 (Spring): 1–18.

——. 2007. *God Needs No Passport: Immigrants and the Changing American Religious Landscape.* New York: New Press: Distributed by W. W. Norton & Company.

Lindenberg, Marc & Coralie Bryant. 2001. *Going Global: Transforming Relief and Development NGOs.* Bloomfield, CT: Kumarian.

Lindo-Fuentes, Hector, Erik Ching, & Rafael A. Lara-Martinez. 2007. *Remembering a Massacre in El Salvador: The Insurrection of 1932, Roque Dalton, and the Politics of Historical Memory.* Albequerque: University of New Mexico Press.

Louw, P. Eric. 2004. *The Rise, Fall, and Legacy of Apartheid.* Westport, CT: Praeger.

Lungo Ucles, Mario. 1996. *El Salvador in the Eighties. Counterinsurgency and Revolution.* Philadelphia: Temple University Press.

MacLean, John. 1987. *Prolonging the Agony: The Human Cost of Low Intensity Warfare in El Salvador.* London: El Salvador Committee for Human Rights.

MacLeod, Lisa. 2006. *Constructing Peace: Lessons from UN Peacebuilding Operations in El Salvador and Cambodia.* Lanham, MD: Lexington Books.

MacLeod, Murdo. 1973. *Spanish Central America: A Socioeconomic History, 1520–1720.* Berkeley: University of California Press.

Mahler, Sarah J. 1995. *Salvadorans in Suburbia: Symbiosis and Conflict.* Boston: Allyn and Bacon.

——. 1999. "Engendering Transnational Migration: A Case Study of Salvadorans." *American Behavioral Scientist* 42, no. 4: 690–719.

Mandryk, Jason. 2010. *Operation World: The Definitive Prayer Guide to Every Nation.* Seventh Edition. Colorado Springs: Biblica.

Marais, Hein. 2001. *South Africa: Limits to Change: The Political Economy of Transition.* New York: Zed Books Ltd.

Mariz, Cecília Loreto. 1994. *Coping with Poverty: Pentecostals and Christian Base Communities in Brazil.* Philadelphia: Temple University Press.

Marshall-Fratani, Ruth. 2001. "Mediating the Local and Global in Nigerian Pentecostalism." In *Between Babel and Pentecost: Transnational Pentecostalism in Africa and Latin America.* Eds. André Corten & Ruth Marshall-Fratani. Bloomington: Indiana University Press, 80–105.

Martin, Bernice. 2011. "Interpretations of Latin American Pentecostalism." In *Pentecostal Power: Expressions, Impact and Faith of Latin American Pentecostalism.* Ed. Calvin L. Smith. Boston: Brill, 111–136.

Martin, David. 1990. *Tongues of Fire: The Explosion of Protestantism in Latin America.* Oxford: Basil Blackwell.

——. 1991. "The Economic Fruits of the Spirit." In *The Culture of Entrepreneurship.* Ed. Brigitte Berger. San Francisco: ICS Press, 73–85.

——. 2002. *Pentecostalism: The World Their Parish.* Oxford: Blackwell.

Marx, Anthony. 1998. *Making Race and Nation: A Comparison of the United States, South Africa, and Brazil.* New York: Cambridge University Press.

Massey, Douglas. 2007. Panelist in "Debating Immigration." Forum at Woodrow Wilson School, Princeton University. October 3, 2007.

Maxwell, David. 1999. *Christians and Chiefs in Zimbabwe.* Edinburgh: Edinburgh University Press.

Maxwell, John C. 1998. *The 21 Irrefutable Laws of Leadership: Follow Them and They Will Follow You.* Nashville: Thomas Nelson, Inc.

Menjivar, Cecilia. 2000. *Fragmented Ties: Salvadoran Immigrant Networks in America.* Berkeley: University of California Press.

——. 2003. "Religion and Immigration in Comparative Perspective: Catholic and Evangelical Salvadorans in San Francisco, Washington, D.C., and Phoenix." *Sociology of Religion* 64, no. 1 (Spring): 21–45.

Meyer, Birgit. 1998. "Commodities and the Power of Prayer: Pentecostalist Attitudes Towards Consumption in Contemporary Ghana." *Development and Change* 29: 751–776.

Meyer, John & Brian Rowan. 1977. "Institutionalized Organizations – Formal Structure as Myth and Ceremony." *American Journal of Sociology* 83: 340–363.

Miller, Donald E. & Tetsunao Yamamori. 2007. *Global Pentecostalism: The New Face of Christian Social Engagement.* Berkeley: University of California Press.

Miller, Roberta Balstad. 1993. "Science and Society in the Early Career of H.F. Verwoerd." *Journal of Southern African Studies* 19, no. 4 (December): 634–661.

Minimum Wage Rates and Resources. Minimum-Wage.org. http://www.minimum-wage. org/. Accessed May 3, 2012.

Mische, Ann. 2003. "Cross-Talk in Movements: Reconceiving the Culture-Network Link." In *Social Movements and Networks: Relational Approaches in Collective Action.* Eds. Mario Diani & Doug McAdam. New York: Oxford University Press, 258–280.

Moakley, Joe. 1990. *Congressional Record*, May 22, 1990, H2712.

Montgomery, Tommie Sue. 1995. *Revolution in El Salvador: From Civil Strife to Civil Peace.* Boulder: Westview Press.

Mora, G. Cristina. 2008. "Latino Immigrant Educational Success: A Response to the No Margin for Error Report." *Annals of the American Academy of Political and Social Sciences* 620: 295–298.

Moroni Bracamonte, Jose Angel & David E. Spancer. 1994. *Strategy and Tactics of the Salvadoran FMLN Guerrillas.* Westport, CT: Praeger.

National Labor Committee, Columbia University. "U.S. Apparel Companies Hide Starvation Wages Behind Local Minimum Wage Hoax." http://www.nlcnet.org. Accessed February 2008.

Niebuhr, H. Richard. [1929] 1957. *The Social Sources of Denominationalism.* New York: The World Publishing Company.

Noll, Mark. 2002. "The American Contribution to World-Wide Evangelical Christianity in the Twentieth Century." Paper presented at International Conference on Evangelical Protestantism, Groupe de Sociologie des Religions et de la Laicite, Paris.

———. 2009. *The New Shape of Global Christianity: How American Experience Reflects Global Faith.* Downers Grove, IL: IVP Academic.

Nthla, Moss. 2005a. "Our Ten Year Journey: TEASA, a Miracle Transition." In *Looking Back, Moving Forward: Reflections by South Africans.* Eds. Louise Kretzschmar & Moss Ntlha. Johannesburg: Evangelical Alliance of South Africa, 10–18.

———. 2005b. "Evangelicals: Who Do They Think They Are?" In *Looking Back, Moving Forward: Reflections by South African Evangelicals.* Eds. Louise Kretzschmar & Moss Ntlha. Johannesburg: The Evangelical Alliance of South Africa, 19–31.

Nurnberger, Klaus. 1990. "The Impact of Christianity on Socio-Economic Developments in South Africa." In *Christianity Amidst Apartheid: Selected Perspectives on the Church in South Africa.* Ed. Martin Prozesky. New York: St. Martin's Press.

Offutt, Stephen. December 2011. "The Role of Short-Term Mission Teams in the New Centers of Global Christianity." *Journal for the Social Scientific Study of Religion* 50, no. 4, 796–811.

Opp, Karl-Dieter & Christiane Gern. 1993. "Dissident Groups, Personal Networks, and Spontaneous Cooperation: The East German Revolution of 1989." *American Sociological Review* 58, no. 5 (October): 659–680.

Osa, Maryjane. 2003. "Networks in Opposition: Linking Organizations Through Activists in the Polish People's Republic." In *Social Movements and Networks: Relational Approaches in Collective Action.* Eds. Mario Diani & Doug McAdam. New York: Oxford University Press, 77–104.

Oucho, John. 2006. "Cross-Border Migration and Regional Initiatives in Managing Migration in Southern Africa." In *Migration in South and Southern Africa:*

Dynamics and Determinants. Eds. Pieter Kok, Derik Gelderblom, John Oucho, & Johan Van Zyl. Cape Town: HSRC Press.

Parsons, Talcott. 1964. "Religion and Modern Industrial Society." In *Religion, Culture, and Society: A Reader in the Sociology of Religion.* Ed. Louis Schneider. New York: Wiley.

Pederson, David. 2013. *Migrants, Money and Meaning in El Salvador and the United States.* Chicago: University of Chicago Press.

Pendergast, Mark. 1999. *Uncommon Grounds.* New York: Basic Books.

Perez Brignoli, Hector. 1995. "Indians, Communists, and Peasants: The 1932 Rebellion in El Salvador." In *Coffee, Society, and Power in Latin America.* Eds. William Roseberry, Lowell Gudmundson, & Mario Samper Kutschbach. Baltimore: Johns Hopkins University Press, 232–261.

Peterson, Anna L. 1997. *Martyrdom and the Politics of Religion: Progressive Catholicism in El Salvador's Civil War.* Albany: State University Press of New York.

Pew Forum on Religion & Public Life. 2011. "A Report on the Size and Distribution of the World's Christian Population." www.pewforum.org. Accessed May 6, 2013.

Pew Forum on Religion & Public Life. 2006. *Spirit and Power: A 10-Country Survey of Pentecostals.* A Project of the Pew Research Center. www.pewforum.org. Accessed April 12, 2008.

Popkin, Margaret. 2000. *Peace Without Justice: Obstacles to Building the Rule of Law in El Salvador.* University Park: Pennsylvania State University Press.

Portes, A. & Rumbaut, R. 1996. *Immigrant America: A Portrait.* Berkeley: University of California Press.

Powell, Walter. 1990. "Neither Market nor Hierarchy: Network Forms of Organization." *Research in Organizational Behavior* 12: 295–336.

Priest, Robert. 2007. "Peruvian Churches Acquire 'Linking Social Capital' Through STM Partnerships." *Journal of the Latin American Theological Fraternity* 2, no. 2: 175–189.

Priest, Robert, Douglas Wilson, & Adelle Johnson. 2010. "U.S. Megachurches and New Patterns of Global Mission." *International Bulletin of Missionary Research* 34, no. 2: 97–104.

Quebedeaux, Richard. 1974. *The Young Evangelicals.* New York: Harper and Row.

Quispe-Agnoli, Myriam & Elena Whisler. 2006. "Official Dollarization and the Banking System in Ecuador and El Salvador." *Economic Review.* Third Quarter 2006. Federal Reserve Bank of Atlanta.

Reisman, Lainie. 2006. "Breaking the Vicious Cycle: Responding to Central American Youth Gang Violence." *SAIS Review* 26, no. 2 (Summer-Fall): 147–152.

Reynolds, Amy & Stephen Offutt. 2014. "Global Poverty and Evangelical Action." In *The New Evangelical Social Engagement.* Eds. Brian Steensland & Philip Goff. New York: Oxford University Press.

Richardson, Peter & Jean Jacques Van-Helten. 1984. "The Development of the South African Gold-Mining Industry, 1895–1918." *The Economic History Review.* New Series 37, no. 3 (August): 319–340.

Rodriguez, Ana Patricia. 2005. "Departamento 15: Cultural Narratives of Salvadoran Transnational Migration." *Latin Studies* 3: 19–41.

Roth, Guenther & Claus Wittich. 1978. "Introduction." In *Economy and Society: An Outline of Interpretive Sociology.* By Max Weber. Eds. Guenther Roth & Claus Wittich. Berkeley: University of California Press, xxxiii–cx.

Rothschild, Joyce & Raymond Russell. 1986. "Alternatives to Bureaucracy: Democratic Participation in the Economy." *Annual Review of Sociology* 12: 307–328.

Samaritan's Purse. 2012. "Ministry Report." http://media.samaritan.ca/doc/annual-rep ort/2012-annual-report.pdf. Accessed July 23, 2014.

Sandeen, Ernest. 1970. *The Roots of Fundamentalism*. Chicago: University of Chicago Press.

Sanneh, Lamin. 2003. *Whose Religion Is Christianity? The Gospel Beyond the West*. Grand Rapids: Eerdmans.

Sassen, Saskia. 2000. *Cities in a World Economy*. Second Edition. Thousand Oaks, CA: Pine Forge Press.

——. 2012. *Cities in a World Economy: Sociology for a New Century*. Fourth Edition. Los Angeles: Pine Forge Press, an Imprint of Sage Publications, Inc.

Schlemmer, Lawrence. 2005. "Lost In Translation? South Africa's Emerging African Middle Class." A CDE Focus Paper. Johannesburg: Centre for Development and Enterprise.

——. 2006. "Immigrants in South Africa: Perceptions and Reality in Witbank, a Medium-Sized Industrial Town." *CDE Focus*, no. 9 (May). Johannesburg: Centre for Development and Enterprise.

Schmidt, Arthur. 1996. "Introduction: The Continuing Relevance of El Salvador." In *El Salvador in the Eighties*. By Mario Lungo Ucles. Philadelphia: Temple University Press.

Schumpeter, Joseph. 1934. *The Theory of Economic Development; an Inquiry into Profits, Capital, Credit, Interest, and the Business Cycle*. Translated by Redvers Opie. Cambridge, MA: Harvard University Press.

Seria, Nasreen. 2008. "South Africa to Deport Xenophobia Victims, Business Day Says." July 23, 2008. http://www.bloomberg.com/apps/news?pid=20601116&sid=aZy5Dn ucPb9s&refer=afric. Accessed August 2008.

Sewell, William H. 1992. "A Theory of Structure: Duality, Agency, and Transformation." *American Journal of Sociology* 98: 1–29.

Shaw, Mark. 2012. "Robert Wuthnow and World Christianity: A Response to Boundless Faith." *International Bulletin of Missionary Research* 36, no. 4: 179–184.

Sheringham, Olivia. 2013. *Transnational Religious Spaces: Faith and the Brazilian Migrant Experience*. Basingsoke: Palgrave MacMillan.

Smilde, David. 1998. "'Letting God Govern': Supernatural Agency in the Venezuelan Pentecostal Approach to Social Change." *Sociology of Religion* 59, no. 3 (Autumn): 287–303.

——. 2005. "A Qualitative Comparative Analysis of Conversion to Venezuelan Evangelicalism: How Networks Matter." *American Journal of Sociology* 111, no. 3 (November): 757–798.

——. 2007. *Reason to Believe: Cultural Agency in Latin American Evangelicalism*. Berkeley: University of California Press.

Smith, Christian. 1991. *The Emergence of Liberation Theology: Radical Religion and Social Movement Theory*. Chicago: University of Chicago Press.

——. 1994. "The Spirit and Democracy: Base Communities, Protestantism, and Democratization in Latin America." *Sociology of Religion* 55, no. 2 (Summer): 119–143.

——. 1996. *Resisting Reagan: The US Central America Peace Movement*. Chicago: University of Chicago Press.

——. 2003. *Moral, Believing Animals: Human Personhood and Culture*. New York: Oxford University Press.

Snyder, Howard A. 2010. *Yes in Christ: Wesleyan Reflections on Gospel, Mission and Culture*. Toronto: Clements Academic.

Snyder, Howard & Joel Scandrett. 2011. *Salvation Means Creation Healed: The Ecology of Sin and Grace*. Eugene: Cascade Books, an Imprint of Wipf & Stock Publishers.

Sparks, Allister. 2003. *Beyond the Miracle: Inside the New South Africa*. Johannesburg: Jonathan Ball Publishers.

Statistics South Africa. 2011. "Census 2011." http://www.statssa.gov.za/census2011/ Accessed March 2012.

Steele, Liza. 2011. "A Gift from God: Adolescent Motherhood and Religion in Brazilian Favelas." *Sociology of Religion* 72, no. 1: 4–27.

Steigenga, Timothy J., & Edward L. Cleary. 2007. *Conversion of a Continent: Contemporary Religious Change in Latin America*. New Brunswick, NJ: Rutgers University Press.

Stoll, David. 1990. *Is Latin America Turning Protestant? The Politics of Evangelical Growth*. Berkeley and Los Angeles: University of California Press.

Stone, John. 2002. "Ethnonationalism in Black and White: Scholars and the South African Revolution." In *Ethnonationalism in the Contemporary World*. Ed. Daniele Conversi. New York: Routledge, 113–129.

Street, Nick. 2013. *Moved by the Spirit: Pentecostal and Charismatic Christianity in the Global South*. Los Angeles: Center for the Study of Religion & Civic Culture.

Swartz, David. 1996. "Bridging the Study of Culture and Religion: Pierre Bourdieu's Political Economy of Symbolic Power." *Sociology of Religion* 57, no. 1 (Spring): 71–85.

Teichert, Karl. 2005. "A Decade of Growth: Church Growth and Church Planting by Evangelical Churches in South Africa." In *Looking Back Moving Forward: Reflections by South African Evangelicals*. Eds. Louise Kretzschmar & Moss Ntlha, 78–90.

Tennent, Timothy. 2010. *Invitation to World Missions*. Grand Rapids: Kregel Academic.

Thale, Geoff. 2014. "Background Information on the Upcoming Elections in El Salvador." WOLA- Washington Office on Latin America. January 29, 2014. http://www.wola.org/news/background_information_on_the_upcoming_elections_in_el_salvador. Accessed February 15, 2014.

Theal, George McCall. 1904. *History of South Africa: From 1846–1860*. London: Swan Sonnenschein & Co.

Thompson, John B. 1991. "Introduction." In *Language & Symbolic Power*. By Pierre Bourdieu. Ed. John B. Thompson. Cambridge, MA: Harvard University Press, 1–31.

Tilley, Virginia Q. 2005. *Seeing Indians: A Study of Race, Nation, and Power in El Salvador*. Albuquerque: University of New Mexico Press.

Tilly, Charles. 2007. "Trust Networks in Transnational Migration." *Sociological Forum* 22, no. 1: 3–25.

Tiryakian, Edward. 1967. "Sociological Realism: Partition for South Africa?" *Social Forces* 46, no. 2 (December): 208–221.

Trading Economics. 2014a. "El Salvador GDP Annual Growth Rate." http://www.tradingeconomics.com/el-salvador/gdp-growth-annual. Accessed February 2014.

——. 2014b. "South Africa GDP Growth Rate." http://www.tradingeconomics.com/south-africa/gdp-growth. Accessed February 2014.

Troeltsch, Ernst. [1931] 1992. *The Social Teachings of the Christian Churches.* Volume 2. Translated by Olive Wyon. Louisville: Westminster/John Knox Press.

Truth & Reconciliation Commission. 1998. Final Report. Chairperson DM Tutu. http:// www.polity.org.za/polity/govdocs/commissions/1998/trc/index.htm. Accessed July 2008.

Tutu, Desmond. 1999. *No Future Without Forgiveness.* New York: Doubleday.

United Nations. 2006. *Human Development Report.* New York: United Nations.

United Nations Development Programme. 2005. *Informe sobre desarrollo humano El Salvador 2005: Una Mirada al Nuevo nosotros. El impacto de las migraciones.* San Salvador: UNDP.

——. 2007. *Annual Report: Making Globalization Work for All.* New York: United Nations.

United Nations Population Fund. 2013. "Linking Population, Poverty and Development." http://unfpa.org/pds/migration.html. Accessed May 9, 2013.

UNODC Global Study on Homicide 2011. United Nations Office on Drugs and Crime. http://www.unodc.org/unodc/en/data-and-analysis/statistics/crime/global-study-on-hom icide-2011.html. Accessed May 3, 2012.

U.S. Department of State. 2010. "International Religious Freedom Report 2010." http:// www.state.gov/j/drl/rls/irf/2010/. Accessed February 16, 2014.

Van-Helten, Jean Jacques. 1982. "Empire and High Finance: South Africa and the International Gold Standard 1890–1914." *The Journal of African History* 23, no. 4: 529–548.

Varela, Karla. 1990. *La Familia Salvadorena: Análisis Antropológico-Social.* San Salvador: Fundación Salvadorena para el Desarrollo Económico y Social, Departamento de Estudios Económicos y Sociales.

Wallerstein, Immanuel. 1974. *The Modern World-System.* New York: Academic Press.

——. 1979. *The Capitalist World-Economy: Essays.* New York: Cambridge University Press.

Walls, Andrew. 1996. *The Missionary Movement in Christian History.* Maryknoll, NY: Orbis.

——. 2002. *The Cross-Cultural Process in Christian History: Studies in the Transmission and Appropriation of Faith.* Maryknoll, NY: Orbis Books.

Warner, Stephen. 1993. "Work in Progress toward a New Paradigm for the Sociological Study of Religion in the United States." *American Journal of Sociology* 98: 1044–1093.

Warren, Rick. 2002. *The Purpose-Driven Life.* Grand Rapids: Zondervan.

Weber, Max. [1920] 2002. "Prefatory Remarks to Collected Essays in the Sociology of Religion." In *The Protestant Ethic and the Spirit of Capitalism.* Translated by Stephen Kalberg. Los Angeles: Roxbury Publishing Company, 149–165.

——. 1946. "Social Psychology of World Religions." In *From Max Weber: Essays in Sociology.* Translated by and Eds. H. H. Gerth & C. Wright Mills. New York: Oxford University Press, 267–301.

——. 1978. *Economy and Society: An Outline of Interpretive Sociology.* Translated by Guenther Roth & Claus Wittich. Berkeley: University of California Press.

——. [1904] 2002. *The Protestant Ethic & the Spirit of Capitalism.* Translated by Stephen Kalberg. Los Angeles: Roxbury Publishing Company.

Wellman Barry & Scot Wortley. 1990. "Different Strokes from Different Folks: Community Ties and Social Support." *The American Journal of Sociology* 96, no. 3: 558–588.

Whitfield, Teresa. 1995. *Paying the Price*. Philadelphia: Temple University Press.

Wilkinson, Bruce. 2000. *The Prayer of Jabez*. Sisters, OR: Multnomah Publishers.

Willems, Emílio. 1967. *Followers of the New Faith; Culture Change and the Rise of Protestantism in Brazil and Chile*. Nashville: Vanderbilt University Press.

Williams, Philip. 1997. "The Sound of Tambourines: The Politics of Pentecostal Growth in El Salvador." In *Power, Politics & Pentecostals in Latin America*. Eds. Edward L. Cleary & Hannah W. Stewart Gambino. Boulder: Westview Press, 179–200.

Williams, Philip J. & Guillermina Seri. 2003. "The Limits of Reformism: The Rise and Fall of Christian Democracy in El Salvador and Guatemala." In *Christian Democracy in Latin America*. Eds. Scott Mainwaring & Timothy R. Scully. Stanford: Stanford University Press, 301–329.

Williams, Philip J. & Ana L. Peterson. 1996. "Evangelicals and Catholics in El Salvador: Evolving Religious Responses to Social Change." *Journal of Church and State* 38: 873–897.

Williams, Philip J. & Knut Walter. 1997. *Militarization and Demilitarization in El Salvador's Transition to Democracy*. Pittsburgh: University of Pittsburgh Press.

Williams, Robert G. 1994. *States and Social Evolution: Coffee and the Rise of National Governments in Central America*. Chapel Hill: University of North Carolina Press.

Wood, Elisabeth Jean. 2000. *Forging Democracy from Below: Insurgent Transitions in South Africa and El Salvador*. New York: Cambridge University Press.

——. 2003. *Insurgent Collective Action and Civil War in El Salvador*. New York: Cambridge University Press.

Woodberry, Robert. 2012. "The Missionary Roots of Liberal Democracy." *American Political Science Review* 106, no. 2: 244–274.

Woodward, Ralph Lee. 1996. "The Liberal-Conservative Debate in the Central American Federation, 1823–1840." In *Liberals, Politics and Power: State Formation in Nineteenth-Century Latin America*. Eds. Vincent C. Peloso & Barbara A. Tenenbaum. Athens: University of Georgia Press, 59–89.

——. 1999. *Central America: A Nation Divided*. Third Edition. New York: Oxford University Press.

World Bank. 2009. *World Bank Data Indicator 2009*. The World Bank. http://data.world bank.org/indicator Accessed May 3, 2012.

——. 2013. "World Development Indicators." The World Bank. http://data.worldbank. org/indicator/bx.trf.pwkr.cd.dt. Accessed July 8, 2013.

World Vision. 2013. "Annual Review." https://www.worldvision.org/sites/default/fil es/2013-annual-report-brochure-new.pdf. Accessed July 23, 2014.

Wuthnow, Robert. 1987. *Meaning and Moral Order*. Berkeley: University of California Press.

——. 1992. *Rediscovering the Sacred: Perspectives on Religion in Contemporary Society*. Grand Rapids: W.B. Eerdmans.

——. 2009. *Boundless Faith: The Global Reach of American Churches*. Berkeley: University of California Press.

Wuthnow, Robert & Stephen Offutt. 2008. "Transnational Religious Connections." *Sociology of Religion* 69, no. 2 (Summer): 209–232.

Yang, Fenggang, & Helen Rose Ebaugh. 2001. "Transformation of New Immigrant Religions and Their Global Implications." *American Sociological Review* 66: 269–288.

Yelvington, Kevin. 2004. "Foreword." In *Salvadoran Migration to Southern California: Redefining El Hermano Lejano*. Ed. Beth Baker-Cristales. Gainesville: University of Florida, ix–xii.

Young, Michael P. 2002. "Confessional Protest: The Religious Birth of U.S. National Social Movements." *American Sociological Review* 67, no. 5 (October): 660–688.

Index

Made in United States
North Haven, CT
26 November 2022

27281185R00126